ICS 01. 080. 10

CCS A 22

浙 江 省 杭 州 市 地 方 标 准

DB3301／T 0423—2023

杭州市公共服务领域外文译写规范

杭州市人民政府外事办公室 主编

浙江工商大学出版社 | 杭州
ZHEJIANG GONGSHANG UNIVERSITY PRESS

图书在版编目(CIP)数据

杭州市公共服务领域外文译写规范 / 杭州市人民政府外事办公室主编. --杭州:浙江工商大学出版社,2024.4

ISBN 978-7-5178-5985-7

Ⅰ. ①杭… Ⅱ. ①杭… Ⅲ. ①公共服务—外文—翻译—杭州②公共服务—外文—写作—杭州 Ⅳ. ①C916.2

中国国家版本馆 CIP 数据核字(2024)第066978号

杭州市公共服务领域外文译写规范
HANGZHOU SHI GONGGONG FUWU LINGYU WAIWEN YIXIE GUIFAN

杭州市人民政府外事办公室　主编

责任编辑	张莉娅
责任校对	王　英
封面设计	望宸文化
责任印制	包建辉
出版发行	浙江工商大学出版社
	(杭州市教工路198号　邮政编码310012)
	(E-mail:zjgsupress@163.com)
	(网址:http://www.zjgsupress.com)
	电话:0571-88904980,88831806(传真)
排　版	杭州朝曦图文设计有限公司
印　刷	杭州宏雅印刷有限公司
开　本	710mm×1000mm　1/16
印　张	23.75
字　数	380千
版 印 次	2024年4月第1版　2024年4月第1次印刷
书　号	ISBN 978-7-5178-5985-7
定　价	65.00元

前　言

　　本文件按照 GB/T 1.1—2020《标准化工作导则　第 1 部分:标准化文件的结构和起草规则》的规定起草。

　　请注意本文件的某些内容可能涉及专利。本文件的发布机构不承担识别专利的责任。

　　本文件由杭州市人民政府外事办公室提出、归口并组织实施。

　　本文件起草单位:杭州市人民政府外事办公室

　　　　　　　　　　浙江外国语学院

　　　　　　　　　　浙江大学

　　　　　　　　　　浙江工商大学

　　　　　　　　　　浙江海洋大学

　　　　　　　　　　浙江越秀外国语学院

　　本文件主要起草人:赵　伐　陈　刚　刘法公　徐剑锋　辛献云

　　　　　　　　　　　刘晓杰　徐雪英　张建青　杨　平　陈科芳

　　　　　　　　　　　姚明发　朱武汉　刘继华　郁伟伟　王晓露

　　　　　　　　　　　赵芳贤　李　乐　董　科　贾临宇　关冰冰

　　　　　　　　　　　金　艳　张学莲　陈　澄　李翔宇　王晓露

目　录

1 范围

本文件规定了公共服务领域英文以及旅游领域日、韩文译写的术语和定义、译写原则、译写方法和书写要求。

本文件适用于公共服务领域场所和机构名称、设施及功能信息、公共服务信息的英文以及旅游领域日、韩文译写。

2 规范性引用文件

下列文件中的内容通过文中的规范性引用而构成本文件必不可少的条款。其中,注日期的引用文件,仅该日期对应的版本适用于本文件,不注日期的引用文件,其最新版本(包括所有的修改单)适用于本文件。

GB/T 10001(所有部分)　公共信息图形符号

GB/T 16159　汉语拼音正词法基本规则

GB 17733　地名　标志

GB/T 30240.1—2013　公共服务领域英文译写规范　第1部分:通则

3 术语和定义

下列术语和定义适用于本文件。

3.1 场所和机构名称　names of public places and institutions

公共服务领域中具有对外服务功能的公共场所(包括道路及设施)、场馆、服务机构、经营机构、管理机构、企事业单位等的名称。

[来源:GB/T 30240.1—2013,有修改]

3.2 专名　specific terms

场所和机构名称中用于与同类别、同属性的其他场所或机构相区别,具有唯一性特征的部分。

[来源:GB/T 30240.1—2013]

3.3 通名 generic terms

场所和机构名称中标示场所或机构的类别和属性,不具有唯一性特征的部分。

[来源:GB/T 30240.1—2013]

3.4 设施及功能信息 facilities and functional information

为满足人们在公共场所活动需要所提供的基础设施、保障设施和服务设施的名称及功能信息。

3.5 公共服务信息 public service information

为满足人们在公共场所活动需要所提供的说明提示、指示指令、警示警告和限令禁止信息。

4 译写原则

4.1 规范性

符合英、日、韩文使用规范和书写要求。宜使用英、日、韩文国家同类信息的习惯用语和常用表达。

4.2 服务性

根据对外服务的实际需要进行译写。使用通俗易懂、便于理解的词语,避免使用生僻、过时的词语和表达方式。

4.3 文明性

有利于塑造文明城市形象,避免使用带有歧视色彩或损害社会公共利益的词语和译法。

4.4 人文性

反映杭州的历史文化内涵,传达江南名城的人文特色。

5 英文译写方法和要求

5.1 场所和机构名称

5.1.1 总则

场所和机构名称区分专名、通名、修饰或限定成分,分别使用汉语拼音和英文进行拼写或译写。

5.1.2 专名

5.1.2.1 专名宜使用汉语拼音拼写,不标声调符号(见示例)。

示例:同德医院 Tongde Hospital

5.1.2.2 来源于英文的专名,直接使用英文原文(见示例)。

示例:杭州香格里拉饭店 Shangri-La Hotel, Hangzhou

5.1.2.3 有实际含义并需要向服务对象说明其含义的专名,可使用英文译写(见示例)。

示例:天王殿 Hall of Heavenly Kings 或 Heavenly Guardians Hall

5.1.3 通名

5.1.3.1 通名宜使用英文译写(见示例)。

示例:黄龙体育中心 Huanglong Sports Center

5.1.3.2 专名是单音节时,其通名部分可视作专名的一部分,先与专名一起用汉语拼音拼写,然后用英文重复译写(见示例)。

示例:湘湖 Xianghu Lake(若"湘湖"用作地名、公交或地铁站名,则译作 Xianghu。)

5.1.3.3 通名在原文中省略时,可视情况补译(见示例)。

示例:楼外楼(饭店名)Louwailou Restaurant(若"楼外楼"用作地名、公交或地铁站名,则译作 Louwailou。)

5.1.4 修饰或限定成分

5.1.4.1 行政区划限定成分

5.1.4.1.1 行政区划限定成分用汉语拼音拼写(见示例)。

示例:富阳 Fuyang

5.1.4.1.2 行政区划名中的"市、区、县、乡(镇)、街道"等可省去不译。但在党政组织机构名称中应译出(见示例)。

示例:富阳区教育局 Education Bureau of Fuyang District

5.1.4.1.3 常用行政区名称按表1规定译写。

表1 常用行政区名称译法一览表

行政区名称	英文译法	示例
村	Village	双峰村 Shuangfeng Village
镇/乡	Town/ᵃTownship	塘栖镇 Tangqi Town;上官乡 Shangguan Township
街道	Subdistrict	武林街道 Wulin Subdistrict
区	District	西湖区 Xihu District
县	County	淳安县 Chun'an County
(县级)市	Cityᵇ	建德市 Jiande City
市(省会)	Municipality/City	杭州市 Hangzhou Municipality/Hangzhou City
省	Province	浙江省 Zhejiang Province
ᵃ 表示"/"符号前后的两个译文可任选其一使用。 ᵇ 在特殊正式语境下,可使用municipality。		

5.1.4.1.4 与上级政府有隶属关系的部门或机构,应译出上级政府所在行政区划的限定词(见示例)。

示例:杭州市政府侨务办公室 Hangzhou Municipal Office for Overseas Chinese Affairs

5.1.4.1.5 属于政府主管或分管但无行政级别或不具有行政职能的企事业单位,如学校、医院、研究机构、企业和公共服务机构等,其名称中的行政区划限定词不译出(见示例)。

示例:杭州市残疾人就业服务中心 Hangzhou Center for Disabilities Employment Services

5.1.4.1.6 含有两个及以上行政层级并按由高到低的层级顺序翻译时,高一级行政层级的行政区划限定词不译出(见示例)。

示例:杭州市临安区商务局 Hangzhou Lin'an District Bureau of Commerce

5.1.4.2 序列、方位、属性、特点等修饰成分

5.1.4.2.1 序列词用英文序数词译写(见示例1),也可采用"No.+数字"形式(见示例2)。部门或单位的内部处室,可用处室名+罗马数字I、II、III等形式译写(见示例3)。

示例1:杭州市第七人民医院 Hangzhou Seventh People's Hospital

示例2:杭州市第一人民医院 Hangzhou No.1 People's Hospital

示例3:一处 Division I;二处 Division II

5.1.4.2.2 方位词含有指示方向的意义时,应意译(见示例1)。但当方位词本身固化为地名的一部分时,该方位词采用汉语拼音拼写(见示例2)。

示例1:西广场 West Square;东广场 East Square

示例2:临平东湖公园 Linping Donghu Park

5.1.4.2.3 属性词宜用英文译写(见示例1)。属性词已失去原属性特点的,用汉语拼音拼写(见示例2)。

示例1:杭州国画院 Hangzhou Traditional Chinese Painting Academy

示例2:青年路社区 Qingnianlu Community

5.1.5 例外情况

现用英文译名不符合前述规定,但已经约定俗成的,或符合实际情况的,可沿用其习惯的或与实际情况相符的译写方法(见示例)。

示例:西湖 West Lake(但道路名"西湖大道"则译作 Xihu Ave。)

5.1.6 实体名称

5.1.6.1 实体名称按冠名、专名、序列名、属性名和通名进行译写(见示例1)。冠名和专名用汉语拼音拼写,表示国际、国家、地区等的名称可用英文译写(见示例2)。序列名、属性名和通名按照第5.1.3和5.1.4条的要求用英文译写。属

性词英译时可采用顺译法,置于通名之前(见示例3)。当属性词较多时,可将其置于通名之后,使用of或for连接(见示例4)。

注:实体名称指公共服务领域有关企事业单位和其他具有实体性质的机构和单位的名称。党政组织机构名称的外文译写只用于对外交流,不应用于组织机构名称的标牌。

示例1:杭州市(冠名)第二(序列名)社会福利(属性名)院(通名) Hangzhou No. 2 Social Welfare Institute

示例2:中国美术学院 China Academy of Art

示例3:杭州市经济建设发展公司 Hangzhou Economic Construction and Development Company

示例4:西湖区发展改革和经济信息化局 Xihu District Bureau of Development, Reform and Economic Informatization

5.1.6.2 多层级机构名称译写规则

a)含两个行政层级的,可按照由高到低的层级顺序翻译(见示例1);

b)含两个以上行政层级的,可将需要翻译的主体层级置于最前,其余按照由高到低的层级顺序翻译(见示例2);

c)具有隶属关系的内设机构,可将该机构名称前置,用介词of 或标点符号",连接所隶属的主体部门或机构名称(见示例3)。

示例1:杭州市公安局临安区分局 Hangzhou Municipal Public Security Bureau, Lin'an District Branch

示例2:中共杭州市萧山区义桥镇委员会 Yiqiao Township Committee of the Communist Party of China, Hangzhou Xiaoshan District 或 CPC Yiqiao Township Committee of Hangzhou Xiaoshan District

示例3:中共杭州市委杭州市人民政府信访局 Public Complaints and Proposals Bureau of CPC Hangzhou Municipal Committee and Hangzhou Municipal People's Government 或 Public Complaints and Proposals Bureau, CPC Hangzhou Municipal Committee and Hangzhou Municipal People's Government

5.1.7 城市道路名称

5.1.7.1 由"专名+通名"构成的城市道路或设施名称,专名用汉语拼音拼写,通名用英文译写(见示例1)。用汉语拼音拼写的专名应符合汉语拼音字母拼写规则中有关连写和分写的规定(见示例2)。不含通名、只有专名的城市道路,先用汉语拼音拼写专名,再根据道路性质补充通名的英文(见示例3)。

示例1:留和(专名)路(通名) Liuhe Rd

示例2:钱江隧道 Qianjiang Tunnel

示例3:直大方伯 Zhidafangbo Rd

5.1.7.2 城市道路在某一区域内按序列命名时,可采用序数词译写(序数词可以简写)(见示例1)。街道编号为13及以上的,可书写为13th St或13 St(见示例2)。城市道路名称中含具有序列性质的序数词,使用英文序数词译写(序数词可简写)(见示例3)。城市道路名称中的序数词已固化为道路专名的一部分的,采用汉语拼音拼写(见示例4)。

示例1:1号(大)街 1st St

示例2:43号街 43rd St或43 St

示例3:建设二路 Jianshe 2nd Rd 或 Jianshe Second Rd

示例4:文一路 Wenyi Rd

5.1.7.3 城市道路名称中的方位词用英文缩略语译写,置于道路名之后的括弧中(见示例1)。地铁、公交车在用语音播报站名时,为突出站名中方位词的重要信息,可采用英文方位词前置的惯用法(见示例2)。

示例1:天目山西路 Tianmushan Rd (W)

示例2:枫桦西路站 West Fenghua Road(书写时Road不缩写。)

5.1.7.4 城市道路名称中的通名按表2规定用英文译写。

表2 城市道路名称通名译法一览表

通名	英文译法	示例
街	St	北山街 Beishan St
路	Rd	中山路 Zhongshan Rd
大道	Ave	江南大道 Jiangnan Ave
巷(弄、里弄)	Alley	百井坊巷 Baijingfang Alley
线	Hwy/Highway^{a}	红十五线 Hongshiwu Hwy

通名	英文译法	示例
支路[b]	Branch Rd	潮王支路 Chaowang Branch Rd
高架道路(快速路)	(Elevated)[c] Expwy/ Expressway	中河高架 Zhonghe (Elevated) Expwy
立体交叉口(互通)	Interchange	上德立交 Shangde Interchange
隧道	Tunnel	西湖隧道 Xihu Tunnel
桥[d]	Bridge	复兴大桥 Fuxing Bridge
运河	Canal	京杭大运河 (the) Beijing-Hangzhou Grand Canal
绕城高速	Beltway	杭州绕城高速 Hangzhou Beltway

[a] 视道路等级或实际情况还可译作 Expwy/Expressway,或 Rd/Road。
[b] 其他译法见表 A.1。
[c] "( )"表示括弧中的单词可根据实际情况选用,后同。
[d] 道路名中的"桥"失去原属性特点,固化为道路名的一部分时,则使用汉语拼音拼写,如沈塘桥 Shentangqiao。

5.1.7.5 其他道路交通设施及服务信息的译写示例见表 A.1。

5.1.8 旅游景区景点、文化娱乐场所名称

5.1.8.1 景区景点名称中的专名使用汉语拼音拼写,通名按表 3 规定用英文译写。

表3 景区景点名称通名译法一览表

通名	英文译法	示例
山	Mountain(高山)、Hill(小山) 或 Mount/Mt(须放在专名前)	小和山 Xiaohe Mountain 宝石山 Baoshi Hill (Precious Stone Hill)
峰	Peak	五老峰 Wulao Peak

通名	英文译法	示例
岭	Ridge	万松岭 Wansong Ridge (Myriad Pines Ridge)
坞	Valley	梅家坞 Meijia Valley^a
寺	Temple 或 Monastery(佛寺)	灵隐寺 Lingyin Temple (Monastery of the Soul's Retreat)
	Mosque(清真寺)	凤凰寺 Fenghuang Mosque (Phoenix Mosque)
庙	Temple(城隍庙、太庙)	岳庙 Yue Fei's Temple
祠	Temple、Ancestral Temple、Shrine 或 Memorial Temple (根据实际含义选用)	钱王祠 Qianwang Temple 或 Temple to King Qians 白苏二公祠 Memorial Temple of Bai Juyi and Su Shi
宫、观（道教）	Daoist 或 Taoist Temple^b	福星观 Fuxing Daoist Temple (Lucky Star Temple)
洞	Cave	紫来洞 Zilai Cave
塔	Pagoda(佛塔)	雷峰塔 Leifeng Pagoda
	Stupa 或 Dagoba(舍利塔)	神尼塔 Shenni Stupa
	Tower(普通的塔)	广播电视塔 Radio and TV Tower
湖	Lake	里西湖 the West Inner Lake
溪	Stream、Creek 或 Brook	九溪 Jiuxi Creeks (Nine Creeks)
桥	Bridge	玉带桥 Yudai Bridge (Jade Belt Bridge)
堤	Causeway	赵公堤 Zhaogong Causeway
院	Courtyard、Yard、Garden 或 Temple（根据实际含义选用）	金竹院 Jinzhu Courtyard 大石佛院 Dashifo (Big Stone Buddha) Temple

通名	英文译法	示例
牌楼	Arch、Archway、Pailou 或 Ceremonial/Memorial/Decorative/Monumental Gateway	杨家牌楼 The Yang Family Arch
牌坊	Memorial Gateway 或 Memorial Arch/Archway	"万松书院"牌坊 Memorial Gateway of Wansong Academy
湿地	Wetland	西溪湿地 Xixi Wetland
名人故居	Former Residence/Mansion of XXX	司徒雷登旧居 Former Residence of J. L. Stuart 胡雪岩故居 Former Mansion of Hu Xueyan
遗址	Site 或 Ruins	南宋皇城遗址 Site of the Southern Song (Dynasty) Imperial City 良渚古城遗址 Archaeological Ruins of Liangzhu City 或 Archaeological Site of Liangzhu City

a "梅家坞"用作机构或场所名称的修饰语时,可译写为 Meijiawu,如梅家坞茶文化村 Meijiawu Tea Culture Village。

b 特指某一宫、观时,Daoist 或 Taoist 可省略。

5.1.8.2 "亭、台、楼、阁、榭、阙"等与专名一起使用汉语拼音拼写。根据对外服务的需要,可后加英文予以解释(见示例)。

示例:湖心亭 Huxinting Isle (Midlake Pavilion)

5.1.8.3 "馆、殿、堂"可译作 Hall,如某一场所具备明确功能或用途,则需根据其实际功能或用途进行译写(见示例1至4)。

示例1:星象馆 Hall of Astrology

示例2:蚕学馆 Sericulture Academy

示例3:闻莺馆 Wenying Teahouse

示例4:述古堂 Shugu Hall (Hall of Historical Records)

5.1.8.4 景区景点名称中的专名如只包含一个汉字,则专名与通名一并使用汉语拼音拼写,再用英文翻译通名(见示例)。约定俗成的例外。

示例:葛岭 Geling Ridge

5.1.8.5 景区景点名称具有地理信息和人文内涵的,可采用"音译+意译"的方式译写,对名称较长的,音译时按照 GB/T 16159 规定的以词或语节为书写单位拼写(见示例)。

示例:断桥残雪 Duanqiaocanxue(音译)(Lingering Snow on the Broken Bridge)(意译)

5.1.8.6 其他旅游景区景点名称的译写示例见表 B.1。

5.1.8.7 "电影院、电影厅、影都、放映公司"及以放电影为主的"影剧院"均译作 Cinema。"影城"宜译作 Cinema,如规模特别大,或者有同名的电影院需要区分的可译作 Cinema City 或 Cineplex。在博物馆、展览馆内部的影厅译作 Movie Hall。

5.1.8.8 "剧场、剧院、舞台、戏院、戏苑"等均译作 Theater。"音乐厅"译作 Concert Hall。

5.1.8.9 "文化馆、文化中心"译作 Cultural Center。如同一区域内文化中心与文化馆需加以区别,"文化中心"可译作 Cultural Complex 或 Cultural Complex Center。(见示例)"社区文化(活动)中心"译作 Community Cultural Center。文化宫的"宫"可沿用 Palace。"文化(大)礼堂"译作 Cultural Auditorium。"文化驿站"译作 Cultural Station 或 Cultural Commons。

示例:余杭区文化中心 Yuhang Cultural Complex;余杭区文化馆 Yuhang Cultural Center

5.1.8.10 其他文化场馆、娱乐场所和文化旅游管理机构名称的译写示例见表 B.3。

5.1.9 会展赛事场馆、场所和相关机构名称

5.1.9.1 "展览馆、陈列馆、展览中心"等具有展示、陈列功能的场馆译作 Exhibition Center 或 Exhibition Hall(见示例)。

示例:杭州市城市规划展览馆 Hangzhou City Planning Exhibition Hall

5.1.9.2 "会展中心"译作 Convention & Exhibition Center。"博览中心"译作 Exposition Center 或 Expo Center(见示例)。

示例:杭州国际博览中心 Hangzhou International Expo Center

5.1.9.3 "展馆"可译作 Pavilion，特指临时建造的大型展馆(见示例1)，也可译作 Hall 或 Exhibition Hall(见示例2)。"展(示)区"译作 Exhibition Floor/Space/Section 或 Stand/Booth/Display Area。"多功能展厅"译作 Multi-function Hall。"会展服务区"译作 Service Area。"交易洽谈区"译作 Negotiation Zone/Area。"餐饮区"译作 Food & Beverage。"行政办公区"译作 Administration Area。"休闲区"译作 Snack Lounge。"茶歇区"译作 Tea Break Area。

示例1：(世博会)中国馆 China Pavilion

示例2：3号展馆 Hall 3

5.1.9.4 "美术馆、艺术馆"均译作 Art Gallery 或 Art Museum。"画廊"译作 Gallery。

5.1.9.5 "博物馆"译作 Museum。"科技馆"译作 Science Museum。"纪念馆"译作 Memorial Hall 或 Memorial Museum。文史馆译作 Research Institute of Culture and History。

5.1.9.6 "体育馆"译作 Indoor Stadium、Gymnasium 或 Sports Hall(见示例)。

示例：杭州体育馆 Hangzhou Gymnasium

5.1.9.7 "体育场"应区分其不同的情况采用不同的译法：包括观众席在内的整个体育场译作 Stadium。面积较大，可用于足球、橄榄球、曲棍球、田径等比赛和训练的场地译作 Field。面积较小，仅用于篮球、网球等比赛和训练的场地译作 Court。

5.1.9.8 "体育中心"译作 Sports Center(见示例1)。大型体育中心译作 Sports Complex。社区体育活动场所可译作 Community Sports Center 或 Community Sports Ground(见示例2)。

示例1：杭州奥林匹克体育中心 Hangzhou Olympic Sports Center

示例2：五常街道文化体育中心 Wuchang Community Culture and Sports Center

5.1.9.9 水上运动场馆应区分不同的情况采用不同的译法：可用于游泳、跳水、水球等项目比赛和训练的大型室内游泳场馆译作 Natatorium。一般的游泳池译作 Swimming Pool 或 Indoor Swimming Pool。用于赛艇、皮划艇等水上项目比赛和训练的可译作 Water Sports Center(见示例)。

示例:富阳水上运动中心 Fuyang Water Sports Center

5.1.9.10 其他会展赛事场馆及机构名称的译写示例见表C.1。

5.1.10 教育及管理机构名称

5.1.10.1 综合性大学译作 University。大学的二级学院可译作 School、College 或 Faculty。独立设置或具有相对独立办学资格的二级学院译作 College。"研究生院"译作 Graduate School。

5.1.10.2 专科性学院和尚未升格为大学的学院译作 College 或 Institute(见示例1)。艺术类院校和含研究性质的教育机构译作 Academy(见示例2)。音乐类院校译作 Conservatory(见示例3)。"职业技术学院"译作 Polytechnic、Polytechnic College 或 Vocational and Technical College(见示例4)。

示例1:杭州医学院 Hangzhou Medical College

示例2:中国美术学院 China Academy of Art

示例3:浙江音乐学院 Zhejiang Conservatory of Music

示例4:浙江长征职业技术学院 Zhejiang Changzheng Vocational and Technical College

5.1.10.3 "党校"译作 Party School 或 Party Institute。"社会主义学院"译作 Institute of Socialism。"行政学院"宜译作 Administration Institute。"干部学院"宜译作 Cadre Institute。

5.1.10.4 中小学用 School 译写:"初中"译作 Junior Middle School 或 Junior High School。"高中"译作 Senior Middle School 或 Senior High School。同时设有初中部和高中部的"完全中学"译作 High School 或 Secondary School(见示例1)。职业高中、中等专业或职业学校均译作 Vocational School(见示例2)。"小学"译作 Primary School 或 Elementary School。小学和初中的九年一贯制学校直接译作 School。特殊教育类学校译作 Special School 或 Special Education School(见示例3)。

示例1:杭州东方中学 Hangzhou Dongfang High School

示例2:杭州市闲林职业高级中学 Hangzhou Xianlin Vocational School

示例3:萧山区特殊教育学校 Xiaoshan Special Education School

5.1.10.5 作为校外教育机构的青少年活动中心、基地等均可译作 Youth Center 或 Youth and Children's Center(见示例1)。少年宫、青年宫的"宫"可沿用 Palace(见示例 2)。

示例 1:杭州青少年活动中心 Hangzhou Youth and Children's Center

示例 2:杭州富阳青少年宫 Hangzhou Fuyang Youth and Children's Palace

5.1.10.6 成人教育体系中的业余大学、继续教育学院等可译作 College of Continuing Education。"社区学校"译作 Community School。"开放大学"译作 Open University(见示例)。

示例:浙江开放大学 Zhejiang Open University

5.1.10.7 "教育局"译作 Education Bureau 或 Bureau of Education(见示例)。

示例:杭州市教育局 Education Bureau of Hangzhou Municipality 或 Hangzhou Municipal Bureau of Education

5.1.10.8 教育管理机构下设的"处"译作 Division(见示例 1),"科"译作 Subdivision 或 Section(见示例 2)。

示例 1:高等教育处 Higher Education Division

示例 2:教材科 Textbook Procurement Section

5.1.10.9 其他学校及管理机构名称的译写示例见表 D.1。

5.1.11 医疗卫生机构名称

5.1.11.1 "医院"译作 Hospital。"诊所、防治所、卫生室、医务室、门诊"等译作 Clinic。"疗养院"可译作 Convalescent Hospital/Home,不译作 Sanatorium(除非特指传染病医院)。

5.1.11.2 "职工医院"译作 Workers' Hospital 或 Hospital for Staff and Workers。"中心医院"译作 Central Hospital。"人民医院"译作 People's Hospital。"中医院"译作 Traditional Chinese Medicine Hospital 或 TCM Hospital。"妇产科医院"译作 Women's Hospital 或 Obstetrics and Gynecology Hospital。"儿童医院"译作 Children's Hospital。"牙科医院/诊所"译作 Dental Hospital/Clinic。

5.1.11.3 "疾病防治中心/院/所"译作 Center for Disease Control and Prevention(CDC)。

5.1.11.4 "社区卫生服务中心"译作 Community Health Center 或

Community Healthcare Center。

5.1.11.5 医院的分院译作 Branch Hospital,用 of 连接所隶属的总院名称;也可采用"总院名称,专名+Branch"的译写方法(见示例)。

示例:浙江省人民医院望江山分院 Zhejiang People's Hospital, Wangjiangshan Branch

5.1.11.6 大学附属医院需要译出隶属关系时,可按表 4 规定的译法译写。如某附属医院英文名称的译法一经选定,应固定为该医院的唯一英译名。

表4　大学附属医院英文译法一览表

中文名	英文译法	示例
XX 大学医学院第一附属医院	序数词+Affiliated/Affiliate Hospital+of+大学及医学院名(医学院名,大学名)	(the) First Affiliated Hospital of XX University School of Medicine 或 (the) First Affiliated Hospital of School of Medicine, XX University
XX 大学医学院第二附属医院	将大学及其医学院名称置于医院名称之后,中间用","隔开	(the) Second Hospital, School of Medicine, XX University 或 (the) Second Hospital, XX University School of Medicine
XX 大学医学院第三附属医院	按"大学名+医学院名+医院名"的方式	XX University School of Medicine Third Hospital
XX 大学医学院附属医院	University-Affiliated Hospital	XX University-Affiliated Hospital

5.1.11.7 医保定点医院译作 Medical Insurance Designated Hospital。医保定点诊所译作 Medical Insurance Designated Clinic。医保定点药房译作 Medical Insurance Designated Pharmacy。

5.1.11.8 从事疾病防控、卫生健康指导等工作的"健康驿站"译作 Health Station。

5.1.11.9 其他医疗卫生、科研、管理、服务机构及科室名称的译写示例见表 E.1。

5.1.12 商业金融、邮电机构和场所名称

5.1.12.1 商业、金融机构名称应区分专名和通名,分别使用汉语拼音和英文进行拼写或译写(见示例1)。专名如来源于英文,则直接使用英文原文(见示例2)。有的商业场所名称采用专名和通名全部英译的方式,如能形象传达名称设计者的原意,且译文正确,符合英语表达习惯,可采用意译的方式(见示例3)。

示例1:华联(专名)超市(通名) Hualian Supermarket

示例2:山姆会员店 Sam's Club

示例3:(龙湖)天街 Paradise Walk

5.1.12.2 "中央商务区、中央商业区、商务中心区"译作 Central Business District(CBD)。"商业副中心"译作 Sub-CBD。"商圈"译作 Business Zone。"金融区"译作 Financial District 或 Financial Zone。"商业街"译作 Commercial Street。"商业街区"译作 Commercial Street Area。"步行街"译作 Pedestrian Street(见示例)。

示例:湖滨步行街 Hubin Pedestrian Street

5.1.12.3 商业性写字楼可译作 Tower、Building 或 Mansion。主要功能为购物、餐饮和商业活动的大型场所或大楼、大厦译作 Plaza(见示例)。

示例:万达广场 Wanda Plaza

5.1.12.4 集购物、休闲、娱乐、餐饮等于一体,包括百货店、大卖场以及众多专业连锁零售店在内的商业中心译作 Shopping Mall 或 Shopping Center。大型百货商店译作 Department Store。如该中心或百货商店已有自己固定的官方译名,可根据"名从主人"的原则使用其官方译名(见示例)。

示例:银泰百货 Intime Department Store

5.1.12.5 只针对货品进行分类销售、不具有休闲娱乐等多种功能的较小规模的商店、店铺译作 Store 或 Shop。除 Barber Shop 等习惯用法或固定搭配外,通常情况下 Store 和 Shop 可互换使用。专卖店采用"品牌名+Store/Shop"的方式译写,Store 或 Shop 可省略。如该店已有自己固定的官方译名,可根据"名从主人"的原则使用其官方译名(见示例)。

示例:七次元艺术商店 Seven Dimensions Artistic Shop

5.1.12.6 "银行"译作 Bank。各银行在杭州的分行均译作 Hangzhou Branch,置于所属总行译名之后(见示例1)。"支行"译作 Sub-Branch,可置于所属总行、分行译名之后,用逗号隔开,或将支行前置,在介词 of 后跟上总行和支行名称,如"分行"一词在中文名称中省略,则可将分行与支行名称并列译出(见示例2至3)。银行的"营业部"译作 Banking Center 或 Banking Department。"分理处"译作 Office。"储蓄所"译作 Savings Agency。

示例1:中国光大银行杭州分行 China Everbright Bank Hangzhou Branch

示例2:华夏银行杭州分行滨江支行 Huaxia Bank Hangzhou Branch, Binjiang Sub-Branch 或 Binjiang Sub-Branch of Huaxia Bank Hangzhou Branch

示例3:中国银行杭州三墩支行 Bank of China, Hangzhou Sandun Sub-Branch

`5.1.12.7` 保险、证券、期货、财务管理与服务类的公司译作 Company 或 Corporation。通常情况下,Company 和 Corporation 可互换使用,具体根据"名从主人"和"约定俗成"的原则选择使用。"交易所"译作 Exchange。"证券交易所"译作 Stock Exchange。"期货交易所"译作 Futures Exchange。"证券公司(股份有限公司、有限责任公司)"译作 Securities Limited Company。"保险公司(股份有限公司、有限责任公司)"译作 Insurance Limited Company。Limited Company 可缩写为 Co., Ltd.(见示例)。

示例:民生人寿保险股份有限公司 Minsheng Life Insurance Co., Ltd.

`5.1.12.8` "邮政局"译作 Post Office。"邮政支局"译作 Branch Post Office。"邮政代办所"译作 Postal Agency。邮政、电信的营业网点、营业厅等窗口服务机构均可译作 Customer Service Center/Hall/Counter(见示例)。

示例:中国电信营业厅 China Telecom Customer Service Hall

`5.1.12.9` 其他商业金融、邮电行业机构和场所名称的译写示例见表F.1。

`5.1.13` 餐饮业、住宿业服务场所和机构名称

`5.1.13.1` 宾馆酒店名称的译写可区分专名和通名,分别使用汉语拼音和英文进行拼写或译写(见示例1)。有实际含义并需要向服务对象特别说明其含义的专名,可使用英文译写(见示例2)。专名如来源于英文,则直接使用英文原文(见示例3)。

示例1:西溪(专名)宾馆(通名) Xixi Hotel

示例2:西湖国宾馆 West Lake State Guesthouse

示例3:杭州JW万豪酒店 JW Marriott Hotel Hangzhou

5.1.13.2 酒家、酒楼、酒店、菜馆、餐馆、餐厅、饭庄、食府以及饮食店等仅提供餐饮服务的服务机构,可译作 Restaurant。中文名称中含有"阁、轩、府、坊、村、廊、楼、庄、堂、园、苑、居、门、斋、馆"等的,视作专名的一部分,连同专名一起用汉语拼音拼写(见示例)。

示例:楼外楼 Louwailou Restaurant

5.1.13.3 宾馆以及提供住宿的酒店、饭店等译作 Hotel。经济型的连锁旅馆可译作 Motel 或 Inn。"民宿"译作 Homestay 或 Guesthouse/Guest House。

5.1.13.4 百年老店名称的译写,先用汉语拼音拼写其全称,然后用英文译写其性质或产品(见示例1至2)。

示例1:胡庆余堂 Huqingyutang TCM Pharmacy

示例2:采芝斋 Caizhizhai Confectionery

5.1.13.5 其他餐饮业、住宿业场所及机构名称的译写示例见表G.1。

5.1.14 中餐菜名的译写

5.1.14.1 中餐菜名可按表5规定的译法译写。

表5　中餐菜名译法一览表

菜名类别	英文译法	示例
以主料为主,配料或配汁为辅的菜名	主料(名称/形状)+ with/in+配料或配汁	清汤鱼圆 Fish Balls in Light Soup 什锦汤面 Noodle Soup with Meat and Vegetables
以烹饪方法为主,原料为辅的菜名	烹饪方法(动词过去分词)+主料(名称/形状)	拌双耳 Tossed Black and White Fungus
	烹饪方法(动词过去分词)+主料(名称/形状)+ 配料	豌豆炒牛肉 Sautéed Beef and Green Peas
	烹饪方法(动词过去分词)+主料(名称/形状)+ with/in+配料或汤汁	红烧狮子头 Braised Pork Balls in Brown Sauce
以形状、口感为主,原料为辅的菜名	形状/口感+主料	糖醋咕咾肉 Sweet and Sour Pork
	烹饪方法、形状或口感+主料+with/in+配料	豆豉芦笋炒鸭柳 Sautéed Sliced Duck with Asparagus in Black Bean Sauce

菜名类别	英文译法	示例
以人名、地名为主，原料为辅的菜名	人名(地名)+ 主料	东坡肉 Dongpo Pork
	烹饪方法或主辅料+人名/地名+Style	杭州酱鸭 Duck in Brown Sauce, Hangzhou Style

5.1.14.2 中国特有的食品名称，如饺子、包子、粽子、馒头、火烧、煎饼、肉夹馍、油条等，使用汉语拼音拼写。

5.1.14.3 已成为英语外来词并收入权威英语词典的中国菜名和食品名称，保留其原译名(见示例1至3)。

示例1:豆腐 Tofu

示例2:宫保鸡丁 Kung Pao Chicken

示例3:馄饨 Wonton

5.1.14.4 无法体现其烹饪方法及主配料的菜名，使用汉语拼音译写，并在后面的括弧里标注英文注释(见示例)。

示例:片儿川 Pian'erchuan (Noodles with Sliced Pork, Bamboo Shoots, and Pickled Potherb Mustard)

5.1.14.5 部分中餐菜名的译写示例见表G.2。

5.2 设施及功能信息

5.2.1 公共交通设施及功能信息

5.2.1.1 "机场"译作 Airport。"火车站"译作 Railway Station。"轨道交通"译作 Metro。"游客码头"译作 Pier。"轮渡站"译作 Ferry Terminal。"货运码头"译作 Wharf。"装卸码头"译作 Loading/Unloading Dock。

5.2.1.2 "机场航站楼"译作 Terminal。同一机场内有多座航站楼的，用"Terminal+阿拉伯数字"的方式译写(见示例)。

示例:1号航站楼 Terminal 1(可缩写为T1)

5.2.1.3 飞机航班号、列车车次、轮船班次的译写根据行业标准或惯例执行。机场、铁路等服务设施及功能信息可根据行业标准执行。

5.2.1.4 地铁线路译作 Line，具体线路用"Line+阿拉伯数字"的方式译写（见示例）。

示例：(地铁)6号线 Line 6

5.2.1.5 公交车线路译作 Bus Route，指示具体公交线路时 Route 可省略，直接用阿拉伯数字表示（见示例）。

示例：公交63路 Bus 63

5.2.1.6 运河水上巴士线路译作 Line，具体线路用"Line+阿拉伯数字"的方式译写。

5.2.1.7 地铁站点译作 Station，"同台换乘站"译作 Transfer Station 或 Interchange Station。

5.2.1.8 公共汽车"始发站"和"终点站"分别译作 Terminal 和 Station，沿途站点译作 Stop。

5.2.1.9 运河水上巴士"起点站"和"终点站"分别译作 Starting/Start Point 和 End/Ending Point，中间的站点译作 Stop。

5.2.1.10 公交车、地铁、运河水上巴士的站牌、线路图或电子屏在显示具体站点时，"站"字可不必译出（见示例）。

示例：武林门站 Wulinmen

5.2.1.11 其他公共交通服务信息的译写示例见表 A.2。

5.2.2 文化旅游设施及功能信息

5.2.2.1 "电影放映厅"译作 Theater 或 Screen。不同的放映厅用"Theater+阿拉伯数字"或"Screen+阿拉伯数字"的方式进行译写（见示例）。

示例：1号放映厅 Theater 1 或 Screen 1

5.2.2.2 剧场、剧院、舞台、戏院、戏苑等的楼层可采用"序数词+Floor"的方法译写（见示例）。音乐厅、歌剧院等已经习惯使用 Stalls(正厅)、Mezzanine(楼厅)、Balcony(像阳台一样的包厢)、Box(一间间隔开的包厢)的，可沿用。

示例：(剧场)一层 First Floor

5.2.2.3 座位的"排"译作 Row，"座"译作 Seat(见示例)。

示例：3排5座 Row 3, Seat 5

5.2.2.4 "文物"可译作 Cultural Object/Relic，专指古董时也可译作 Antique。"文物保护单位"可译作 Monument 或 Cultural Heritage Site(见示例)。

示例:国家级文物保护单位 National Monument

5.2.2.5 文物的级别可采用"序数词+Grade"的方法译写,也可采用"Grade+阿拉伯数字或罗马数字"的方法译写(见示例)。

示例:一级文物 First Grade Cultural Object/Relic 或 Grade 1 Cultural Object/Relic 或 Grade I Cultural Object/Relic

5.2.2.6 其他旅游服务信息的译写示例见表B.2。文化场馆、娱乐场所和文化旅游管理机构服务信息的译写示例见表B.3。

5.2.3 会展和体育设施及功能信息

5.2.3.1 "博览会"译作 Exposition 或 Expo。"交易会"译作 Trade Show/Fair/Exhibition。"推介会"译作 Promotional Meeting/Session/ Conference。"产品发布会"译作 Product Presentation/Release Show。"产品品牌展"译作 Brands and Products Exhibition/Expo。"收藏展"译作 Collection Exhibition。"成果展、成就展"译作 Achievement/Accomplishment Show/Exhibition。"图片展"译作 Photograph Show。"联展"译作 Co-exhibition 或 Joint Exhibition(见示例1)。"主题展"译作 Theme Exhibition/Show/Display(见示例2)。

示例1:书画作品联展 Paintings & Calligraphy Co-exhibition

示例2:"红船精神"主题展 Theme Exhibition of "Red Boat Spirit"

5.2.3.2 "展台、展位、摊位"译作 Stand 或 Booth。"展示墙"译作 Display Wall。"展示窗"译作 Display Window。"展台布局"译作 Stand/Booth Layout。"展位平面图"译作 Floor Plan。"导视图、指示图"译作 Directory/Guide。"展馆分布图"译作 Pavilion Layout/Distribution (Map) 或 Exhibition Hall Layout。"展商分布图"译作 Exhibitor Distribution Map 或 Exhibitor Map。"展位图、展场图"译作 Stand/Booth/Site Plan。"展位区隔"译作 Stand/Booth Partition。

5.2.3.3 "展期"译作 Exhibition Period/Duration 或 Show Days。"开幕式"译作 Opening Ceremony。"闭幕式"译作 Closing Ceremony。"倒计时"译作 Countdown 或 ____ Days to Go。"论坛"译作 Forum。"文化互动"译作 Cultural Interaction。"日程安排(表)"译作 Agenda。"酒会"译作 Cocktail Party。"专题活动"译作 Special Event。"欢迎晚宴"译作 Welcome Dinner。"颁奖晚会"译作 Award Evening。"媒体吹风会"译作 Media Briefing/Release 或 News Briefing。

5.2.3.4 "会议日程、议程"译作 Conference Agenda。"主旨演讲"译作 Keynote Speech。"开幕式/闭幕式致辞"译作 Opening/Closing Remarks。"欢迎辞"译作 Welcome/Welcoming Speech/Address。"答谢辞"译作 A Vote of Thanks 或 A Thank You Speech。

5.2.3.5 体育场馆的入场门应区分不同的情况采用不同的译法:以数字或字母命名的入场门用"Gate+阿拉伯数字或字母"的方式译写(见示例1)。以方位词命名的入场门用"方位词+Gate"的方式译写(见示例2)。

示例1:一号门 Gate 1;B口 Gate B

示例2:东门 East Gate

5.2.3.6 体育场馆的座位分区应区分不同的情况采用不同的译法:以数字或字母命名的分区用"Zone+阿拉伯数字或字母"或"Section+阿拉伯数字或字母"的方式译写(见示例1)。以方位词命名的分区用"方位词+Section"的方式译写(见示例2)。

示例1:一区 Zone 1或Section 1;B区 Zone B或Section B

示例2:东区 East Section

5.2.3.7 包含多个项目比赛的"综合性运动会"译作 Games 或 Sports Games。"单项运动比赛、邀请赛和锦标赛"等译作 Tournament 或 Championship。一个单位内部举行的"多项目综合性运动会"译作 Sports Meet。

5.2.3.8 其他会展赛事服务信息的译写示例见表C.2。体育运动项目和比赛名称的译写示例见表C.3。

5.2.4 医疗设施及功能信息

5.2.4.1 门诊部总称译作 Outpatient Department。住院部总称译作 Inpatient Department 或 Inpatient Ward。急诊部总称译作 Emergency Department。译写较大规模的门诊部、急诊部和住院部时可采用复数(见示例)。

示例:门诊部 Outpatient Departments

5.2.4.2 门诊部、急诊部的分科诊室宜译作 Department(见示例1)。住院部的分科病房或科室宜译作 Ward,也可译作 Department(见示例2)。

示例1:(门、急诊部)血液科 Hematology Department

示例2:(住院部)血液科 Hematology Ward 或 Hematology Department

5.2.4.3 门诊部、急诊部及分科诊室名称中的 Department 在用于指示处所时可省略,但在用于指示方位时应译出,如"血液科",在设置血液科诊室门口的标识时可简单译作 Hematology,但在设置于候诊区域指示血液科诊室所处方位的标识时则应完整译作 Hematology Department。如果是用于集中指示诊室等部门的标牌,如电梯指示牌等,则可省略 Department。

5.2.4.4 针对特殊疾病或特殊需求而设立的不同类别的门诊译作 Clinic,且不能省略(见示例1至3)。

示例1:发热门诊 Fever Clinic

示例2:专家门诊 Expert Clinic 或 Specialist Clinic

示例3:名医门诊 Famous Doctor Clinic

5.2.4.5 设施名称在英文中已习惯使用其缩写形式的,应采用相应的英文缩写(见示例)。

示例:耳鼻喉科 ENT Department

5.2.4.6 其他医疗卫生服务信息的译写示例见表 E.2。

5.2.5 通用类设施及功能信息

5.2.5.1 无障碍设施、残疾人专用设施可译作 Wheelchair Accessible、Accessible+具体设施或 Accessible+残疾人图标(见示例1至3)。

示例1:无障碍坡道 Wheelchair Accessible Ramp(Ramp 可以省略)

示例2:残疾人电梯 Accessible Elevator

示例3:残疾人专用设施 Accessible Facilities 或 Accessible+残疾人图标

5.2.5.2 厕所、洗手间、卫生间、盥洗室应根据不同场合采用不同译法。飞机和列车上的厕所或洗手间译作 Lavatory。公共厕所、洗手间或卫生间可译作 Toilet、Restroom 或 Washroom,但在同一场所内应保持统一。在导览图中用于标示男女厕所的位置时,Toilet、Restroom、Washroom 可使用复数。

5.2.5.3 男厕所可译作 Men 或 Gents。女厕所译作 Women 或 Ladies。第三卫生间译作 Family Restroom/Toilet,或省略为 Family。不同译法在同一场所内应保持统一。

5.2.5.4 其他通用类设施及功能信息的译写示例见表 H.1。

5.3 公共服务信息

5.3.1 总则

公共服务信息使用英文译写。

5.3.2 说明提示和指示指令信息

5.3.2.1 宜用祈使句或短语译写(见示例)。

示例:紧急时击碎玻璃 Break Glass in Emergency

5.3.2.2 由设施名称和指示信息两部分内容组成的语句,宜以译出指示信息为主,如"旅客通道,请勿滞留",其中"请勿滞留"必须译出,"旅客通道"可不必译出(见示例)。

示例:旅客通道,请勿滞留 Keep Walking 或 No Lingering/Loitering

5.3.2.3 安全保障设备应简要译出其使用方法(见示例)。

示例:求助按钮 Press for Help

5.3.2.4 应注意语气得当,如"请勿……"可用 Please Do Not...(见示例)。

示例:请勿触摸 Please Do Not Touch 或 Hands off

5.3.2.5 以译出功能信息为主,次要信息可省去不译(见示例1),或宜将需要采取的行动放前,理由或原因放后(见示例2)。

示例1:背包向前,文明你我(地铁车厢内使用) Wear backpacks on your front.

示例2:施工请绕行 Detour // Construction Ahead

注:"//"表示书写时应当换行的断行处。

5.3.2.6 直接关系人身和财产安全、需要强令执行的事项可使用 must 译写(见示例)。

示例:请勿让孩子独自搭乘电梯 Children must be accompanied by an adult.

5.3.2.7 含有否定意义的提示信息宜使用肯定句式译写(见示例)。

示例:衣冠不整者谢绝入内 Proper Attire Required

5.3.2.8 设置有监控设备的场所,应进行说明提示(见示例)。

示例:本商场设有视频监控 This Area Is Under Video Surveillance

5.3.3 警示警告信息

5.3.3.1 一般性警示宜用祈使句或短语译写，使用动词 Mind... 或 Watch... 或 Beware of...（见示例）。

示例：当心碰头 Mind Your Head

5.3.3.2 为强调可能导致人身伤害而语气较强的警示使用 CAUTION 译写（见示例）。

示例：小心烫伤（指开水）CAUTION // Hot Water

5.3.3.3 直接关系生命财产安全需引起高度注意的警示使用 WARNING 或 DANGER 译写（见示例）。

示例：当心触电 DANGER // High Voltage

5.3.3.4 应明确信息所警示、提示的对象主体（见示例）。

示例：旅游车辆禁止入内 No Admittance for Tourist Vehicles（不宜简单译作 No Admittance）

5.3.4 限令禁止信息

5.3.4.1 劝阻性的信息用 Please Do Not... 或 Thank You for Not v-ing 译写（见示例）。

示例：请勿打扰 Please Do Not Disturb

5.3.4.2 禁止性的信息用 Do Not... 或 No v-ing 或 ...Not Allowed 译写（见示例）。

示例：切勿酒后驾车 Do Not Drink and Drive

5.3.4.3 直接关系生命财产安全、需严令禁止的信息用 ... (be) Forbidden 或… (be) Prohibited 译写（见示例）。

示例：严禁携带危险物品上船 Dangerous articles are forbidden on board.

5.3.4.4 禁止停车应区分不同的情况采用不同的译法："禁止长时间停车"（但可临时停靠以让乘客上下车或装卸货物）译作 No Parking。"禁止临时停车、停留"译作 No Stopping。

5.3.4.5 其他通用类公共服务信息的译写示例见表H.2。

5.4 词语选用和拼写方法

5.4.1 同一场所中的词语选用和英文拼写应保持一致，如："剧场、剧院、舞台、戏院、戏苑"等可在 Theater 或 Theatre 中任选一种拼写；"卫生间"可在 Toilet

或 Restroom 中任选一个词语,但在同一场所内应该保持统一。

5.4.2 汉语拼音拼写应符合 GB/T 16159 和 GB 17733 的规定。约定俗成的人名和地名沿用原有拼写(见示例)。

示例:西湖 West Lake

5.5 语法和格式

5.5.1 冠词

可不使用冠词(见示例)。

示例:火警时按下 Press Button in Case of Fire

5.5.2 单复数

5.5.2.1 名词特指一类人或事物时,使用单数(见示例1),泛指时,使用复数(见示例2)。

示例1:医患沟通中心 Doctor-Patient Communication Center

示例2:意见箱 Suggestions & Complaints

5.5.2.2 可数名词用在指示处所的标志里宜用复数形式(见示例1),用在指示实物的标志里宜用单数形式(见示例2)。

示例1:当场票购票窗口 Rush Tickets

示例2:当场票 Rush Ticket

5.5.2.3 用交通工具名称指示乘车点或停车点方位的标志应用复数,不用单数(见示例)。GB/T 10001 对公共信息图形中英文单复数形式另有规定的,按该国家标准执行。

示例:Coaches (机场、火车站标识牌上用于指示长途车站)

5.5.2.4 车、船、机票应根据具体场合使用单复数形式,指示售票窗口的标志应用复数(见示例)。

示例:民航售票(厅) Airline Tickets

5.5.2.5 指示服务项目中的 Service 应根据服务项目的多少选择使用单数或复数,如"礼宾服务",只提供单一项目的服务时使用单数 Concierge Service,提供多项目的服务时使用复数 Concierge Services。

5.5.3 缩写

5.5.3.1 采用缩写形式应符合国际惯例。来自外来概念的中文缩略语,应使用外来概念原词的英文缩写(见示例)。

示例:快速公交(系统或车道) BRT

5.5.3.2 道路名中的通名和方位词可用英文缩写(见示例)。

示例:延安西路 Yan'an Rd (W);西湖大道 Xihu Ave

5.5.3.3 使用序数词的,可缩写为 1st、2nd 或 1st、2nd 等。

6 日文译写方法和要求

6.1 旅游景区景点信息

6.1.1 旅游景区景点需要用日文对其功能和性质予以解释。原则上专名部分转写为日文常用汉字,通名采用日文译写(见示例)。

示例:西湖(专名)隧道(通名) 西湖トンネル

6.1.2 如果日文中有相对应的同形同义的表述时,宜首选同形同义的日文表述。比如"山"在日文中有同形同意的日文表述,因此译写为"山"。

6.1.3 如果日文中没有同形同义的日文表述时,采用对应翻译(见示例)。

示例:步行街 步行者天国

6.1.4 如果日文中没有相对应的表述时,用与中文相对应的日文汉字进行标示并在后面加括号进行简单的说明(见示例)。

示例:牌坊 牌坊(記念アーチ、メモリアルアーチ)

6.1.5 其他旅游景区景点名称的译写示例见表 I.1。

6.2 公共旅游服务设施信息

6.2.1 公共旅游服务设施信息需要用日文对其功能和性质予以解释,宜采用日文直接译写(见示例)。

示例:售票窗口 チケット販売窓口

6.2.2 少部分公共旅游服务设施根据日文习惯以表达信息的方式译写(见示例)。

示例:手机充电处 充電スポット

6.2.3 宜保持统一原则。比如"售票窗口"中的"票"在日文中既可译写为

"チケット"，也可译写为"切符"。本书附录中与"票"有关的译写全部使用"チケット"一词。

6.2.4 其他旅游服务设施的译写示例见表 I.2。

6.3 公共旅游服务相关告知、提示及警示类信息

6.3.1 告知类信息用日文直接译写，在表达信息核心内容的前提下，宜保持译文简洁（见示例）。

示例：残疾人服务　障がい者向けサービス

6.3.2 提示及警示类信息用日文直接译写，结合使用环境，在表达信息核心内容的前提下，宜保持译文简洁（见示例）。

示例：不准擅入（观众止步、请勿入内、游人止步）立ち入り禁止

6.3.3 警示类信息分为建议、提倡类信息、提示类信息、警示类信息以及一般性劝阻类信息、限令禁止类信息等。属于建议和提倡类信息的，宜用"ましょう"或"お（ご）—ください"的形式来译写（见示例1）。属于提示类信息的，宜译写为"ご注意ください"（见示例2）。属于警示类信息的，宜采用"必ずお（ご）-ください"的形式译写（见示例3）。属于一般性劝阻类信息的，宜译写为"—ないでください"或"ご遠慮ください"（见示例4）。属于限令禁止类信息的，宜译写为"禁止"或"お断りします"（见示例5）。译写时，在上述基础上同时也需考虑日文的使用习惯。

示例1：爱护树木　木を大切にしましょう（为保持译文简洁也可省略为"木を大切に"）

示例2：注意脚下　足元にご注意ください（为保持译文简洁也可省略为"足元に注意"）

示例3：请务必戴头盔　必ずヘルメットをご着用ください

示例4：请不要进入草坪　芝生に入らないでください

示例5：禁止拍照　撮影禁止

6.3.4 其他告知、提示和警示信息的译写示例见表 I.3。

7 韩文译写方法和要求

7.1 旅游景区景点信息

7.1.1 景区景点需要用韩文对其功能和性质予以解释。景区景点名称的专名采用韩文汉字音译写,通名采用韩文常用词汇译写,包括韩文中的汉字词和固有词(见示例1至5)。

示例1:西湖 서호

示例2:灵隐寺 영은사

示例3:德寿宫 덕수궁

示例4:茶俗体验街区 차 풍속 체험 거리

示例5:烈士陵园 열사 묘역

7.1.2 如果在韩文中常用汉字词表达,则首选汉字词进行译写(见示例1至5)。

示例1:山 산

示例2:河、桥、峰分别为하、교、봉

示例3:龙山河 용산하

示例4:拱宸桥 공신교

示例5:飞来峰 비래봉

7.1.3 如果仅用韩文汉字词进行表述,意思不够明确时,可在汉字词后加括号进行补充解释,也可直接采用释义性翻译(见示例1至2)。

示例1:故居 고거(옛집, 고택, 생가);胡雪岩故居 호설암 옛집

示例2:纤道 염도(배 끄는 인부 전용 도로);雷家桥古纤道 뇌가교 옛 염도(배 끄는 인부 전용 도로)

7.1.4 如果韩文中没有对应的汉字词或者使用汉字词容易产生歧义,则直接进行释义性翻译(见示例1至2)。

示例1:弄、巷均为골목;吉祥寺弄 길상사 골목

示例2:清真寺 이슬람교 사원;杭州清真寺 항주 이슬람교 사원

7.1.5 其他旅游景区景点的译写示例见表J.1。

7.2 公共旅游服务设施信息

7.2.1 公共旅游设施服务信息需要用韩文对其功能和性质予以解释,采用韩文常用的表达进行译写(见示例1至4)。

示例1:宾馆 호텔

示例2:停车场 주차장

示例3:售票口 매표소

示例4:观光船 유람선

7.2.2 部分词汇虽有对应的韩文表达,但在韩文中有更常用的外来词汇时,首选更常用的外来词汇进行译写(见示例1至3)。

示例1:餐饮区 푸드코트

示例2:度假村 리조트

示例3:亲子区 키즈존

7.2.3 部分公共旅游服务设施信息根据韩文的表达习惯,可采取解释或增译的方式进行译写(见示例1至2)。

示例1:开水间 뜨거운 물 받는 곳

示例2:行李提取 짐 찾는 곳

7.2.4 其他公共旅游服务设施信息的译写示例见表 J.2。

7.3 公共旅游相关告知、提示及警示类信息

7.3.1 告知类信息按照韩文常用表达方式直接译写,在表达信息核心内容的前提下,宜保持译文简洁(见示例1至3)。

示例1:残疾人服务 장애인 서비스

示例2:故障 수리 중

示例3:欢迎光临 어서 오세요.

7.3.2 涉及"请勿……、禁止……"等限令类信息时,根据具体语境可采用"-지 마세요"的敬语方式或者更为简洁的"...금지"进行译写。部分限令禁止类信息根据韩文的表达习惯,应改为提示类信息进行译写。

示例:此处不准遛狗 애완견 산책 금지 구역입니다.

7.3.3 涉及"请……"等提示及警示类信息时,可采用"-아/어/여 세요"或者

"-아/어/여 주십시오"의 形式译写。但考虑到简洁性原则,宜首选前者(见示例1至2)。

示例1:请系好安全带 안전벨트를 착용하세요.

示例2:先下后上 승객이 내린 후에 승차하세요.

7.3.4 涉及建议或提倡类信息时可采用"-ㅂ시다/읍시다"的敬语方式或者更为礼貌的"-아/어/여 주시기 바랍니다"。但考虑到简洁性原则,宜首选前者(见示例)。

示例:请爱护洞内景观 동굴 내 경물을 보호합시다.

7.3.5 根据韩文常用表达方式及前后用词(汉字词、固有词)的搭配与简洁性原则,部分提示和警示类信息采用删掉语尾的方式进行译写(见示例1至2)。

示例1:请保持整洁 청결 유지

示例2:可以信用卡支付 신용카드 사용 가능

7.3.6 其他告知、提示和警示信息的译写示例见表J.3。

8 英文书写要求

8.1 总则

公共服务领域中场所和机构名称、设施及功能信息、公共服务信息的英文书写应符合英语国家公共标识中的书写规范和使用习惯。英文大小写、标点符号、字体、空格、换行等的用法应符合GB/T 30240.1—2013中的要求。

8.2 大小写

8.2.1 短语、短句字母全部大写或者所有单词的首字母大写(见示例)。

示例:下车通道,请勿站人　EXIT // KEEP CLEAR 或 Exit // Keep Clear

8.2.2 句子中第一个单词的首字母应大写(见示例1),或所有实义词和4个及以上字母组成的虚词首字母应大写(见示例2)。

示例1:严禁携带易燃易爆等危险品进站 Flammable, explosive and other dangerous articles are prohibited.

示例2:请随手关灯 Turn off Lights Before You Leave

8.2.3 需要特别强调的警示性、提示性独词句,字母全部大写(见示例)。

示例:禁止通行 STOP

8.2.4 依据国际惯例,独词路标的英文可全部大写(见示例)。

示例:绕行 DETOUR

8.2.5 由警示语和警示内容两部分组成的语句,警示语字母全部大写(见图1)。

涌潮危险!
DANGER!
Tidal Surge.

图1

8.2.6 使用连字符"-"连接两个单词时,连字符后面的单词如果是实词则其首字母大写,如果是虚词则其首字母小写(见示例)。

示例:送货上门(直销) Door-to-Door Delivery

8.3 标点符号

8.3.1 宜不使用标点符号。但长句结尾处可用英文点号,并且全句首词的首字母大写,其余单词首字母不大写(见示例1)。分句或平行短语之间应使用逗号(见示例2)。如前面的分句或短语使用了标点符号,后面的分句和短语也应使用点号(见示例3)。

示例1:遛狗要牵绳,粪便及时清。 Please leash and clean up after your dog.

示例2:严禁携带易燃、易爆、有毒物等违禁品 Flammable, Explosive, Poisonous and Other Illegal Articles Strictly Prohibited

示例3:前面施工,请绕行 Construction Ahead. Detour.

8.3.2 需要加以警示、强调时可使用感叹号。感叹号后面如跟有短语或句子,短语或句子后使用英文点号(见示例)。

示例:请勿靠近,有电危险 Keep Out! Hazardous Voltage Inside.

8.3.3 作为缩写形式的 St、Rd、Hwy、Expwy 等道路称谓和 E、W、S、N 方向词的后面统一不加"."。

8.4 空格

8.4.1 单词内部的字母之间不空格。单词与单词之间空一格。道路指示牌上英文单词的位置不必与相关的汉字一一对应,而应按照英文书写要求保持英文单词之间正确的间隔。

8.4.2 地名、道路名等中的专名在使用汉语拼音字母拼写时,应以词或语节为单位使用空格(见示例)。

示例:紫之隧道 Zizhi Tunnel

8.4.3 英文的逗号、点号、感叹号、分号后须空一格,双引号前后须空一格。

8.4.4 撇号(')出现在一个单词中间时前后均不空格(见示例1)。出现在词末时,后空一格(见示例2)。

示例1:旅客的车票(单数) Passenger's Ticket

示例2:女子高中 Girls' High School

8.4.5 汉语拼音中以 a、o、e 开头的零声母音节连接在其他音节后面时,将隔音符号(')标在音节开头字母 a、o、e 的左上方,该符号前后不加空格(见示例)。

示例:淳安 Chun'an

8.4.6 连字符"-"前后不空格。

8.5 换行

8.5.1 宜不换行。但由警示语和警示内容两部分组成的语句,警示语和警示内容可分行书写。

8.5.2 按8.2.2大写规则书写的标识语如需换行,断行时应保持单词以及意群的完整,在两个意群之间断行。句子换行后行首单词的首字母不大写(见图2)。实义词首字母均大写的标识语换行后,行首虚词的首字母应大写(见图3)。

Please lock and secure your vehicle
and remove all valuables.

图2

图 3

8.5.3 需要换行的长句排版时不应使用两端对齐。

9 日文书写要求

9.1 总则

9.1.1 日文书写应符合日本公共标识中的书写规范和使用习惯。

9.2 日文汉字

9.2.1 日文汉字一律不标注读音。

9.3 标点符号

9.3.1 宜不使用标点符号,但长句可使用。

9.4 换行

9.4.1 宜不换行。

10 韩文书写要求

10.1 总则

10.1.1 韩文书写应符合韩国公共标识中的书写规范和使用习惯。按照韩国文化体育观光部《韩文书写法》正文及附录中的规定进行韩文书写。

10.2 空格

10.2.1 遵守韩文空格书写规则,必要时名词词组可不空格。词与词之间可空格也可不空格时,宜采用不空格方式,但在同一场所内应保持统一。

附录 A

（资料性）

交通服务信息英文译写示例

A.1 道路交通设施及服务信息英文译写示例见表A.1。表A.1按中文汉语拼音排序。

表 A.1　道路交通设施及服务信息英文译写示例

序号	中文	英文
	A	
1	安全岛；交通岛	Island 或 Refuge Island 或 Pedestrian Refuge
	B	
2	傍山险路	Steep Mountain Road 或 Cliff Road
3	保持车距	Keep Distance 或 Keep a Safe Distance
4	避让行人	Yield to Pedestrians
5	避险车道	Truck Escape Ramp
6	标线	Marking
7	步行道	Walkway
	C	
8	超车道	Passing Lane〔美语〕 或 Overtaking Lane〔英语〕
9	超限检测站	Weigh Station
10	潮汐车道	Tidal Lane/Lanes〔视车道数选用〕 或 Reversible Lane/Lanes〔视车道数选用〕
11	长下坡慢行	Slow Down // Long Descent

序号	中文	英文
12	车道封闭	Lane Closed
13	车道数变少	Fewer Lanes Ahead
14	车道数增加	More Lanes Ahead
15	车距确认	Check Your Following Distance
16	车辆慢行	SLOW 或 Slow Down
17	车辆绕行	Detour
18	车辆上下客区	Passenger Pick-up and Drop-off Area〔Area 可以省略〕
19	车站控制室	Station Control Room
20	城市道路	Urban Road
21	乘客服务中心	Passenger Service Center
22	除公共汽车外(其他车辆不得进入或停靠)	Buses Only 或 Except Buses
23	此道临时封闭	Temporarily Closed
24	此路不通	No Through Road 或 Dead End
25	此路封闭	Road Closed
26	村庄	Village
27	错车道	Passing Bay
	D	
28	大型车靠右	Large Vehicles Keep Right
29	单行路(直行、向左或向右)	One Way〔需标示单行路"直行""向左"或"向右"方向时,使用此译文并辅以相应箭头图形符号〕
30	道路变窄;车道变窄	Road Narrows

序号	中文	英文
31	道路封闭;此路封闭	Road Closed
32	道路交通信息	Traffic Information
33	堤坝路	Embankment Road
34	地面道路	Ground-Level Road
35	地面交通	Ground Transportation
36	地下通道;高架桥下通道	Underpass
37	电动汽车充电站	EV Charging Station
38	电子收费(通道)	ETC Lane〔Lane 可以省略〕 或 Electronic Toll Collection
39	掉头车道	U-Turn Lane〔Lane 可以省略〕
40	掉头和左转合用车道	Left or U-Turn Lane〔Lane 可以省略〕
41	丁字交叉路口	〔使用图形标志,见 GB 5768.2〕
42	陡坡	Steep Descent Ahead
43	陡坡减速;陡坡慢行	Slow Down // Steep Descent
44	多乘员(专用)车道	HOV Lane 或 Carpools Only 或 Car Pools Only
45	多雾路段	Foggy Area
	F	
46	反向弯路	Reverse Curve
47	非机动车车道	Non-Motor Vehicle Lane 或 Non-Motor Vehicles〔用于 Lane 可以省略的场合〕
48	非机动车行驶	Non-Motor Vehicles Only
49	分向行驶车道	Road Divides Ahead

序号	中文	英文
50	辅路	Relief Road 或 Side Road
	G	
51	干路先行	Yield to Main Road Traffic
52	高架道路(快速路)	Elevated Road/Expwy 或 Elevated Highway 或 Expressway 或 Expwy
53	高架桥	Overpass〔指城市中的高架桥〕〔美语〕 或 Flyover〔英语〕 Viaduct〔指横跨河流或山谷的高架桥〕
54	(高速公路)服务区	Service Area
55	公共汽车优先	Bus Priority
56	公交车道	Bus Lane 或 Buses Only〔用于 Lane 可以省略的场合〕
57	公路	Highway
58	国道	National Highway
59	过水路面	Low Water Crossing 或 Low Level Crossing
	H	
60	横路	Cross Road
61	环岛;环形交叉路口	Roundabout
62	环岛行驶	Roundabout
63	会车让行	Give Way to Oncoming Vehicles
64	会车先行	Priority Over Oncoming Vehicles
65	货车	Trucks〔美语〕 或 Lorries〔英语〕

序号	中文	英文
	J	
66	机动车	Motor Vehicles
67	机动车车道	Motor Vehicle Lane 或 Motor Vehicles〔用于 Lane 可以省略的场合〕
68	机动车行驶	Motor Vehicles Only
69	急弯路	Sharp Bend/Curve
70	计重收费	Toll-by-Weight
71	加气站	Natural Gas Station 或 Gas Station
72	加油站	Petrol/Gas/Service/Filling Station 〔在同一场所内应保持统一〕
73	驾培学校	Driving School
74	驾驶考试路线	Driving Test Route
75	减速带;减速路面;减速丘	Speed Bumps/Humps
76	减速让行	YIELD
77	建议速度:____千米/小时(千米/小时可以省略) 前方有拍照	Speed Limit: _____ km/h // Photo Enforced Ahead〔km/h 可以省略〕 或 Suggested Speed: _____ km/h // Photo Enforced Ahead〔km/h 可以省略〕
78	交叉路口	Crossroads 或 Intersection
79	交通监控设备	Traffic Surveillance
80	交通信号灯	Traffic Lights
81	教练车行驶路线	Learner Driver Training Route
82	解除禁止超车	END // No-Overtaking Zone 或 End of No-Overtaking Zone

序号	中文	英文
83	解除限制速度:____千米/小时	End // ____ km/h Speed Limit
84	紧急电话	Emergency Call
85	紧急停车带	Emergency Stop Area
86	谨防追尾	WARNING // Rear End Collision
87	禁止超车	No Overtaking
88	禁止超高	Do Not Exceed Height Limit
89	禁止超速	No Speeding 或 Do Not Exceed Speed Limit
90	禁止超越;禁止越线	Stay in Lane
91	禁止超载	Do Not Overload 或 Do Not Exceed Weight Limit
92	禁止大型客车驶入	No Large Buses
93	禁止电动三轮车驶入	No Electric Tricycles
94	禁止掉头	No U-Turn
95	禁止二轮摩托车驶入	No Motorcycles
96	禁止非机动车驶入	Motor Vehicles Only 或 No Entry for Non-Motor Vehicles
97	禁止挂车、半挂车驶入	No Trailers or Semi-Trailers
98	禁止行人进入	No Pedestrians
99	禁止货车及小型客车直行	No Straight Thru for Trucks or Minibuses
100	禁止机动车驶入	No Motor Vehicles
101	禁止酒后开车	Do Not Drink and Drive 或 Driving After Drinking Is Prohibited by Law
102	禁止开车使用手机	Do Not Use Cellphone While Driving

序号	中文	英文
103	禁止鸣喇叭	No Honking 或 Do Not Honk
104	禁止摩托车驶入	No Motorcycles
105	禁止某两种车驶入	No Entry for _____ and _____
106	禁止疲劳驾驶	Do Not Drive Tired
107	禁止骑自行车下坡	Do Not Cycle Downhill
108	禁止汽车拖、挂车驶入	No Trailers
109	禁止三轮机动车驶入	No Motor Tricycles
110	禁止三轮汽车、低速货车驶入	No Tricars or Low-Speed Motor Vehicles
111	禁止驶入	Do Not Enter 或 No Entry
112	禁止停车	No Stopping 或 No Stopping at Any Time
113	禁止通道两侧停车	No Parking on Either Side
114	禁止通行	Do Not Enter 或 No Entry
115	禁止拖拉机驶入	No Tractors
116	禁止向右转弯	No Right Turn
117	禁止向左向右转弯	No Left or Right Turn 或 No Turns
118	禁止向左转弯	No Left Turn
119	禁止小型客车驶入	No Minibuses
120	禁止小型客车右转	No Right Turn for Minibuses
121	禁止运输危险物品车辆驶入	Vehicles Carrying Hazardous Materials Prohibited

序号	中文	英文
122	禁止载货货车和拖拉机向左向右转弯	No Left or Right Turn for Trucks or Tractors 或 No Turns for Trucks or Tractors
123	禁止载货货车及拖拉机左转弯	No Left Turn for Trucks or Tractors
124	禁止载货货车左转	No Left Turn for Trucks
125	禁止载货汽车驶入	No Trucks
126	禁止长时停车	No Parking
127	禁止直行	No Straight Thru
128	禁止直行和向右转弯	No Straight Thru or Right Turn
129	禁止直行和向左转弯	No Straight Thru or Left Turn
130	救援电话	First Aid Call
	K	
131	卡车停靠点	Truck Parking Only 或 Trucks Only
132	靠右侧道路行驶	Keep Right
133	靠左侧道路行驶	Keep Left
134	快速公交系统专用车道	Bus Rapid Transit Lane 或 BRT Lane 或 BRT Only〔用于 Lane 可以省略的场合〕
	L	
135	里街	Inner Street
136	立交桥(车行)	Highway Interchange〔Highway 可以省略〕 或 Flyover〔英语〕 或 Overpass〔美语〕
137	立体交叉直行和右转弯行驶	Overpass Ahead // Straight or Right Turn
138	立体交叉直行和左转弯行驶	Overpass Ahead // Straight or Left Turn

序号	中文	英文
139	连续弯路	Winding Road Ahead 或 Curves Ahead
140	连续下坡	Long Descent
141	两侧变窄	Road Narrows on Both Sides
142	两侧通行	Pass on Either Side
143	林荫大道;风景区干道	Parkway
144	临时停车	Temporary Parking
145	＿＿路与＿＿路路口	＿＿ Rd and ＿＿ Rd Intersection/Crossing 或＿＿ Rd and ＿＿ Rd
146	路侧停车点	Roadside Parking
147	路口优先通行	Priority at Intersection
148	路面不平	Rough Road Ahead
149	路面低洼	Low-Lying Road Ahead
150	路面高突	Bumpy Road Ahead 或 Humps Ahead
	M	
151	慢行	Slow Down 或 Slow
152	免费通行	Toll Free
153	鸣喇叭;鸣笛	Honk
	P	
154	爬坡车道	Climbing Lane
155	爬坡车道结束	End of Climbing Lane
156	平稳驾驶,注意安全	Drive Safely

序号	中文	英文
	Q	
157	汽车修理	Garage 或 Auto Repair 或 Automobile Maintenance
158	汽车租赁	Car Rental
159	前方出口	Exit Ahead
160	前方____米进入无路 灯路段	No Road Lights ____ m Ahead
161	前方服务区	Service Area Ahead
162	前方路面不平	Rough Road Ahead
163	前方桥低	Low Bridge Ahead
164	前方施工	Road Work Ahead
165	前方弯道	Curve Ahead
166	前方弯路慢行	SLOW // Bend Ahead 或 Bend Ahead // Slow Down
167	前方学校,减速慢行	Slow Down // School Ahead
168	前方拥堵	Congestion Ahead
169	前方有事故,减速行驶	Slow Down // Accident Ahead
170	前方右侧绕行	Detour Ahead Right 或 Detour Right
171	前方右急转弯	Sharp Right Turn Ahead
172	前方左侧绕行	Detour Ahead Left 或 Detour Left
173	前方左急转弯	Sharp Left Turn Ahead
174	前方左右绕行	Detour Ahead Left or Right

序号	中文	英文
175	桥梁	Bridge
176	请按车道行驶;分道行驶	Stay in Lane
177	区域禁止停车	No Stopping in This Area
178	区域禁止停车解除	END // No Stopping Zone 或 End of No Stopping Zone
179	区域禁止长时停车	No Parking in This Area
180	区域禁止长时停车解除	End // No Parking Zone 或 End of No Parking Zone
181	区域限制速度:____千米/小时	____ km/h // Speed Zone
182	区域限制速度解除:____千米/小时	END // ____ km/h // Speed Zone 或 End of ____ km/h Speed Limit
	R	
183	让车道	Yield Lane
184	绕城公路;环路	Beltway 或 Ring Road
185	绕行	Detour
186	人工(收费)通道(用于收费站)	Manual Lane 或 Attended Lane
187	人行道	Sidewalk〔美语〕 或 Pedestrians〔英语〕
188	人行道封闭	Sidewalk Closed
189	人行地下通道	Underpass 或 Pedestrian Underpass
190	人行过街,请走天桥	Please Use the Footbridge
191	人行横道(线)	Pedestrian Crossing
192	人行天桥;天桥	Footbridge 或 Pedestrian Overpass 或 Overpass

序号	中文	英文
193	入口预告	Entrance Ahead
194	软基路段	Weak Subgrade 或 Soft Roadbed
195	软路肩	Soft Shoulder
	S	
196	省道	Provincial Highway
197	施工;道路作业	Road Work
198	施工请绕行	Detour // Construction Ahead
199	十字交叉路口	〔使用图形标志,见 GB 5768.2〕
200	市区(指示市区方向)	To City 或 To Downtown
201	事故易发路段	CAUTION // Accident Black Spot
202	收费停车场	Pay Parking
203	收费站	Toll Station 或 Toll Gate
204	双向交通	Two-Way Traffic
205	隧道	Tunnel
206	隧道开车灯	Turn on Headlights Before Entering Tunnel
	T	
207	塌方	Landslide
208	特殊天气建议速度	Suggested Speed Under Special Weather
209	铁路道口	Railway Crossing
210	停车场收费处	Parking Booth
211	停车港湾	Parking Bay

序号	中文	英文
212	停车检查;停车接受检查	Stop for Inspection
213	停车领卡	Stop for Toll Card
214	停车让行	STOP
215	停车位	Parking Space
216	驼峰桥	Camel-Back Bridge 或 Hump-Back Bridge 或 Hump Bridge
217	拖拉机	Tractors
	W	
218	弯道建议速度：____千米/小时	Suggested Speed on Curves: ____ km/h 或 KMH
219	往地铁站(指示地铁站方向)	To Metro
220	未经允许货车禁止通行	No Trucks Unless Authorized
221	无路灯路段全长____米	No Road Lights Next ____m
222	无人看守铁道路口	Unguarded Railway Crossing
	X	
223	行人绕行	Pedestrians Detour
224	洗车	Car/Auto Wash
225	下一出口预告	Next Exit
226	县道	County Highway
227	限制高度：____米	Maximum Clearance: ____ m
228	限制宽度：____米	Maximum Width: ____ m

序号	中文	英文
229	限制速度：____千米/小时	Speed Limit: ____ km/h 或 KMH
230	限制质量：____吨	Weight Limit: ____ t
231	限制轴重：____吨	Axle Weight Limit: ____ t
232	向前200米	200 Meters Ahead
233	向右急转弯路	Sharp Curve to Right
234	向右转弯	Turn Right
235	向左和向右转弯	Turn Left or Right
236	向左急转弯路	Sharp Curve to Left
237	向左转弯	Turn Left
238	小心滑坡	Landslide Hazard Area
239	小心驾驶	Drive with Caution
240	小心雪天路滑	Road May Be Icy
241	校车停靠站点	School Bus Stop
242	休息区	Rest Area
243	学校	School
	Y	
244	易滑	CAUTION // Slippery Surface
245	应急车道	Emergency Lane
246	硬路肩	Hard Shoulder
247	有人看守铁道路口	Guarded Railway Crossing
248	右侧变窄	Road Narrows on Right

序号	中文	英文
249	右侧通行	Keep Right
250	右转车道	Right-Turn Lane〔Lane可以省略〕
251	雨雪天气请慢行	Drive Slowly in Rain or Snow
252	允许掉头	U-Turn
	Z	
253	窄路	Narrow Road
254	窄桥	Narrow Bridge
255	支路	Feeder Road〔支路;公路支线〕 Slip Road〔与快车道或高速公路相连的支路〕 Branch Road 或 Access Road〔进入某处的通道〕
256	直街	Straight Street
257	直行	Go Straight
258	直行车道	Straight Lane〔Lane可以省略〕
259	直行和向右转弯	Straight or Right Turn
260	直行和向左转弯	Straight or Left Turn
261	直行和右转合用车道	Straight and Right-Turn Lane〔Lane可以省略〕
262	直行和左转合用车道	Straight and Left-Turn Lane〔Lane可以省略〕
263	注意保持车距	Keep Distance
264	注意残疾人	Yield to People with Disabilities
265	注意潮汐车道	Reversible Lane Ahead〔车道有多条时应使用复数Lanes〕
266	注意动物	Watch for Animals 或 Yield to Animals

序号	中文	英文
267	注意儿童	Watch for Children
268	注意非机动车	Watch for Non-Motor Vehicles
269	注意分离式道路	Split Road Ahead
270	注意行人	Watch for Pedestrians
271	注意合流	Roads Merge 或 Lanes Merge
272	注意横风	Beware of Crosswind
273	注意火车	Beware of Trains
274	注意路面结冰	CAUTION // Icy Road
275	注意落石	DANGER // Falling Rocks
276	注意前方车辆排队	Queues Likely
277	注意前方人行横道	Pedestrian Crossing Ahead
278	注意牲畜	Watch for Livestock
279	注意危险	Drive with Caution
280	注意雾天	Drive Carefully in Foggy Weather
281	注意信号灯	Traffic Lights Ahead
282	注意雨雪天气	Drive Carefully in Rain or Snow
283	注意障碍物	Watch out for Obstacles 或 CAUTION // Obstacles Ahead
284	____专用(车)道	____ Only Lane/Lanes〔视车道数选用；Lane 可以省略〕
285	转弯慢行	Slow Down // Turn Ahead
286	最低限速:____千米/小时	Minimum Speed:____ km/h 或 KMH
287	左侧变窄	Road Narrows on Left

序号	中文	英文
288	左侧通行	Keep Left
289	左转车道	Left-Turn Lane〔Lane可以省略〕

注1:"〔　〕"中的内容是对英文译法的解释说明。

注2:"/"表示可选择该组词语中的一种。

注3:"//"表示书写时应当换行的断行处。需要同行书写时"//"应改为句点".",警示词后加惊叹号"!"。

注4:"___"表示使用时应根据实际情况填入具体内容。

注5:"或"前后所列出的不同译法可任意选择一种使用。

注6:解释说明中指出某个词"可以省略"的,省略该词的译文只能用于设置在该设施上的标志中,如"应急车道"应译作 Emergency Lane,在设置于该车道上的标志中可以省略 Lane,译作 Emergency。

A.2 公共交通服务信息英文译写示例见表 A.2。表 A.2 按中文汉语拼音排序。

表 A.2　公共交通服务信息英文译写示例

序号	中文	英文
	A	
1	IC卡查询业务	IC Card Inquiry Service
2	爱心专座(用于车厢内)	Courtesy Seating/Seat 或 Priority Seat 或 Reserved Seating/Seat
3	"XX"站首末车时间	First/Last Train from "XX" Station〔用于地铁〕 First/Last Bus from "XX" Stop/Station〔用于公共汽车〕
4	"XX"站综合资讯图	"XX" Station Information
5	安检执勤	Security Supervision
6	安全出口	Exit

序号	中文	英文
7	安全出口,请勿阻塞	Exit // Please Do Not Block
8	安全检查；安全检查通道:请接受安全检查	Security Check
9	安全设备,请勿擅动	Safety Equipment // Authorized Use Only
	B	
10	班车乘车地点	Shuttle Bus Pick-up Point〔Point可省略〕或 Commuter Bus Pick-up Point〔Point可省略〕
11	班车服务	Shuttle Bus Service 或 Commuter Bus Service
12	办理乘机手续	Check-in
13	办理国际登机手续	International Check-in
14	办理国内登机手续	Domestic Check-in
15	办理临时身份证明	Temporary-ID Service
16	办票;票务	Ticket Services 或 Ticketing
17	半价	Half Fare
18	本班列车停止服务。请等候下一班列车。（地铁广播）	This train will be taken out of service. Please wait for the next train.
19	本班列车已经抵达终点站,请所有乘客带齐您的随身物品下车,多谢搭乘杭港地铁。（地铁广播）	This is the terminal station. Please take all your belongings with you and exit from the train. Thank you for taking Hangzhou Metro.
20	本班列车已经十分拥挤,请等候下一班列车。（地铁广播）	This train is very crowded. Please wait for the next train.

序号	中文	英文
21	本站部分照明发生故障,请您注意安全,如需帮助,请及时联系工作人员。（地铁广播）	Your attention, please! There is a power supply problem. Please remain calm and ask station staff if you need assistance.
22	本站的列车服务已经恢复正常。	Train service from this station is now normal.
23	本站因客流较多,须采取临时限流措施,请您配合我们的工作,耐心排队等候或选择其他交通工具,不便之处,敬请谅解。（地铁广播）	Crowd management plans are now in place as the station is very busy. Please be patient and wait, or use other transport. We apologize for any inconvenience this might cause.
24	本站因设备故障停止售票,请使用储值卡或电子支付方式进站,不便之处,敬请谅解。（地铁广播）	The ticket vending machines are not in use because of a technical fault. Please use stored value tickets or scan a QR code to enter. We apologize for any inconvenience this might cause.
25	本站因设备故障无法刷卡进站/出站,请您听从工作人员的指挥有序进站/出站,不便之处,敬请谅解。（地铁广播）	The entry/exit gates are not in use because of a technical fault. Please follow our staff's directions to enter/exit the station. We apologize for any inconvenience this might cause.
26	本站运营即将结束,现停止进站乘车,请您换乘其他交通工具,谢谢配合!（地铁广播）	Train service for today has ended. Please leave the station and use other transport. Thank you.
27	必须系安全带	Seat Belt Must Be Fastened 或 Fasten Safety Belt
28	边防检查;边检	Immigration Inspection
29	边检民警 为您服务	Immigration Officers at Your Service

序号	中文	英文
30	边检咨询	Immigration Information
31	步行____米,约____分钟(用于机场航站楼、车站等地)	About/Approx ____ Meters & ____ Minutes' Walk
	C	
32	餐车	Dining Car
33	厕所(飞机或列车上)	Lavatory
34	厕所位于"X出口"(用于地铁站内)	Toilets at Exit X
35	插入公共交通卡	Insert Your Public Transportation Card
36	超大行李	Oversize Baggage/Luggage
37	超大行李托运处	Oversized Baggage/Luggage Check-in
38	超规行李	Excess Baggage/Luggage
39	超规行李登记	Oversize and Overweight Baggage/Luggage Check-in
40	超重行李	Overweight Baggage/Luggage
41	长途汽车	Coach〔英语〕 或 Long Distance Bus〔美语〕
42	长途汽车站	Coach Station/Terminal〔英语〕 或 Long Distance Bus Station〔美语〕
43	车门关闭 请勿上下车	Do not exit or board when doors are closing.
44	车门将延时打开,不便之处,敬请谅解。(地铁广播)	There will be a short delay before the train doors open. We apologize for any inconvenience this might cause.
45	车内发生紧急情况时,请按按钮报警。	Press Button in Case of Emergency 或 Press the button in case of emergency.

序号	中文	英文
46	车厢里严禁饮食	Eating or drinking is not allowed on trains.
47	车站出入口、车站和车厢里严禁摆卖或行乞	Hawking or begging is not allowed in the metro system.
48	车站大厅	Station Concourse/Hall
49	车站和车厢里严禁抽烟	Smoking is not allowed in stations or on trains.
50	乘客专用	For Passengers Only
51	持IC卡乘客,请上车刷卡	Swipe Your Card Here 或 Swipe Your IC Card 或 Swipe Your Transport Card Here 〔如是非接触式的,Swipe 改为 Tap〕
52	冲水(用于厕所抽水马桶)	Flush
53	充值、储值(地铁站内使用)	Value-Adding 或 Top up
54	充值机	Add-Value Machine 或 Top-up Machine
55	出发大厅	Departures Hall/Lounge 或 Departures
56	出发航班信息	Departure Flight Information〔可简作 Departure Flights 或 Departure Information 或 Departures〕
57	出境登记卡	Departure Card
58	出口请慢行	Slow Down at Exit
59	出站检查;出站验票	Exit Ticket Check
60	出租车	Taxi
61	出租车发票	Taxi Receipt
62	出租车计价器	Taxi Meter

序号	中文	英文
63	出租车起步价;起步费	Flag-Down Fare 或 Base Fare 或 Initial Fare
64	出租车投诉电话	Taxi Service Complaints Hotline
65	出租车扬招点;出租车停靠站;出租车停车点	Taxi Stand〔美语〕 或 Taxi Rank〔英语〕 或 Taxi 〔在同一场所内应保持统一〕
66	出租车预约电话	Taxi Booking
67	磁卡票	Magnetic Card Tickets
68	此票不能使用(检票机上提示信息)	This Ticket Is Invalid 或 Ticket Invalid
69	从早上6:00到晚上6:30,每10分钟一班(车)	6:00 am – 6:30 pm // Departing Every 10 Minutes
	D	
70	大件行李	Large Baggage/Luggage
71	当心火车	Beware of Trains 或 Watch out for Train
72	当心悬空高压电缆	DANGER! // Live Wires Overhead
73	当心站台空隙	Mind the Gap
74	到达出口	Exit for Arrivals
75	到达大厅	Arrivals Hall/Lounge 或 Arrivals
76	到达航班信息	Arrival Flight Information〔可简作 Arrival Flights 或 Arrival Information 或 Arrivals〕
77	到达时间	Arrival Time
78	灯亮铃响,请勿上下车。	No boarding or disembarking while the light is flashing and the bell is ringing.

序号	中文	英文
79	登机	Boarding
80	登机口	Gate
81	登机桥	Boarding Bridge
82	登机信息	Boarding Information
83	一等座	First Class
84	地铁	Metro
85	地铁 _____ 号线	Metro Line _____
86	地铁换乘查询	Metro Transfer Information
87	地铁换乘站	Transfer Station〔美语〕 或 Interchange Station〔英语或欧洲用法〕
88	（地铁进/出口） 南 1、2、3、4……口 北 1、2、3、4……口 东 1、2、3、4……口 西 1、2、3、4……口	South Entrance/Exit 1, 2, 3, 4... North Entrance/Exit 1, 2, 3, 4... East Entrance/Exit 1, 2, 3, 4... West Entrance/Exit 1, 2, 3, 4...
89	地铁人工售票	Manual Ticketing
90	地铁站	Metro Station 或 Station
91	地铁智能导向综合信息系统	Metro Service Information Query System
92	地铁终点站	Terminus 或 Terminal
93	地下通道	Underpass
94	第 _____ 航站楼	Terminal _____
95	电车;无轨电车	Trolleybus
96	电梯位于"X入口"	Elevator at Entrance X

序号	中文	英文
97	电子机票	Electronic Tickets 或 e-Tickets
98	电子监控区域	This Area Is Under Electronic Surveillance
99	动植物检疫	Animal and Plant Quarantine
100	渡船	Ferry Boat
101	兑零（地铁站内使用）	Money Change
	E	
102	儿童票适用身高： ____米——____米	Height Limits for Children's Tickets: ____ – ____m
103	二等座	Second Class
	F	
104	方便你我，背包向前 （地铁车厢内使用）	To make room for others, wear backpacks on your front. 或 Wear/Carry backpacks on your front.
105	方向引导	Direction Guide
106	防爆检查，请予配合	Please Comply with Explosive Inspection
107	非付费区（地铁站内使用）	Non-Paid Area
108	非紧急情况请勿开启	For Emergency Use Only
109	非紧急情况使用将负法律责任	Passengers shall bear legal liability for non-emergency use.
110	服务监督电话	Service and Complaints Hotline 或 Passenger Complaints Hotline
111	付费区（地铁站内使用）	Paid Area

序号	中文	英文
	G	
112	高铁站	HSR Station
113	公共交通卡充值（窗口）	Add-Value Card Only 或 Public Transportation Card Only
114	公共汽车	Bus
115	公共汽车路线图	Bus Route
116	公交换乘	Bus Transfer
117	公交换乘信息	Bus Transfer Information
118	公交卡售卡点；市政交通一卡通售卡点	Transport Pass Vendor 或 Transport Card Vendor
119	公交枢纽站	Public Transport Hub
120	公交信息	Public Transport Information
121	公交站点	Bus Stop
122	公交中心站	Central Bus Station/Terminal
123	公交专用出口	Bus Exit Only
124	公务舱候机室	Business Class Lounge〔Lounge 可以省略〕 或 Airlines Lounge
125	购票须知	Ticketing Information
126	关站时间	Closing Time
127	观光船码头	Sightseeing Cruise Dock
128	广播服务	Broadcast Service
129	柜台关闭	Counter Closed
130	贵宾通道	VIP Passage〔Passage 可以省略〕
131	国际、港澳台出发	International and Hong Kong/Macao/Taiwan Departures

序号	中文	英文
132	国际、港澳台到达	International and Hong Kong/Macao/Taiwan Arrivals
133	国际、港澳台航班	International and Hong Kong/Macao/Taiwan Flight (s)
134	国际出发	International Departures
135	国际到达	International Arrivals
136	国际航班通道	International Flight Passage 或 International Flights〔用于 Passage 可以省略的场合〕
137	国际转机	International Transfer
138	国内出发	Domestic Departures
139	国内到达	Domestic Arrivals
140	国内航班通道	Domestic Flight Passage 或 Domestic Flights〔用于 Passage 可以省略的场合〕
141	国内转机	Domestic Transfer
142	过站旅客;过境旅客	Transit Passenger/Passengers
	H	
143	杭州火车东站	Hangzhoudong Railway Station〔采用铁路系统的译法〕
144	杭州火车南站	Hangzhounan Railway Station〔采用铁路系统的译法〕
145	杭州火车西站	Hangzhouxi Railway Station〔采用铁路系统的译法〕
146	杭州火车站(杭州城站火车站)	Hangzhou Railway Station〔采用铁路系统的译法〕
147	杭州汽车(九堡)客运中心	Hangzhou Coach Center
148	杭州汽车北站	Hangzhou North Coach Station

序号	中文	英文
149	杭州汽车东站	Hangzhou East Coach Station
150	杭州汽车南站	Hangzhou South Coach Station
151	杭州汽车西站	Hangzhou West Coach Station
152	杭州萧山国际机场	Hangzhou International Airport〔可缩写为HIA〕
153	航班号	Flight No.＿＿
154	航班信息	Flight Information
155	航空货运	Air Freight
156	航站楼	Terminal
157	航站楼出发层平面图	Departures Floor Map
158	航站楼到达层平面图	Arrivals Floor Map
159	航站楼间旅客免费摆渡车	Free Inter-Terminal Shuttle Bus
160	红色通道(有申报物品)(机场用)	Red Channel // Goods to Declare
161	＿＿号登机口	Gate ＿＿
162	＿＿号屏蔽门	Safety Door No. ＿＿
163	候车楼;候车厅	Passenger Terminal 或 Waiting Hall/Lounge
164	候船室	Waiting Room
165	候机区域	Waiting Area
166	换乘 ＿＿ 号线	Transfer to Line ＿＿
167	换乘、中转大厅(机场用)	Transfer/Transit Lounge〔Lounge可以省略〕

序号	中文	英文
168	换乘2号线的乘客，请上楼。(地铁站内使用)	Passengers transferring to Line 2 please go up one level.
169	会合大厅(车站内使用)	Waiting Lounge 或 Waiting Hall 或 Station Concourse
170	火车售票	Railway/Train Tickets
171	货物查询	Freight Inquiry
172	货物检查	Freight Check
173	货物交运	Freight Check-in
174	货物提取	Freight Collection
175	货运卡车	Truck〔美语〕 或 Lorry〔英语〕
176	货运列车	Freight/Cargo Train
177	货运码头	Wharf
	J	
178	机舱服务员专用通道	Crew Passage 或 Crew Only〔用于Passage可以省略的场合〕
179	机场巴士	Airport Bus 或 Airporter 或 Shuttle Bus 或 Airporter Express 〔在同一场所内应保持统一〕
180	机场巴士站	Airport Shuttle Bus Station
181	机场摆渡	Ferry 或 Airport Shuttle 〔在同一场所内应保持统一〕
182	机场控制区;口岸限定区域	Restricted Area

序号	中文	英文
183	稽查管理（机场用）	Inspection Management
184	即停即走（限时5分钟）；（接送区）限时停车	Kiss and Ride // Max 5 min. 或 Park and Ride〔也可指停放私家车后改用公共交通的停车场〕
185	检票通道	Ticket Check Passage
186	交通卡余额	Card Balance
187	交通卡原额	Previous Card Balance
188	交通信息查询机	Inquiry Machine
189	接客止步	Entry for Staff and Crew Only
190	今日运营已结束（公交、地铁用）	Closed
191	紧急时,击打玻璃边缘,敲碎玻璃。（公共汽车车厢内使用）	Hit the glass edge to break the window in emergency. 或 In emergency, hit the glass edge to break the window.
192	紧急手柄（指拉手）	Emergency Handle
193	紧急制动	Emergency Braking
194	紧握扶手	Hold Handrail 或 Please Hold Handrail
195	进站检票；检票口	Ticket Check
196	禁止摆卖（地铁站内使用）	No Hawking
197	禁止冲门 顾己及人（地铁站内使用）	Be safe and considerate. Never force your way into the train.
198	禁止存储危险货物	Dangerous Freight Prohibited
199	禁止机动车通行	No Motor Vehicles
200	禁止跳下站台	Do Not Jump off the Platform

序号	中文	英文
201	禁止停车或堆放杂物	No Parking or Stacking
202	禁止(携带)物品	Prohibited Articles
203	经济舱	Economy Class
204	经停	Transit
205	经停航班	Stopover Flight/Flights
	K	
206	开往XX方向的列车因故晚点到达,请您耐心等候,不便之处,敬请谅解。(地铁广播)	There is a short delay in train service towards XX. Please wait. We apologize for any inconvenience this might cause.
207	开往XX方向的列车因故预计延误15分钟以上,请您耐心等候或选择其他交通方式,不便之处,敬请谅解。(地铁广播)	There is a delay of more than 15 minutes in train service towards XX. Please wait, or consider using other transport. We apologize for any inconvenience this might cause.
208	开站时间	Opening Time
209	可接收纸币面额:____	Banknotes Acceptable:____
210	客运码头	Passenger Dock/Pier
	L	
211	连廊(机场航站楼)	Connecting Corridor
212	列车门蜂鸣声响,请勿上下列车。(地铁用)	Do not get on or off the train when the door-bell buzzes.
213	列车门关闭,请立刻退到安全线以内。(地铁广播)	Stay behind the yellow line when the door is closing.

序号	中文	英文
214	临时旅客列车	Extra Passenger Train
215	临停接送区	Pick-up & Drop-off Parking〔Parking 可以省略〕 或 Kiss and Ride 或 Kiss 'n' Ride Zone〔Zone 可以省略〕 或 Kiss & Ride
216	轮船售票	Boat Tickets
217	轮渡	Ferry
218	旅客出口	Passenger Exit
219	旅客等候区	Passenger Waiting Area
220	旅客禁止随身携带和托运物品目录	List of Prohibited Articles for Carry-on and Checked Baggage
221	旅客留言	Passengers' Messages
222	旅客通道,请勿滞留	Please Keep Passage Clear 或 Busy Passage // Keep Clear
223	旅客投诉接待	Passenger Complaints
224	旅客须知	Notice to Passengers
225	旅游列车	Tourist Train
226	绿色通道(无申报物品)(机场用)	Green Channel // Nothing to Declare
	M	
227	码头(游客、旅客上下用)	Pier
228	门灯闪烁时禁止上下车。(地铁车厢内使用)	Do not get on or off the train when the door-light is flashing.
229	门对门送货车	Door-to-Door Delivery
230	免费行李重量	Baggage/Luggage Allowance

序号	中文	英文
231	民航售票	Airline Tickets 或 Ticketing
232	末班车	Last Train〔用于火车、地铁〕 Last Bus〔用于公共汽车〕
233	末班车进站前3分钟停售该末班车车票（地铁用）	Ticket Sales Stop 3 Minutes Before Last Train Arrives
234	末车时间（地铁用）	Last Train Departure Time
235	母婴室;母婴休息室	Nursery Room 或 Baby Care Lounge〔Lounge 可以省略〕
236	目的地车站	Terminal Station
	N	
237	逆时针方向扳动手柄90度（用于车厢紧急制动装置）	Turn the Handle 90 Degrees Counterclockwise
	P	
238	票价	Ticket Rates〔Ticket 可以省略〕 或 Fares
239	凭证通行	Permits Required
240	普通席(机舱、车厢内使用)	Economy Class
	Q	
241	起飞前40分钟停止办理乘机手续	Check-in Closes 40 Minutes Before Departure
242	起飞时间	Departure Time
243	汽车客运中心站	Coach Center Station
244	前方到站;下一站	Next Station〔用于轨道交通站点〕 Next Stop〔用于公共汽车、水上巴士站点〕

序号	中文	英文
245	前往XX的末班车即将到达,请在黄线外排队,先下后上,当心脚下空隙。(地铁广播)	The last train to XX is arriving. Please stand behind the yellow line and let passengers exit first. Please mind the gap when boarding.
246	切勿倒置（指货物、行李的摆放）	This Side Up
247	切勿挤压（指货物、行李的摆放）	Fragile
248	切勿倾倒（指货物、行李的摆放）	Keep Upright
249	请保留车票待检	Please Retain Your Ticket for Inspection
250	请出示登机牌和身份证件	Please Show Your Boarding Pass and ID
251	请从后门下车	Please Get off From Rear Door
252	请到售票处办理	Please Go to the Ticket Office for Help
253	请到售票处换硬币	Coin Change at Ticket Office
254	请留意您乘坐航班的登机时间,以免误机	Please Pay Attention to Your Boarding Time
255	请您保管好磁票,出站验票收回	Please Keep Your Magnetic Ticket to Exit
256	请您别遗忘放在手推车上的物品	Please Do Not Leave Any of Your Baggage/Luggage on Trolley
257	请您向下按手柄,松开刹车后推行(用于行李手推车)	Press Down Handle to Move the Trolley
258	请您由此进入,依次候检	Please Line Up Here
259	请使用其他通道	Please Use Another Passage

序号	中文	英文
260	请投入现金,然后按下确认按钮(用于售票机等)	Please Insert Cash and Press Button____〔"____"应视不同情况填入不同的按钮名称,如OK键或Enter键〕
261	请往人少的区域候车(地铁站台上使用)	For easier boarding, please move along the platform.
262	请为您的交通卡充值	PLS Top Up Your Card 或 Please Add Value to Your Card
263	请维护好车厢的清洁卫生,谢谢合作	Thank You for Helping Us Keep This Bus Clean〔用于公共汽车〕 Thank You for Helping Us Keep This Car Clean〔用于火车、地铁〕
264	请勿打扰司机;请勿与司机闲谈(公共汽车上使用)	Do Not Distract the Driver
265	请勿将行李手推车推入自动扶梯	No Baggage/Luggage Cart Allowed on Escalator
266	请勿阻止车门关闭	Keep Clear of Closing Doors
267	请勿坐卧停留;禁止坐卧停留(用于车站内)	No Loitering
268	请选择起始站(售票机上使用)	Select Departure Station
269	请选择线路(售票机上使用)	Select Line
270	请选择要查询的线路	Please Select Line
271	请选择张数(售票机上使用)	Select Number of Tickets
272	请选择终点站(售票机上使用)	Select Your Destination

序号	中文	英文
273	请在安全黄线内候车，车门未完全打开或关闭，不得触摸车门。	Please stand behind the yellow line. Do not touch the door before it is fully opened or closed.
274	请在此排队候车	Please Wait in Line for Boarding
275	请在前门上车	Please Get on From Front Door
276	请注意，本站因故暂停服务，请听从指挥，有序疏散出站，不便之处，敬请谅解。（地铁广播）	Your attention, please! Train service is suspended. Please follow our staff's directions and exit from the station. We apologize for any inconvenience this might cause.
277	请注意，由于车站发生火警，工作人员正在进行处理，请保持镇定，尽快疏散出站。（地铁广播）	Your attention, please! There is a critical situation. Please follow our staff's directions and exit from the station immediately!
278	请注意换乘线路的首末班车时间，以免耽误您的出行。（地铁用）	Please be aware of the departure time of the first and last trains to ensure a smooth connection.
279	请自觉遵守乘车秩序	Please Observe Passenger Rules
280	取票，找零	Take Your Ticket and Change
281	去往____号门仅需____分钟	Only ____ Minutes to Gate ____ 或 Only ____ Minutes Walking to Gate ____
	R	
282	如身体不适，请在下一站寻求车站人员协助。（用于地铁车厢内）	If you feel unwell, please contact staff at the next station.
283	如需人工服务，请至____号窗口	Please Go to Window ____ for Staff Assistance

序号	中文	英文
284	入境登记卡	Arrival Card
285	软卧车厢	Soft Sleeper/Berth
286	软席候车室	Soft-Seat Passenger Waiting Lounge 或 Soft-Seat Passengers〔用于 Waiting Lounge 可省略的场合〕
287	软纸票	Soft Paper Tickets
288	软座车厢	Soft Seat
	S	
289	商务座	Business Class
290	上车乘客请尽量往里走,下车乘客请提前准备,谢谢配合!(地铁广播)	Please move inwards on the train after boarding, and prepare to exit before arriving at your station. Thank you!
291	上车后请往车厢中部移动。(地铁广播)	Please move down the train after boarding.
292	上客点	Passenger Pick-up
293	上一站	Previous Station〔用于地铁〕 Previous Stop〔用于公共汽车、水上巴士〕
294	设备间(地铁站内使用)	Equipment Room
295	设备区(地铁站内使用)	Equipment Area
296	设施服务时间	Service Hours
297	失物招领	Lost and Found
298	使用自动扶梯时,请照顾同行的儿童和帮助有需要的长者。	When riding escalators, please look after young children and offer help to the elderly.
299	始发站	Departure Station

序号	中文	英文
300	手提行李规格	Size and Weight Limits for Carry-on Baggage/Bags
301	首、末班车时间	Time for First/Last Train of This Line〔用于地铁〕 Time for First/Last Bus of This Route〔用于公共汽车〕
302	首班车	First Train〔用于火车、地铁〕 First Bus〔用于公共汽车〕
303	首车时间	First Train Departure Time〔用于地铁〕 First Bus Departure Time〔用于公共汽车〕
304	售卡(地铁站内使用)	Card Selling 或 Card Vending
305	售票处(厅)	Ticket Office/Hall 或 Tickets
306	售全线票;通售所有站点车票	Tickets for All Stations
307	枢纽站	Junction Station
308	水路货运	Water Freight
309	水上巴士	Water Bus 或 River Bus
310	送客止步	Passengers Only
	T	
311	特快列车	Express Train
312	提取行李,请注意安全	Please Be Careful When Claiming Baggage/Luggage
313	天桥	Overpass
314	铁路出发	Railway Departures
315	铁路达到(北1)	Railway Arrivals (North Gate 1)
316	铁路货运	Rail Freight

序号	中文	英文
317	停机坪摆渡车	Airside Transfer Bus 或 Apron Bus
318	停止办票	Check-in Closed
319	停止登机	Boarding Closed
320	通道禁止停留	Do Not Block Access 或 Do Not Block Passage
321	头等舱	First Class
322	头等舱/商务舱服务	First/Business Class Service
323	头等舱候机室	First Class Lounge〔Lounge 可以省略〕 或 Airlines Lounge
324	投入硬币、纸币或插入公共交通卡	Insert Coins, Banknotes or Public Transportation Card
325	投诉台	Complaints
326	团队集合点	Group Gathering Point
327	团队通道	Groups Passage〔Passage 可以省略〕
328	推杆开启	Push to Open
	W	
329	外国人通道(机场用)	International Visitors Passage〔Passage 可以省略〕
330	外交礼遇通道(机场用)	Diplomats Passage〔Passage 可以省略〕 或 Diplomatic Visa Holders Passage〔Passage 可以省略〕
331	网约车	Online Ride Hailing〔Online 可以省略〕 或 Ride-Hailing Car
332	往 XX 方向的末班车已经开出,前往该方向的乘客,请改用其他交通方式。(地铁广播)	The last train to XX has already departed. Please use other transport.

序号	中文	英文
333	往返票	Return Ticket 或 Round-Trip Ticket 或 Two-Way Ticket
334	为方便上车,请乘客前往站台中部人较少的位置候车,谢谢配合。(地铁用)	For easier boarding, please move along the platform. Thank you.
335	为了您的安全,请不要靠近打开的屏蔽门。(地铁用)	For safety reasons, please keep away from the open platform screen doors.
336	为确保安全,换乘时请勿奔跑。(地铁站台用)	For safety reasons, please don't run when changing trains.
337	为确保安全,请不要在站厅或站台上奔跑。	For safety reasons, please don't run in the concourse or on the platform.
338	为确保安全,车门正在关上的时候,请不要冲进车厢或妨碍车门关闭。(地铁广播)	For safety reasons, please do not rush into the train or block the train doors when they are closing.
339	为营造良好的乘车环境,请在车厢内降低音量,低声言语,谢谢配合!(地铁广播)	Please lower your voice or the volume of your electronic device when inside the train compartment. Thank you!
340	卫生间位于"X入口"(地铁站内使用)	Toilets at Entrance X
341	未经授权禁止进入轨行区(地铁用)	No Track Access Without Authorization
342	文明乘车 先出后进	Please let other passengers get off before you get in. 或 Manner Matters. Exit First.
343	问询	Enquiry 或 Information

序号	中文	英文
344	无人陪伴儿童	Unaccompanied Children
345	勿放潮湿处（指货物、行李的摆放）	Store in Dry Place
	X	
346	＿＿小时过境免签	＿＿ Hours Transit Without Visa
347	行李安检;行李检查	Baggage/Luggage Security Check 或 Baggage/Luggage Check/Inspection
348	行李查询	Baggage/Luggage Inquiry
349	行李寄存	Baggage/Luggage Deposit
350	行李寄存须知	Notice of Baggage/Luggage Deposit
351	行李检查	Baggage/Luggage Check
352	行李提取	Baggage/Luggage Claim
353	行李托运	Baggage/Luggage Check-in
354	行李专用,请勿载人（行李手推车用）	For Baggage/Luggage Only // No Riding
355	下车请勿忘物品	Please Do Not Leave Your Belongings Behind
356	下车通道 请勿站人	Exit // Keep Clear
357	下一站	Next Station〔用于地铁〕 Next Stop〔用于公共汽车〕
358	先下后上	Yield to Alighting Passengers 或 Exit First
359	现在是高峰时段,如需服务请稍候。	Rush Hours. Please Wait a Moment. 或 Peak Hour. Please Wait a Moment.
360	限乘15人	Maximum Capacity: 15 Persons
361	限乘人数	Maximum Capacity
362	限紧急时使用	For Emergency Use Only

序号	中文	英文
363	限制（携带）物品	Restricted Articles
364	限制重量	Maximum Weight
365	小心脚下间隙落差；注意站台缝隙	Mind the Gap
366	休息处	Rest Area 或 Lounge
367	休息大厅；等候大厅	Waiting Hall
368	选择充值交易（充值机上使用）	Select Add-Value
369	选择票价（售票机上使用）	Select Fare
	Y	
370	严禁携带易燃易爆等危险品进站	Dangerous Articles Prohibited 或 Flammable, explosive and other dangerous articles are prohibited.
371	氧气罩	Oxygen Mask
372	夜间滞留旅客请在此休息	Rest Area for Overnight Passengers
373	液态物品	Liquids
374	1号线的列车服务已恢复正常。（地铁用）	Train service on Line 1 is now normal.
375	1号线的列车已暂停服务，前往1号线的乘客请改用其他交通工具。（地铁用）	Train service on Line 1 is suspended. If you are intending to travel on Line 1, please use other transport.
376	已驶过车站（地铁用）	Stations Passed
377	应急门	Escape/Emergency Door
378	硬币兑换处	Coin Change

序号	中文	英文
379	硬卧车厢	Hard Sleeper/Berth
380	硬纸票	Hard Paper Tickets
381	硬座车厢	Hard Seat
382	优先登机	Priority Boarding
383	逾重行李收费处	Overweight Baggage/Luggage Charge〔Charge 可以省略〕
384	预售10日内全国各线车票	10-Day Advance Booking for All Destinations
385	月票无效(刷卡机上使用)	Monthly Pass Invalid
386	月票有效(刷卡机上使用)	Monthly Pass Valid
	Z	
387	____ 站示意图	Map of ____ Station
388	暂停售票;暂停服务;临时关闭	Temporarily Closed
389	站层图	Station Floor Map
390	站间转乘(地铁用)	Transfer Between Stations
391	站内空间示意图	Station Layout
392	站区图(公交、地铁用)	Station Map
393	站台;月台	Platform
394	站台轨行区(地铁站内使用)	Rail Line Area
395	站长室(指值班站长)(公交、地铁用)	Station Master Office〔Office 可以省略〕
396	招手即停	Hail and Ride〔指路边临时停车点〕

序号	中文	英文
397	证照检查	ID Check 或 Documents Check
398	直达车	Non-Stop Bus〔公共汽车〕 Non-Stop Coach〔长途汽车〕
399	直达航班	Direct Flight/Flights
400	直达特快列车	Non-Stop Express Train 或 Through Train
401	值机柜台;办票柜台;办理乘机手续柜台	Check-in Counters〔Counters 可以省略〕
402	值机区域;办理登机区	Check-in Area〔Area 可以省略〕
403	中国边检	China Immigration Inspection
404	中国边检检疫	China Inspection and Quarantine
405	中国人通道	Chinese Citizens Passage〔Passage 可以省略〕
406	中转柜台(机场用)	Transfer Counter
407	中转联程(机场用)	Connecting Flights
408	中转旅客免费乘车点(机场用)	Free Shuttle for Transfer Passengers
409	中转旅客休息室(机场用)	Transfer Passenger Lounge
410	中转值机(机场用)	Transfer Check-in
411	终点;终点站(公交、地铁用)	Destination 或 Terminus
412	终点站 请勿上车(公交、地铁用)	This is the last stop. Please don't get on the train/bus.
413	注意安全,抓好扶手	Please Hold Handrail
414	注意车辆	Watch for Vehicles 或 Beware of Moving Vehicles
415	注意强风	CAUTION! // Strong Gust

序号	中文	英文
416	注意通风	Use with Adequate Ventilation
417	注意转弯车辆	Watch for Turning Vehicles
418	驻站民警室	Police Office〔Office可以省略〕
419	专用候车室	Designated Waiting Room
420	转乘港澳台航班	Transfer to Hong Kong/Macao/Taiwan 或 Hong Kong/Macao/Taiwan Transfer
421	转乘国内（国际）航班	Domestic (International) Transfer
422	转机;换乘	Transfer 或 Flight Connections
423	转机旅客	Transfer Passenger/Passengers
424	装卸码头	Loading/Unloading Dock
425	自动步行道	Automatic/Moving Walkway 或 Travelator
426	自动寄包柜	Self-Service Locker
427	自动检票	Automatic Check-in
428	自动售票（机）	Ticket Vending Machine
429	自助行李寄存	Self-Service Baggage/Luggage Deposit
430	自助值机;乘机手续自助办理机	Self Check-in

注1:"〔 〕"中的内容是对英文译法的解释说明。

注2:"/"表示可选择该组词语中的一种。

注3:"//"表示书写时应当换行的断行处。需要同行书写时"//"应改为句点".",警示词后加惊叹号"!"。

注4:"___"表示使用时应根据实际情况填入具体内容。

注5:"或"前后所列出的不同译法可任意选择一种使用。

注6:解释说明中指出某个词"可以省略"的,省略该词的译文只能用于设置在该设施上的标志中,如"出发大厅"应译作 Departure Lounge,在设置于出发大厅门口的标志中可省略 Lounge,译作 Departure。

附录B

(资料性)

文化和旅游服务信息英文译写示例

B.1 旅游景区景点名称英文译写示例见表B.1。表B.1按中文汉语拼音排序。

表B.1 旅游景区景点名称英文译写示例

序号	中文	英文
	A	
1	爱国主义教育基地	Patriotic Education Base
2	庵	Nunnery
	B	
3	白马湖生态创意城	Baimahu Eco-Creative Town
4	半山国家森林公园	Banshan National Forest Park
5	宝石流霞	Baoshiliuxia (Rosy Clouds Floating Over the Precious Stone Hill)
6	碑记	Tablet Inscription 或 Stele
7	北街梦寻	Beijiemengxun (Seeking the Dreams at Historical Beishan Street)
8	不可移动文物	Immovable Cultural Heritage
9	步行街	Pedestrian/Walking Street 或 Pedestrian Zone
	C	
10	长乔极地海洋公园	Changqiao Polar Ocean Park
11	超山风景名胜区	Chaoshan Scenic Area
12	城市公园	City/Urban Park

序号	中文	英文
13	祠(纪念性)	Memorial Temple 或 Temple
	D	
14	大慈岩风景区	Daciyan Scenic Area
15	大兜路历史文化街区	Dadoulu Historical and Cultural Street Area
16	大明山景区	Damingshan Scenic Area
17	岛	Island 或 Isle
18	殿;堂	Hall
19	雕像	Sculpture 或 Statue
20	东方文化园	Oriental Cultural Park
21	动物园	Zoo 或 Zoological Park
22	度假村	Resort 或 Holiday Resort 或 Holiday Village〔美语〕
23	断桥残雪	Duanqiaocanxue (Lingering Snow on the Broken Bridge)
	E	
24	儿童公园	Children's Park
25	儿童游乐场;儿童乐园	Children's Playground
26	二级文物	Grade 2/Grade II Cultural Object/Property〔通称 并指具体文物〕 Grade 2/Grade II Cultural Heritage〔统称〕〔不可数〕 Grade 2/Grade II Cultural/Historical Relic〔指遗迹、遗物、遗存〕

序号	中文	英文
	F	
27	风景名胜;风景名胜区;旅游景区	Tourist Attraction〔泛指多处景点时译作 Tourist Attractions〕
28	峰	Peak 或 Mountain Peak
29	富春桃源景区	Fuchun Taoyuan Scenic Area
	G	
30	皋亭山景区	Gaotingshan Scenic Area
31	工业旅游示范点	Industrial Tourism Demonstration Site
32	工业遗产公园	Industrial Heritage Park
33	公墓	Cemetery
34	公园	Park
35	宫;观〔道教〕	Daoist/Taoist Temple
36	宫〔皇宫〕;行宫	Palace
37	古城	Ancient/Heritage City
38	古迹	Historic/Historical/Heritage Site
39	古建筑	Ancient/Listed/Heritage Building
40	古墓	Ancient Tomb
41	古桥	Ancient Bridge
42	古塔	Ancient Pagoda
43	古镇	Ancient/Old/Heritage Town
44	故居	Former Residence
45	故里	Hometown
46	国家级景区	National Park

序号	中文	英文
47	国家级文物保护单位;全国重点文物保护单位	National Monument 或 National Cultural Heritage Site
48	国家森林公园	National Forest Park
	H	
49	海洋馆;海洋公园	Marine/Ocean Park
50	杭州乐园	Hangzhou Amusement Park
51	杭州临安太湖源景区	Hangzhou Lin'an Taihuyuan Scenic Area
52	杭州市余杭山沟沟景区	Hangzhou Yuhang Shangougou Scenic Area
53	杭州野生动物园	Hangzhou Safari Park
54	杭州之江国家旅游度假区	Hangzhou Zhijiang National Holiday Resort
55	湖;泊	Lake
56	湖滨地区商贸旅游特色街居	Hubin Commercial and Tourist Streets and Buildings
57	湖滨晴雨	Hubinqingyu (Sunny and Rainy Views From the Lakeside)
58	虎跑梦泉	Hupaomengquan (Dreaming of Tiger Spring at the Hupao Valley)
59	花港观鱼	Huagangguanyu (Viewing Fish at the Flower Pool)
60	黄公望隐居地	Huang Gongwang Hermitage
61	黄龙洞景区	Huanglongdong Scenic Area
62	黄龙吐翠	Huanglongtucui (Yellow Dragon Cave Dressed in Green)
63	会址(会议地点)	Venue of ____ Conference/Meeting〔"____"中填入具体会议名称〕

序号	中文	英文
	J	
64	纪念馆;纪念堂	Memorial Hall/Museum
65	建德航空小镇	Jiande Aviation Town
66	江;河	River
67	江南古村落	Jiangnan Ancient Villages
68	教堂	Church〔指基督教堂,常用〕 或 Cathedral〔指教区总教堂、主教座堂〕
69	京杭大运河(杭州段)	The Beijing-Hangzhou Grand Canal (Hangzhou Section)
70	京杭大运河杭州景区	The Grand Canal (Hangzhou Section) Scenic Area
71	景点	Scenic Spot 或 Tourist Attraction
72	景观	Landscape 或 Scenery 或 Scene 或 View
73	景区	Scenic Area 或 Nature Park
74	九溪烟树	Jiuxiyanshu (Nine Creeks Meandering Through Misty Woods)
75	旧址	Site
	K	
76	口袋公园(城市内具有游憩功能的小公园)	Pocket Park
77	跨湖桥遗址	Kuahuqiao Site
	L	
78	廊;长廊	Corridor

序号	中文	英文
79	浪石金滩	Langshi Jintan (Langshi Cobblestone Beach)
80	老街	Old/Ancient Street
81	乐园	Amusement Park
82	雷峰夕照	Leifengxizhao (Leifeng Pagoda at Sunset)
83	历史建筑	Historic Building
84	历史名园	Historic Garden
85	历史文化名城（名镇、名村、街区）	Famous Historical and Cultural City (Town, Village, Street Area)
86	良渚古城遗址公园	Archaeological Ruins of Liangzhu City
87	烈士陵园	Martyrs Cemetery
88	灵隐禅踪	Lingyinchanzong (Zen Retreat at Lingyin Temple)
89	陵;墓	Mausoleum 或 Tomb
90	陵园;墓园	Cemetery
91	岭	Ridge
92	柳浪闻莺	Liulangwenying (Orioles Singing in the Willows)
93	六和听涛	Liuhetingtao (Listening to the Tidal Roar at the Six Harmonies Pagoda)
94	龙井问茶	Longjingwencha (Rediscovering Tea at Longjing)
95	龙门古镇	Longmen Ancient Town
96	龙坞茶镇	Longwu Tea Town
97	陇	Village
98	楼;塔楼;阁	Tower 或 Tower Building 或 Storied Pavilion

序号	中文	英文
99	绿道	Greenway
100	绿地	Green Land
101	旅游城	Tourist/Tourism Town
102	旅游度假区	Resort Area
	M	
103	满陇桂雨	Manlongguiyu (Sweet Osmanthus Blossoming at Manjuelong Village)
104	梅坞春早	Meiwuchunzao (Early Spring at Meijiawu Tea Village)
105	梦想小镇	Dream Town
106	庙;寺(佛教)	Temple 或 Monastery
107	民俗园	Folk/Folklore Park
108	民宿	Homestay 或 Guesthouse/Guest House
109	民族特色街	Ethnic Culture Street
110	名胜古迹	Scenic Spots and Historical Sites〔泛指多处景点〕
	N	
111	南屏晚钟	Nanpingwanzhong (Evening Bell Ringing on the Nanping Hill)
112	南宋御街	Southern Song Imperial Street
113	农家乐	Agritainment
114	农业旅游示范点	Agricultural Tourism Demonstration Site
	P	
115	牌坊;牌楼	Memorial Gateway 或 Arch 或 Ceremonial/Memorial Archway

序号	中文	英文
116	盆景园	Potted/Miniature Landscape Garden 或 Bonsai Garden
117	平湖秋月	Pinghuqiuyue (Autumn Moon Over the Calm Lake)
118	圃（花圃）	Garden 或 Flower Nursery
119	瀑布	Falls 或 Waterfall
	Q	
120	七里扬帆景区	Qili Yangfan Scenic Area
121	千岛湖风景名胜区	Qiandao Lake Scenic Area
122	千岛湖乐水小镇·文渊狮城	Qiandao Lake Leshui Town—Wenyuan Shicheng Holiday Resort
123	千岛湖旅游度假区	Qiandao Lake Tourist Holiday Resort
124	千岛湖石林景区	Qiandao Lake Stone Forest Scenic Area
125	钱祠表忠	Qiancibiaozhong (King Qians' Temple of Loyalty)
126	桥西历史文化街区	Qiaoxi Historical and Cultural Street Area
127	青山湖国家森林公园	Qingshanhu National Forest Park
128	清河坊历史街区	Qinghefang Historical Street Area
129	清凉峰国家级自然保护区	Qingliangfeng National Nature Reserve
130	清凉峰旅游度假区	Qingliangfeng Holiday Resort
131	清真寺	Mosque
132	区级文物保护单位	District Monument 或 District Cultural Heritage Site
133	曲院风荷	Quyuanfenghe (Breeze-Rustled Lotus in the Quyuan Garden)

序号	中文	英文
134	全域旅游	All-for-One Tourism 或 Holistic Tourism
135	泉	Spring
	R	
136	阮墩环碧	Ruandunhuanbi (Ruangongdun Isle Swathed in Greenery)
137	溶洞	Karst/Limestone Cave
	S	
138	三级文物	Grade 3/Grade III Cultural Object/Property〔通称并指具体文物〕 Grade 3/Grade III Cultural Heritage〔统称〕〔不可数〕 Grade 3/Grade III Cultural/Historical Relic〔遗迹/物/存〕
139	三台云水	Santaiyunshui (Crisscross Lakes Against the Cloudy Santai Hill)
140	三潭印月	Santanyinyue (Three Pools Mirroring the Moon)
141	森林;林地	Forest 或 Woods
142	森林公园	Forest Park
143	山	Mountain 或 Hill〔已习惯使用 Mount 的可沿用〕
144	山洞	Cave
145	山谷	Valley
146	山脉	Mountains 或 Mountain Range
147	生态公园	Ecopark 或 Ecological Park
148	省级文物保护单位	Provincial Monument 或 Provincial Cultural Heritage Site

序号	中文	英文
149	湿地	Wetland
150	湿地公园	Wetland Park
151	石碑	Stele〔竖立的石碑〕 Stone Tablet〔横放的石碑〕
152	石刻	Stone Inscription〔文字〕 Stone Carving〔非文字〕
153	石窟	Grottoes
154	世界文化遗产	World Cultural Heritage〔泛指〕 或 World Cultural Heritage Site〔特指一处遗产〕
155	市级文物保护单位	Municipal Monument 或 Municipal Cultural Heritage Site
156	双峰插云	Shuangfengchayun (Twin Peaks Piercing the Clouds)
157	双溪漂流	Shuangxi Rafting
158	水利风景区	Water Conservancy Scenic Area 或 Water Park
159	水上乐园	Water Park
160	水族馆;海洋馆	Aquarium
161	泗洲造纸作坊遗址	Sizhou Paper Mill Site
162	苏堤春晓	Sudichunxiao (Spring Dawn on the Su Causeway)
	T	
163	塔	Pagoda 或 Stupa 或 Dagoba〔舍利塔〕 或 Tower
164	潭;池	Pond 或 Pool〔已习惯使用 Lake 的可沿用〕
165	体育公园	Sports Park
166	天目山风景区	Tianmushan Scenic Area

序号	中文	英文
167	天目山国家级自然保护区	Tianmushan National Nature Reserve
168	天文馆	Planetarium
169	天子地景区	Tianzidi Scenic Area
170	桐庐垂云通天河景区	Tonglu Chuiyun Tongtianhe Scenic Area
	W	
171	湾	Bend 或 Bay
172	万松书缘	Wansongshuyuan (A Love Legend at Wansong Academy)
173	温泉	Hot Spring
174	文物保护点	Cultural Relic Site Under Protection
175	吴山天风	Wushantianfeng (Heavenly Wind Over the Wushan Hill)
176	坞	Valley
	X	
177	西湖风景名胜区	West Lake Scenic Area
178	西溪国家湿地公园	Xixi National Wetland Park
179	溪	Creek 或 Brook 或 Stream
180	下姜景区	Xiajiang Scenic Area
181	湘湖跨湖桥景区	Xianghu Kuahuqiao Scenic Area
182	湘湖国家旅游度假区	Xianghu National Tourist Holiday Resort
183	小河历史文化街区	Xiaohe Historical and Cultural Street Area

序号	中文	英文
	Y	
184	杨堤景行	Yangdijingxing (Historical Reflections on the Governor Yang Causeway)
185	严子陵钓台	Yan Ziling Angling Terrace
186	瑶琳仙境	Yaolin Wonderland
187	野生动物园	Wildlife Park/Zoo 或 Safari Park
188	一级文物	Grade 1/Grade I Cultural Object/Property〔通称并指具体文物〕 Grade 1/Grade I Cultural Heritage〔统称〕〔不可数〕 Grade 1/Grade I Cultural/Historical Relic〔遗迹/物/存〕
189	遗址	Site 或 Ruins〔存有废墟的〕
190	遗址公园	Heritage Park
191	游乐园	Amusement Park
192	余杭径山景区	Yuhang Jingshan Scenic Area
193	玉皇飞云	Yuhuangfeiyun (Scurrying Clouds Over the Jade Emperor Hill)
194	玉皇山南基金小镇	Yuhuang Shannan Fund Town
195	园;苑	Garden
196	院;大院	Courtyard 或 Compound
197	岳墓栖霞	Yuemuqixia (General Yue's Tomb at the Cloud-Lingering Hill)
198	云栖竹径	Yunqizhujing (Clouds Lingering on the Bamboo-Lined Path)
199	运河·塘栖古镇	The Grand Canal—Tangqi Ancient Town

序号	中文	英文
	Z	
200	沼泽（地）	Marsh 或 Marshland 或 Moor
201	浙西大峡谷	West Zhejiang Grand Canyon
202	植物园	Botanical Garden
203	中国优秀旅游城市	China Top Tourist City
204	洲	Isle
205	主题公园	Theme Park
206	自然保护区	Natural Reserve 或 Nature Reserve
207	宗祠	Ancestral Temple 或 Clan Temple

注1："〔 〕"中的内容是对英文译法的解释说明。
注2："/"表示可选择该组词语中的一种。
注3："＿＿"表示使用时应根据实际情况填入具体内容。
注4："或"前后所列出的不同译法可任意选择一种使用。

B.2 旅游服务信息英文译写示例见表B.2。表B.2按中文汉语拼音排序。

表B.2 旅游服务信息英文译写示例

序号	中文	英文
	B	
1	半价（门票等）	50% Off 或 Half Price 或 50% Discount
2	半票（门票、车票等）	Half-Price Ticket〔Ticket可以省略〕 或 Half Rate

序号	中文	英文
3	闭馆时间;闭园时间	Closing Time
4	表演区	Performance Area
5	表演时间	Show Time
6	布告栏;公告栏	Bulletin/Notice Board
7	步行游客在此下车	Hikers Disembark Here
	C	
8	参观通道;游客通道	Visitors Passage〔Passage 可以省略〕
9	参观路线	Visitor Route
10	残疾人服务	Service for People with Disabilities 或 Service for Disabled
11	残疾人证	Disability Certificate
12	成人票	Adult Ticket〔Ticket 可以省略〕
13	乘缆车入口	Cable Car Entrance
14	冲浪	Surfing
15	触摸区(可触摸体验)	Hands-on Area
16	垂钓区	Angling Area
17	瓷器;青花瓷	Porcelain Celadon Porcelain
	D	
18	淡季	Low/Slack Season 或 Off-Season
19	当日使用,逾期作废	Valid on Day of Issue Only〔指购票当日有效〕 Valid for the Date Displayed on the Ticket〔指票面上印刷的日期当日有效〕

序号	中文	英文
20	当心动物伤人	CAUTION // Animals May Attack
21	当心划船区域	CAUTION // Boating Area
22	当心机械伤人(用于游乐设施)	DANGER // Machinery May Cause Injuries
23	当心落水	WARNING // Deep Water 或 DANGER // Deep Water
24	导览册	Guides 或 Guide Book
25	导览机	Audio Guide
26	导游服务;讲解服务	Tour Guide Service 或 Guide Service
27	登山	Mountain Climbing
28	登山避险处	Mountain Refuge
29	电子检票口	e-Ticket Check-in 或 e-Ticket Entrance
	E	
30	儿童票	Child Ticket〔Ticket可以省略〕
31	儿童浅水活动区	Wading Pool
	F	
32	帆板冲浪	Windsurfing
33	返回验印	Visitors Re-Entry Sticker Check
34	房车营地	RV Camp 或 RV Campground/Park 或 RV Campsite/Resort 或 RV Camping Site
35	风力较大,勿燃香,请敬香	WINDY // No incense burning. Please offer incense sticks.
36	服装出租	Costumes Rental

序号	中文	英文
37	浮潜	Snorkeling
38	抚摸区（可抚摸动物）	Petting Area
39	复制品;仿制品	Duplicate 或 Replica
40	副券自行撕下作废	Invalid Without Stub
	G	
41	古旧图书	Antique Books
42	观光船	Sightseeing Boat/Ship
43	观光电梯	Sightseeing/Observation/Glass Elevator 〔在同一场所内应保持统一〕
44	观光廊	Sightseeing Corridor
45	观光索道	Sightseeing Cableway
46	观光线路	Sightseeing Route
47	观光小火车	Sightseeing Train 或 Sightseeing Mini Train
48	观景台	Observation Deck/Platform 或 Viewing Platform
49	观赏区	Viewing Area
50	贵宾通道	VIP Passage〔Passage 可以省略〕
51	贵重物品请自行妥善保管	Please Keep Your Valuables with You
52	过山车	Roller Coaster
	H	
53	杭州丝绸	Hangzhou Silk
54	杭州织锦	Hangzhou Brocade

序号	中文	英文
55	划船	Rowing 或 Boating
56	滑冰	Skating
57	滑草	Grass Skiing/Sliding
58	滑道戏水	Water Sliding
59	滑沙	Sand Skiing
60	滑水	Water Skiing/Ski
61	滑雪	Skiing
62	滑雪坡道	Ski Slope
63	滑雪区;滑雪场	Ski Resort
64	滑雪者在此下车	Skiers Disembark Here
65	货币兑换	Currency Exchange
	J	
66	纪念品店	Souvenir Store/Shop 或 Souvenirs
67	检票口	Check-in 或 Entrance 或 Ticket Gate 或 Ticket-Checking Entrance〔Entrance 可以省略〕
68	剪纸	Paper Cutting〔指具体剪纸艺术品时可用复数 Cuttings〕 或 Papercutting
69	郊游;远足	Outing 或 Excursion
70	金属制品(旅游纪念品)	Metalware
71	禁止采摘	Do Not Pick Flowers or Fruits

序号	中文	英文
72	禁止垂钓	No Angling
73	禁止带火种;禁止放置易燃物	No Flammable Objects
74	禁止放风筝	Do Not Fly Kites
75	禁止滑冰	No Skating
76	禁止露营	No Camping
77	禁止狩猎	No Hunting
78	禁止无照经营	Licensed Vendors Only
79	禁止下水	Stay out of Water
80	禁止游客车辆入内	Authorized Vehicles Only
81	景点管理处	Administration/Management Office
82	景区简介;解说牌	Introduction
83	景泰蓝	Cloisonné
84	敬畏英雄,请勿攀爬(用于烈士陵园、墓碑等)	Respect the Heroes. Do Not Climb. 或 Respectable Heroes Here. No Climbing.
85	救生圈	Life Buoy/Ring
	K	
86	卡丁车	Go-Kart 或 Go-Karting
	L	
87	缆车;索道缆车;空中缆车	Cable Car 或 Telpher Ski Lift〔滑雪场专用〕
88	老年证	Senior Citizen ID

序号	中文	英文
89	老人票	Senior Ticket〔Ticket 可以省略〕
90	礼品店	Gift Store/Shop
91	留言板	Message Board
92	龙井茶	Longjing Tea
93	露营地	Camping Area
94	旅游大巴停车场	Tour Bus Parking 或 Tour Buses〔用于 Parking 可以省略的场合〕
95	旅游观光车	Sightseeing/Tour Bus 或 Sightseeing Car
96	旅游观光车车站	Sightseeing/Tour Bus Stop〔沿途小站〕 Tour/Sightseeing Bus Station〔大站、起点或终点站〕
97	旅游观光车发车时间	Departure Time for Sightseeing/Tour Buses
98	旅游行程表	Itinerary
99	旅游纪念品	Souvenirs
100	旅游投诉	Complaints
	M	
101	门票;普通票	Ticket〔多张门票时用 Tickets〕
102	棉麻制品（旅游纪念品）	Cotton and Linen
103	免票	Free Admission
104	免税商店	Duty Free Store/Shop〔设置在商店门面上时，Store/Shop 可以省略〕
105	民族歌舞	Folk Dancing
106	模型	Models〔作为商品类名时使用复数〕
107	摩托艇	Motorboat

序号	中文	英文
	N	
108	泥沙浴	Mud and Sand Bathing
109	泥塑	Clay Figurines
110	年票	Annual Pass
	P	
111	攀岩	Rock Climbing
112	碰碰车	Bumper Car
113	皮影	Shadow Play 或 Shadow Puppets/Puppetry
114	漂流	Drifting 或 Rafting〔使用竹筏或皮筏〕
115	票价	Ticket Prices/Rates〔Ticket 可以省略〕
116	票务服务	Ticket Service 或 Tickets
117	票已售出,概不退换	No Refunds or Exchanges
118	票已售完	Sold Out
119	凭票入场	Admission by Ticket 或 Ticket Holders Only
120	凭有效证件	Valid ID Required
	Q	
121	漆器	Lacquerware
122	骑行道	Cycle/Cycling/Bicycle/Bike Route 或 Bike Trail
123	骑马	Horse/Horseback Riding
124	潜水	Scuba Diving

序号	中文	英文
125	青铜器	Bronze Ware
126	请爱护洞内景观	Please Respect Sights Inside the Cave 或 Please Show Respect for Sights Inside the Cave
127	请爱护古树	Please Take Care of the Historic/Heritage Tree 〔Tree 应根据实际情况选择单复数〕
128	请爱护景区设施	Please Care for Public Facilities 或 Please Show Respect for Public Facilities
129	请爱护文物	Please Treasure Cultural Objects/Relics 或 Please Show Respect for Cultural Objects/Relics
130	请穿好救生衣	Please Wear Life Vest
131	请等车(船等)停稳后再下	Please Do Not Get off Until the Ride Comes to a Complete Stop
132	请勿触摸;请勿抚摸;请勿手扶	No Touching 或 Please Do Not Touch
133	请勿惊吓、戏弄动物	Do Not Disturb Animals
134	请勿使用扩音器	No Loudspeakers
135	请勿喂食;请勿投食;禁止喂食	Do Not Feed Animals 或 No Feeding
136	请勿摇晃(用于索桥)	Please Do Not Rock the Bridge 或 No Rocking on the Bridge
137	请勿摇晃船只	Do Not Rock the Boat
138	请勿在此进行球类活动	No Ball Games Allowed Here
139	请勿在殿内燃香	Do Not Burn Incense Inside
140	请香处(用于佛教寺庙)	Incense 或 Get Incense Here
141	请沿此路上山	This Way up the Hill

序号	中文	英文
142	请尊重少数民族习俗	Please Respect Ethnic Customs
143	全日制学生证	Full-Time Student ID
	R	
144	日光浴	Sunbathing
145	入园前请提前阅读	Please Read Prior to Entering the Park
	S	
146	森林浴	Forest Bathing
147	射击	Shooting
148	生态小道;游步道	Eco-Trail
149	声讯服务	Audio Guide
150	收费项目	Pay Items〔用于价目牌标题,后列出收费项目及其价格〕 或 Non-Complimentary〔指本项目收费,不免费〕
151	手稿	Manuscripts
152	手工艺品	Handicrafts
153	狩猎区	Hunting Area
154	售票口;售票处;票务处	Ticket Office 或 Tickets〔用于Office可以省略的场合〕
155	书画	Painting and Calligraphy 或 Calligraphy and Painting
156	水果采摘区	Fruit-Picking Area
157	水上运动	Aquatic Sports 或 Water Sports
158	丝毯(旅游纪念品)	Silk Carpet
159	丝织品(旅游纪念品)	Silk Fabrics 或 Silks

序号	中文	英文
	T	
160	探险	Expedition
161	唐三彩(旅游纪念品)	Tang Tri-Color Glazed Ceramics
162	陶器(旅游纪念品)	Pottery
163	套票;联票	Ticket Package
164	徒步旅行	Hiking
165	团体检票口	Group Check-in 或 Group Entrance
166	团体接待	Group Reception
167	团体票	Group Tickets〔Tickets 可以省略〕
168	团体入口	Group Entrance〔Entrance 可以省略〕
169	团体售票口	Group Tickets Office 或 Groups〔用于 Office 可以省略的场合〕
170	退押金处	Deposit Refunding
171	拓片	Rubbing〔指多张拓片时用复数 Rubbings〕
172	拓展区	Outdoor Exercise Area
	W	
173	王星记扇(旅游纪念品)	Wangxingji Fan
174	旺季	Busy/High/Peak Season
175	温泉浴	Hot Spring Bathing
176	无烟景区	Non-Smoking Area
	X	
177	西湖绸伞	West Lake Silk Parasol

序号	中文	英文
178	西湖藕粉	West Lake Lotus Root Powder
179	西湖天竺筷	West Lake Tianzhu Bamboo Chopsticks
180	闲人免入;非请莫入;禁止进入	No Entry Unless Authorized 或 No Trespassing〔用于警告游人勿进入某一特定区域〕
181	谢绝参观	Not Open to Visitors
182	信用卡支付	Credit Cards Accepted
183	休闲区	Leisure Area
184	宣传资料(用于旅游景区景点介绍)	Tourist/Travel Brochure
185	学生票	Student Ticket〔Ticket可以省略〕
	Y	
186	沿此路返回	This Way Back
187	沿运河生态健康步道	(The) Grand Canal Greenwalk
188	野营;露营	Camping
189	艺术品	Artwork
190	营业时间	Business Hours 或 Opening Hours
191	优惠票	Concession Ticket
192	油画	Oil Paintings
193	游步道	Walking Path/Trail
194	游程信息	Itinerary Information 或 Travel Info
195	游船	Rowboat 或 Rowing Boat〔划桨〕 Pedal Boat〔脚踏〕 Electric Boat〔电动〕

序号	中文	英文
196	游船码头	Pier 或 Boat Dock 或 Marina
197	游客报警电话： ————	Police: ____
198	游客服务中心；游客中心	Visitor/Tourist Center
199	游客停车场	Visitor Parking 或 Visitors〔用于 Parking 可以省略的场合〕
200	游客投诉电话： ————	Complaints: ____
201	游客须知	Guest Notice 或 Notice to Tourists
202	游览图	Tourist Map
203	游览指南	Tour Information
204	有佛事活动，请绕行（用于寺庙内）	Service in Progress // Please Take Another Route
205	游园须知	Park Rules 或 Park Rules and Regulations
206	玉器	Jade Ware
207	原路返回	Return the Way You Came 或 Return the Same Way You Came
208	月票	Monthly Pass
	Z	
209	赠票	Complimentary Ticket〔Ticket 可以省略〕
210	张小泉剪刀	Zhangxiaoquan Scissors
211	照相服务	Photo Service
212	中国画	Chinese Paintings
213	主入口	Main Entrance/Gate

序号	中文	英文
214	住宿区	Lodging Area
215	字画店	Painting and Calligraphy Store/Shop
216	租船处	Boat Hire/Rental

注1："〔   〕"中的内容是对英文译法的解释说明。
注2："/"表示可选择该组词语中的一种。
注3："//"表示书写时应当换行的断行处。需要同行书写时"//"应改为句点".",警示词后加惊叹号"!"。
注4："____"表示使用时应根据实际情况填入具体内容。
注5："或"前后所列出的不同译法可任意选择一种使用。
注6:解释说明中指出某个词"可以省略"的,省略该词的译文只能用于设置在该设施上的标识中,如"旅客通道"应译作 Visitors Passage,在设置于该车道上的标识中可以省略 Passage,译作 Visitors。

B.3 文化场馆、娱乐场所和文化旅游管理机构名称及其服务信息英文译写示例见表B.3。表B.3按中文汉语拼音排序。

表B.3 文化场馆、娱乐场所和文化旅游管理机构名称及其服务信息英文译写示例

序号	中文	英文
	B	
1	吧台	Bar Counter
2	办证处(指借书证)	Card Service 或 Reader Registration
3	报刊阅览区	Newspapers & Periodicals Reading Zone
4	闭馆时间	Closing Time
5	博物馆	Museum
	C	
6	畅销书	Bestsellers

序号	中文	英文
7	城市书房	Mini Library 或 Mini City Library
	D	
8	大剧院	Grand Theater
9	大舞台	Grand Stage
10	单号;单号区	Odd 或 Odd Numbers 或 Odd Numbered Seats
11	当场票	Rush Tickets〔Ticket可以省略〕
12	档案室	Archives Room〔Room可依场合省略〕
13	灯光控制室	Lighting Control Room
14	迪吧	Disco Hall
15	典藏文献书库	Collected Literature Stacks〔开放〕 或 Closed Stacks〔不开放〕
16	电竞馆	Esports Hall 或 e-Sports Hall
17	电影放映厅	Theater 或 Screen
18	电影院	Cinema 或 Movie Theater/House
19	电子游戏厅;电子游艺厅	Video Game Center
20	电子阅览室	Digital Reading Room〔Room可依场合省略〕
21	读者服务处	Reader Services
22	读者(观众或游客)止步	Staff Only
23	多媒体视听室	Multimedia Room
24	多语种原版图书区	Multi-Language Book Collections 或 Original Books in Multi-Languages

序号	中文	英文
	E	
25	儿童读物	Children's/Kids' Books 或 Books for Kids/Children
26	儿童阅览室	Children's Reading Room〔Room 可依场合省略〕
	F	
27	非本影城出售的食品请勿带入	Outside Food or Beverages Are Not Allowed Inside
28	非演职人员请勿入内;观众止步	Performers and Staff Only
29	分类目录	Subject Catalog 或 Catalog by Subject
	G	
30	歌厅	KTV 或 Karaoke Bar
31	歌舞剧场	Opera Theater/House
32	歌舞剧团	Song and Dance Troupe
33	公共检索	Catalog Search
34	观众入场门	Entrance
35	观众通道	Audience Passage〔Passage 可以省略〕
36	观众席	Auditorium
37	贵宾间	VIP Box
38	贵宾区	VIP Section
39	贵宾通道	VIP Passage〔Passage 可以省略〕
40	贵宾席	VIP Seats
41	过刊库	Back Periodical Collections 或 Non-Latest Periodical Collections

序号	中文	英文
	H	
42	还书处	Book Drop 或 Book Return
43	杭州博物馆	Hangzhou Museum
44	杭州大剧院	Hangzhou Grand Theatre
45	杭州工艺美术博物馆	Hangzhou Arts and Crafts Museum
46	杭州广播影视周报社	Hangzhou Radio, Film and Television Weekly
47	杭州国画院	Hangzhou Traditional Chinese Painting Academy
48	杭州画院(杭州油画院)	Hangzhou Art Academy (Hangzhou Oil Painting Academy)
49	杭州话剧艺术中心	Hangzhou Dramatic Arts Center
50	杭州江南丝竹南宋乐舞传习院	Hangzhou Teaching Theatre of Jiangnan String and Wind Music and Southern Song Musical Dance
51	杭州青年运动史馆	Hangzhou Youth Movement History Museum
52	杭州青少年活动中心	Hangzhou Youth and Children's Activity Center
53	杭州少年儿童图书馆	Hangzhou Children's Library
54	杭州市富阳公望美术馆	Hangzhou Fuyang Gongwang Art Museum
55	杭州市富阳区郁达夫研究工作室	Hangzhou Fuyang Yu Dafu Research Office
56	杭州市革命烈士纪念馆（蔡永祥烈士事迹陈列馆）	Hangzhou Revolutionary Martyrs Memorial Hall (Exhibition Hall of Martyr Cai Yongxiang's Deeds)

序号	中文	英文
57	杭州市工人文化宫（杭州市职工文化中心）	Hangzhou Workers' Cultural Palace (Hangzhou Cultural Center for Employees)
58	杭州市京杭运河（杭州段）综合保护中心	Hangzhou Beijing-Hangzhou Grand Canal (Hangzhou Section) Comprehensive Protection Center
59	杭州市老年活动中心	Hangzhou Senior Activity Center
60	杭州市旅游形象推广中心（杭州市商务会展旅游促进中心）	Hangzhou Tourism Image Promotion Center (Hangzhou Tourist Promotion Center for MICE)
61	杭州市旅游质量监督管理所	Hangzhou Tourism Quality Supervision and Management Office
62	杭州市市容景观发展中心	Hangzhou Cityscape Development Center
63	杭州市市政设施管理中心	Hangzhou Municipal Facilities Management Center
64	杭州市围棋队	Hangzhou Weiqi Team
65	杭州市文化馆（杭州市非物质文化遗产保护中心）	Hangzhou Cultural Center (Hangzhou Intangible Cultural Heritage Protection Center)
66	杭州市文学艺术创作研究院（杭州中国作协网络文学研究院、《西湖》杂志社）	Hangzhou Institute of Literature and Art Creation (Hangzhou Online Literature Research Academy of China Writers' Association, *West Lake* Magazine Office)
67	杭州市文史研究馆	Hangzhou Literature and History Research Institute
68	杭州市文物保护管理所	Hangzhou Management Office of Cultural Relics Protection
69	杭州市文物考古研究所	Hangzhou Cultural Relics and Archaeology Institute

序号	中文	英文
70	杭州市文物遗产与历史建筑保护中心	Hangzhou Cultural Relic and Historic Building Protection Center
71	杭州市艺术创作研究中心	Hangzhou Art Creation and Research Center
72	杭州市园林绿化发展中心	Hangzhou Landscaping Development Center
73	杭州图书馆	Hangzhou Public Library
74	杭州艺术学校	Hangzhou Art School
75	杭州越剧传习院	Hangzhou Yue Opera Teaching Theatre
76	杭州杂技总团	Hangzhou Acrobatic Troupe
77	化妆间	Dressing/Makeup Room
78	画廊	Gallery
79	会所	Club/Clubhouse〔指会所建筑物或场地〕 或 Entertainment Center〔转义,慎用〕 或 Recreation Center〔转义,慎用〕
80	会员卡充值处	Membership Card Top-up
81	会员售票处	Membership Tickets
82	会员须知	Notice to Members 或 Membership Notice/Guide
83	会员自动售票机	Ticket Vending Machine (Members Only)
84	活动中心	Activity Center
	J	
85	即将上映	Coming Soon 或 Upcoming Movies
86	教育主题书库	Education-Themed Book Collections
87	借书处	Lending Room 或 Circulation 或 Circulation Desk

序号	中文	英文
88	进口片;原版引进	Imported〔依语境,如光碟〕 Imported Films
89	进入场馆请先存包	Please Deposit Your Bag Before Entering
90	旧书	Used Books 或 Second-Hand Books
91	剧院;剧场	Theater〔美语〕 Theatre〔英语〕
	K	
92	咖啡馆	Coffee House/Shop〔House 或 Shop 可以省略〕 或 Café
93	咖啡书店	Coffee & Bookstore
94	开放时间	Opening Time/Hours 或 Business Hours
95	科技馆	Science Museum 或 Science and Technology Museum 或 Museum of Science and Technology
96	KTV 包房	KTV Room
	L	
97	老年活动中心	Senior Citizens' Activity Center
98	历史博物馆	History Museum 或 Museum of History 或 Historical Museum
99	礼品店	Gift Store/Shop 或 Souvenirs
100	良渚博物院	Liangzhu Museum
101	录像资料	Video-Recordings
	M	
102	卖品部	Shop 或 Souvenirs

序号	中文	英文
103	美术馆;艺术馆	Art Gallery/Museum
104	密集书库	Compact Stacks 或 Compact Book Stacks
105	____米以下儿童免票	Free Admission for Children Under ____ m
106	民间艺术;民间工艺	Folk Art Folk Handicrafts
107	民俗博物馆	Folk/Folklore Museum 或 Folk Culture Museum
108	名录;名人录	Directories 或 Who's Who
109	目录咨询	Catalog Information
	P	
110	____ 排	Row ____
111	排练厅	Rehearsal Room
	Q	
112	期刊阅览室	Periodicals Reading Room 或 Periodicals
113	青少年宫	Children's Palace
114	青少年活动中心	Youth Activity Center
115	请(主动)出示(有效)证件/读者证	Please Show Your (Valid) ID/Library Card
116	请爱护书籍	Please Handle Books with Care
117	请出示读者证	Please Show Your Library Card
118	请提前10分钟进场	Please Arrive 10 Minutes Prior to the Show 或 Please Arrive 10 Minutes Before the Show Begins
119	请勿长时间上网	Do Not Stay Online for Too Long

序号	中文	英文
120	请准时入场,对号入座,迟到的观众请待幕间休息时入场,就近入座。	Please arrive on time and take your assigned seat. If you are late, please take the nearest seat during the intermission.
	S	
121	散场时请从指定出口离场	Please Leave by Designated Exit
122	上网登记处	Registration
123	上网前请出示带照片的身份证件	Photo ID Required
124	上网区	Cyber Zone
125	上午场	Morning Shows
126	上线(影片)	Playing in Theaters
127	少年儿童图书馆	Children's Library
128	社区文化馆	Community Cultural Center
129	摄影	Photography
130	身份证登记	Photo ID Required
131	视频转播室	Video Control Room
132	视听室	Audio-Visual Room〔Room可依场合省略〕
133	视障人士书刊借阅处	Service for Readers with Visual Impairment
134	视障人士阅览区	Reading Area for People with Visual Impairment
135	手稿	Manuscripts
136	售票处(用于影剧院等)	Box Office 或 Tickets
137	书法	Calligraphy

續表

序号	中文	英文
138	书名目录	Title Catalog 或 Catalog by Title
139	数字图书馆	Digital Library
140	双号;双号区	Even 或 Even Numbers 或 Even Numbered Seats
141	索引	Indexes
	T	
142	特藏区	Special Collections 或 Special Book Collections
143	体验馆	Exploration/Discovery/Experience Hall
144	体验中心	Exploration/Discovery/Experience Center 〔Center 可译作 Zone〕
145	听障人士书刊借阅处	Service for Readers with Hearing Impairment
146	通宵场	All-Night Shows
147	图书编目室	Cataloging Room
148	图书查询(自助)	Book Search
149	图书查询服务(人工服务)	Book Search Services
150	图书馆	Library
151	图书借阅排行榜	Most Borrowed Books List
152	图书预定	Book Reservation
153	团体票	Group Tickets〔Tickets 可以省略〕
154	推荐图书	Recommended Books〔Books 可依据场合省略〕
	W	
155	网吧	Internet Café/Bar

序号	中文	英文
156	文化(大)礼堂	Cultural Auditorium
157	文化馆	Cultural Center
158	文史馆;文史研究馆	Research Institute of Culture and History
159	文献检索服务	Document Retrieval Service 或 Document Search Service
160	五四宪法历史资料陈列馆	The 1954 Constitution History Exhibition Hall
161	舞蹈	Dance
162	舞厅;歌舞厅	Ballroom 或 Dance Hall
	X	
163	西泠书画院	Xiling Academy of Calligraphy and Painting
164	下午场;午后场	Afternoon Shows 或 Matinée
165	下线(影片)	No Longer Showing
166	欣赏交响乐曲时,乐曲与乐章之间,请不要鼓掌	Please Do Not Applaud Between Movements
167	新刊推荐	New Periodicals
168	新书推荐	New Arrivals 或 Newly Shelved Books〔Books 可以省略〕
169	休息区	Waiting Room 或 Lounge Green Room〔专指演员休息室〕
170	休闲会馆;会所;俱乐部	Recreation Club 或 Club Clubhouse〔指会所建筑物或场地〕
171	学习长廊;学习园地;学习中心(指图书馆内的学习场所)	Learning Commons

序号	中文	英文
	Y	
172	研修空间	Group Study Rooms 或 Rooms for Group Study and Discussion
173	演播厅	Studio
174	演出进行中,请勿大声喧哗或随意走动。	Performance in progress. Please keep quiet and remain seated.
175	演出社	Performing Arts Troupe
176	演员专用通道	Performers Passage 或 Performers Only〔用于 Passage 可以省略的场合〕
177	夜场	Late-Night Shows
178	夜总会	Night Club
179	衣帽寄存;衣帽寄存处	Cloakroom
180	艺术培训中心	Art Education Center 或 Arts Training Center
181	音乐厅	Concert Hall
182	音乐文献室	Musical Documents Collection
183	音乐艺术培训中心	Music and Arts Training Center
184	音响控制室	Sound Control Room
185	音像资料	Audio-Video Recordings
186	影城	Cineplex 或 Cinema 或 Movie Theater
187	影片放映期间请关闭您的手机	Please Switch off Your Cellphone During the Show
188	影片排行榜	Film Ranking 或 Ranking〔依据语境〕

序号	中文	英文
189	影票售出谢绝退换	No Refunds or Exchanges 或 Tickets Are Not Refundable or Exchangeable
190	影院内禁止携带宠物	No Pets Allowed in Theater
191	影院内严禁摄影、录音和录像	No Photography or Recording Is Allowed in Theater
192	优惠票	Concession Tickets
193	有声读物	Audio Books
194	娱乐中心	Entertainment Center
195	____ 元/半小时	____ Yuan/Half-Hour 或____Yuan/30 Minutes
196	院线	Cinema Chain
197	阅后请放回原处	Please Reshelve Books Where You Found Them
198	阅后请放入书车，不要放回原处	Please do not reshelve books. Return them to the book trolley.
199	阅览部;阅览处;阅览室	Reading Room
200	阅览室内请保持安静	Please Keep Quiet 或 SILENCE
	Z	
201	正在上映	Now Showing/Playing
202	只可携带无色无糖饮料进阅览室	No Beverages Allowed Except Plain Water
203	中国茶叶博物馆	China National Tea Museum
204	中国共产党杭州历史馆	Hangzhou Museum for the History of Communist Party of China
205	中国美术学院国家大学科技(创意)园发展中心	Development Center for National University Sci-Tech (Creative) Park of China Academy of Art

序号	中文	英文
206	中国棋院杭州分院	China Chess Academy, Hangzhou Branch (Hangzhou Chess Academy)
207	中国湿地博物馆	China Wetland Museum
208	中国丝绸博物馆	China National Silk Museum
209	中文图书区（A、B类）	Chinese Book Collections (A & B) 或 Books in Chinese (A & B)
210	著者目录	Author Catalog 或 Catalog by Author
211	咨询台	Information Desk
212	自然博物馆	Natural History Museum 或 Museum of Natural History
213	综合阅览室	General Reading Room〔Room 可依场合省略〕
214	总服务台	General Service Counter
215	＿＿＿＿ 座	Seat ＿＿＿＿

注 1："〔 〕"中的内容是对英文译法的解释说明。

注 2："/"表示可选择该组词语中的一种。

注 3："//"表示书写时应当换行的断行处。需要同行书写时"//"应改为句"."，警示词后加惊叹号"!"。

注 4："＿＿＿＿"表示使用时应根据实际情况填入具体内容。

注 5："或"前后所列出的不同译法可任意选择一种使用。

附录 C

（资料性）

会展赛事场馆及机构名称英文译写示例

C.1 会展赛事场馆及机构名称英文译写示例见表C.1。表C.1按中文汉语拼音排序。

表C.1 会展赛事场馆和机构名称英文译写示例

序号	中文	英文
	A	
1	按摩室（体育比赛场地用）	Massage Room
	B	
2	棒球场	Baseball Field
3	保龄球馆（房）	Bowling Alley
4	滨江体育馆	Binjiang Gymnasium
	C	
5	陈列馆	Exhibition Hall/Gallery
6	城市规划展示馆	Urban Planning Exhibition Hall
7	淳安界首体育中心公路自行车赛场	Chun'an Jieshou Sports Centre Cycling Road Course〔Centre 为亚运会官方用法，其他亚运场馆也使用该拼写形式〕
8	淳安界首体育中心山地自行车赛场	Chun'an Jieshou Sports Centre Mountain Bike Course
9	淳安界首体育中心田径训练场	Chun'an Jieshou Sports Centre Athletics Training Field
10	淳安界首体育中心铁人三项赛场	Chun'an Jieshou Sports Centre Triathlon Course
11	淳安界首体育中心小轮车赛场	Chun'an Jieshou Sports Centre BMX Course

序号	中文	英文
12	淳安界首体育中心游泳赛场	Chun'an Jieshou Sports Centre Swimming Course
13	淳安界首体育中心游泳训练场	Chun'an Jieshou Sports Centre Swimming Training Pool
14	淳安界首体育中心自行车馆	Chun'an Jieshou Sports Centre Velodrome
	D	
15	灯光球场	Floodlit Playing Field
16	地掷球场	Bocce Court
	E	
17	2022年第19届亚运会组委会	The 19th Asian Games Hangzhou 2022 Organising Committee
	F	
18	富阳水上运动中心	Fuyang Water Sports Centre
19	富阳体育中心体育馆	Fuyang Sports Centre Gymnasium
20	富阳银湖体育中心	Fuyang Yinhu Sports Centre
	G	
21	高尔夫球场	Golf Course
22	拱墅运河体育公园体育场	Gongshu Canal Sports Park Stadium
23	拱墅运河体育公园体育馆	Gongshu Canal Sports Park Gymnasium
24	国际博览中心	International Expo Center
	H	
25	旱冰场;轮滑场	Roller Skating Rink
26	杭州奥体博览中心	Hangzhou Olympic Sports Expo Center

序号	中文	英文
27	杭州奥体中心	Hangzhou Olympic Sports Center
28	杭州奥体中心国博壁球馆	Hangzhou Olympic Sports Centre Squash Court
29	杭州奥体中心体育场	Hangzhou Olympic Sports Centre Stadium
30	杭州奥体中心体育馆	Hangzhou Olympic Sports Centre Gymnasium
31	杭州奥体中心网球中心	Hangzhou Olympic Sports Centre Tennis Centre
32	杭州奥体中心游泳馆	Hangzhou Olympic Sports Centre Aquatic Sports Arena
33	杭州奥体中心综合训练馆	Hangzhou Olympic Sports Centre Training Hall
34	杭州陈经纶体育学校体育场	Hangzhou Chenjinglun Sports School Athletics Field
35	杭州大关游泳健身馆	Hangzhou Daguan Swim Gym
36	杭州电子科技大学体育场	Hangzhou Dianzi University Athletics Field
37	杭州电子科技大学体育馆	Hangzhou Dianzi University Gymnasium
38	杭州模型无线电运动基地	Hangzhou Model and Radio Sports Base
39	杭州棋院(智力大厦)棋类馆	Hangzhou Qi-Yuan (Zhili) Chess Hall
40	杭州全民健身中心	Hangzhou Public Fitness Centre
41	杭州师范大学(仓前校区)体育场	Hangzhou Normal University Cangqian Athletics Field
42	杭州师范大学(仓前校区)体育馆	Hangzhou Normal University Cangqian Gymnasium
43	杭州市陈经纶体育学校	Hangzhou Chenjinglun Sports School
44	杭州市发展会展业服务中心	Hangzhou MICE Development Service Center

序号	中文	英文
45	杭州市国民体质监测中心	Hangzhou National Physical Monitoring Center
46	杭州市少年儿童业余学校	Hangzhou Children's Amateur School
47	杭州市社会体育指导中心	Hangzhou Social Sports Guidance Center
48	杭州市射击射箭自行车项目管理中心	Hangzhou Shooting Archery and Cycling Management Center
49	杭州市水上运动中心	Hangzhou Aquatic Sports Center
50	杭州市体育彩票管理中心	Hangzhou Sports Lottery Management Center
51	杭州市体育事业发展中心	Hangzhou Sports Development Center
52	杭州市文化创意产业发展中心（杭州市动漫游戏产业发展中心）	Hangzhou Center for Cultural and Creative Industries (Hangzhou Development Center for ACG Industry)
53	杭州市足球运动管理中心	Hangzhou Football Management Center
54	杭州体育场	Hangzhou Stadium
55	杭州体育馆	Hangzhou Gymnasium
56	杭州文汇学校草地掷球场	Hangzhou Wenhui School Lawn Bowls Green
57	杭州游泳健身馆	Hangzhou Swimming Centre
58	杭州游泳馆	Hangzhou Swimming Center
59	杭州之江文化创意中心	Hangzhou Zhijiang Cultural Creative Center
60	黄龙体育中心	Huanglong Sports Centre
61	黄龙体育中心体育场	Huanglong Sports Centre Stadium
62	黄龙体育中心体育馆	Huanglong Sports Centre Gymnasium

序号	中文	英文
63	黄龙体育中心田径训练场	Huanglong Sports Centre Athletics Training Field
64	黄龙体育中心游泳跳水馆	Huanglong Sports Centre Swimming & Diving Centre
65	会展中心	Convention and Exhibition Center 或 Convention Center
	J	
66	健身培训中心	Fitness Training Center
67	健身中心（俱乐部）	Fitness Center 或 Fitness/Health Club
68	举重馆	Weightlifting Gym
	K	
69	卡丁车场	Karting Track 或 Go-Kart Track
	L	
70	篮球场	Basketball Court
71	篮球馆	Basketball Gym
72	垒球场	Softball Field
73	力量训练房	Strength Training Gym
74	临安体育文化会展中心体育馆	Lin'an Sports Culture & Exhibition Centre
75	临平体育中心体育场	Linping Sports Centre Stadium
76	临平体育中心体育馆	Linping Sports Centre Gymnasium
	M	
77	门球场	Gate Ball Court 或 Croquet Court〔Court 均可译作 Field〕

序号	中文	英文
	P	
78	排球场	Volleyball Court
79	排球馆	Volleyball Gym
80	攀岩场	Climbing Gym/Wall
81	乒乓球馆	Table Tennis Gym
	Q	
82	棋牌房(馆)	Chess and Cards Room〔Room 可依场合省略〕
83	棋牌俱乐部	Board Games Club
84	棋院	Chess Institute
85	钱塘轮滑中心	Qiantang Roller Sports Centre
86	曲棍球场	Hockey Field
87	拳击馆	Boxing Gym
	R	
88	柔道馆	Judo Gym
	S	
89	桑拿浴(室)房	Sauna Room〔Room 可依场合省略〕
90	沙滩排球场	Beach Volleyball Court
91	山地自行车赛场	Mountain Bike Racing Field
92	上城体育中心水球馆	Shangcheng Sports Centre Water Polo Arena
93	上城体育中心体育场	Shangcheng Sports Centre Stadium
94	射击馆	Shooting Range
95	射箭场(馆)	Archery Range

序号	中文	英文
96	手球场	Handball Court
97	手球馆	Handball Gym
98	摔跤馆	Wrestling Gym
	T	
99	台球馆；桌球馆	Billiard Hall
100	体操馆	Gymnasium
101	体育场	Stadium
102	体育公园	Sports Park
103	体育馆	Indoor Stadium 或 Gymnasium 或 Sports Hall
104	体育交流中心	Sports Exchange Center
105	体育俱乐部	Sports Club
106	体育中心	Sports Complex/Center
107	天然游泳场	Natural Swimming Pool
108	田径场	Track-and-Field Ground
109	跳水池	Diving Pool
110	桐庐马术中心	Tonglu Equestrian Centre
	W	
111	网球场	Tennis Court
112	网球中心	Tennis Center
113	武术馆	Wushu Gym 或 Martial Arts Gym

序号	中文	英文
	X	
114	西湖国际高尔夫球场	West Lake International Golf Course
115	萧山瓜沥文化体育中心	Xiaoshan Guali Sports Centre
116	萧山临浦体育馆	Xiaoshan Linpu Gymnasium
117	萧山体育中心体育场	Xiaoshan Sports Centre Stadium
118	萧山体育中心体育馆	Xiaoshan Sports Centre Gymnasium
119	训练馆	Training Gym
120	训练基地	Training Center
	Y	
121	游泳馆	Natatorium 或 Indoor Swimming Pool
122	瑜伽馆	Yoga Gym
123	羽毛球馆	Badminton Gym
	Z	
124	展览馆;展示馆	Exhibition Hall
125	展览中心	Exhibition Center
126	浙江财经大学东体育场	Zhejiang University of Finance & Economics East Athletics Field
127	浙江传媒学院(下沙校区)体育场	Communication University of Zhejiang Xiasha Athletics Field
128	浙江大学(紫金港校区)体育馆	Zhejiang University Zijingang Gymnasium
129	浙江工商大学文体中心	Zhejiang Gongshang University Sports Centre
130	浙江工业大学(屏峰校区)板球场	Zhejiang University of Technology Pingfeng Cricket Field

序号	中文	英文
131	浙江建设职业技术学院体能训练场	Zhejiang College of Construction Training Field
132	浙江建设职业技术学院体育场	Zhejiang College of Construction Athletics Field
133	浙江警察学院体育场	Zhejiang Police College Athletics Field
134	浙江理工大学体育场	Zhejiang Sci-Tech University Athletics Field
135	浙江旅游职业学院体育场	Tourism College of Zhejiang Athletics Field
136	浙江师范大学(萧山校区)体育场	Zhejiang Normal University Xiaoshan Athletics Field
137	浙江师范大学(萧山校区)体育馆	Zhejiang Normal University Xiaoshan Gymnasium
138	浙江塘栖盲人门球基地门球馆	China Goalball Training Base
139	浙江体育职业技术学院体操馆	Zhejiang College of Sports Gymnastics Hall
140	浙江体育职业技术学院田径场	Zhejiang College of Sports Athletics Field
141	浙江体育职业技术学院重竞技馆	Zhejiang College of Sports Training Hall
142	浙江中医药大学体育场	Zhejiang Chinese Medical University Athletics Field
143	中国杭州电竞中心	China Hangzhou Esports Centre
144	中国计量大学北体育场	China Jiliang University North Athletics Field
145	中国社区建设展示中心	China Exhibition Center for Community Construction and Development
146	自行车馆	Velodrome 或 Cycling Center
147	自行车赛场	Cycling Track
148	综合房(馆)	General Gym

序号	中文	英文
149	足球场	Football/Soccer Field

注1:"〔 〕"中的内容是对英文译法的解释说明。
注2:"/"表示可选择该组词语中的一种。
注3:"//"表示书写时应当换行的断行处。需要同行书写时"//"应改为句点".",警示词后加惊叹号"!"。
注4:" _____ "表示使用时应根据实际情况填入具体内容。
注5:"或"前后所列出的不同译法可任意选择一种使用。

C.2 会展赛事服务信息英文译写示例见表C.2。表C.2按中文汉语拼音排序。

表C.2 会展赛事服务信息英文译写示例

序号	中文	英文
	B	
1	比赛场馆	Competition Venues
2	闭馆时间	Closing Time
3	标本室	Specimen Room 或 Specimens〔用于 Room 可以省略的场合〕
4	表演区	Performance Area
5	不外售	Not for Sale
	C	
6	裁判区	Referee Area
7	裁判台	Referee Stand
8	裁判员室	Referee/Umpire Room〔用于板球、棒球裁判员室〕
9	参观商(会展用)	Visitors 或 Visiting Businesses 或 Business Visitors

序号	中文	英文
10	参展商(会展用)	Exhibitors
11	场馆区示意图	Schematic Diagram of Venues
12	场馆示意图;导览图	Map 或 Sketch/Site Map 或 Map and Guide 或 Guide Map 或 Venue Map〔用于场馆内部〕
13	承包商(会展用)	Contractor/Contractors〔视承包商数量选用〕
14	储藏室	Storeroom 或 Storage
15	触摸区	Hands-on Area 或 Touch Area
16	瓷器馆	Porcelain Gallery 或 Porcelains〔用于 Gallery 可以省略的场合〕
	D	
17	打印复印室	Printing and Copying
18	当场票	Rush Ticket〔Ticket 可以省略〕
19	当日使用,逾期作废	Valid on Day of Issue Only〔指购票当日有效〕 Valid for the Date Displayed on the Ticket〔指票面上印刷的日期当日有效〕
20	导览册	Guides
21	导览机;语音导览	Audio/Multimedia Guide
22	灯光控制室	Light Control Room
23	等分席(花样滑冰场馆用)	Kiss & Cry 或 Waiting Seats for Coming Scores
24	电气室	Power Supply Room
25	电视评论席	TV Commentary Box 或 TV Commentators

序号	中文	英文
26	动手项目;动手操作	Hands-on Activities
	F	
27	发言讲台;主席台	Rostrum
28	风机房	Ventilator Room
29	复制品;仿制品	Duplicate 或 Replica
	G	
30	更衣室	Locker Room
31	工艺美术品	Arts and Crafts
32	工作人员区	Staff Area
33	供应食品饮料(展馆或展区内用)	Food and Beverages
34	古代家具馆	Ancient Furniture Gallery〔Gallery 可以省略〕
35	古代钱币馆	Ancient Coins Gallery〔Gallery 可以省略〕
36	古代珍宝馆	Historical Treasures Gallery〔Gallery 可以省略〕
37	观赏区	Viewing Area 或 For Viewing
38	观众服务区	Spectator Service Area
39	观众入口	Spectator Entrance 或 Spectators〔用于 Entrance 可以省略的场合〕
40	观众通道	Spectator Passage 或 Spectators〔用于 Passage 可以省略的场合〕
41	观众席	Spectator Seats
42	观众席区	Spectator Area
43	观众止步;员工专用	Staff Only

序号	中文	英文
44	官员区(体育场馆内用)	Officials Area
45	馆藏(指文物)	Museum Collection
46	馆内布展,暂停开放	Temporarily Closed for Remodeling
47	广播室;广播站	Broadcasting Room〔规模较大〕 或 Broadcast Room〔规模较小〕
48	广播寻人寻物	Paging Service
49	贵宾间	VIP Box
50	贵宾通道	VIP Passage〔Passage 可以省略〕
51	贵宾席	VIP Seats
52	贵宾休息室	VIP Lounge〔Lounge 可以省略〕
	H	
53	会员须知	Notice to Members 或 Membership Notice/Guide
54	混合区(媒体自由采访区域)	Mixed Zone
	J	
55	计时控制室	Timing Control Room
56	记者休息室	Press/Media Lounge
57	纪念品商店	Souvenir Store/Shop 或 Gift Store/Shop 或 Gifts & Souvenirs 或 Souvenirs & Gifts
58	技术代表室	Technical Delegates Office 或 Technical Delegates' Office
59	检录处(体育比赛场地用)	Call Room/Area
60	讲解服务	Guide Service

序号	中文	英文
61	进入场馆请先存包	Please Deposit Your Bag Before Entering
62	禁止进入比赛场地	Competition Area // Entry Prohibited
63	禁止跳水	No Diving
64	竞赛办公室	Competition Office
65	竞赛区	Competition Arena
	K	
66	开放时间	Opening Hours
67	开馆时间	Opening Time
68	看台	Spectators Stand 或 Grandstand〔上边有顶、观看露天比赛的大看台〕
69	客队休息室（体育比赛场地用）	Guest Team Lounge〔Lounge 可以省略〕
	L	
70	淋浴室;浴室	Showers
71	（露天)看台	Bleachers〔美语〕 Grandstand〔上边有顶、观看露天比赛的大看台〕
	M	
72	门票价格	Ticket Rates 或 Rates
73	＿＿米以下儿童免票	Free Admission for Children Under ＿＿ m
74	＿＿米以下儿童谢绝入内	No Admittance for Children Under ＿＿ m
75	民间收藏(指文物)	Private Collection

序号	中文	英文
76	模型	Model〔注意根据展出的模型数量选择使用单复数〕
	N	
77	男更衣室	Men's Locker Room
78	男淋浴室	Men's Showers
79	女更衣室	Women's Locker Room
80	女淋浴室	Women's Showers
81	女子通道,男宾止步（游泳馆内用）	Women Only
	P	
82	票已售出,概不退换	No Refunds or Exchanges
83	票已售完	Sold Out
84	凭票入场	Admission by Ticket 或 Ticket Holders Only
	Q	
85	漆器馆	Lacquer Gallery〔Gallery可以省略〕
86	器材室	Equipment Room
87	浅水区	Shallow End
88	浅水区域,禁止跳水	Shallow End // No Diving
89	青铜器馆	Bronze Gallery 或 Bronzes〔用于Gallery可以省略的场合〕
90	请爱护体育器材	Please Take Good Care of Sports Facilities
91	请继续参观;参观由此向前;由此参观	Please Proceed This Way

序号	中文	英文
92	请上楼继续参观	Exhibition Continues Upstairs
93	请提前____分钟进场	Please Enter____ Minutes Ahead of Schedule
94	请勿触摸(展品)	Please Do Not Touch 或 Hands Off
95	请勿在此进行球类活动	No Ball Games Here
	S	
96	散场时请从指定出口离场	Please Leave by Designated Exit
97	散场通道	Exit
98	摄影记者区	Photo Zone
99	深水区	Deep End
100	视听区	Audio-Visual Area
101	视听室	Audio-Visual Room
102	手工艺品	Handicrafts
103	书画馆;字画馆	Painting and Calligraphy Gallery〔Gallery 可以省略〕
104	丝织品	Silk Fabrics 或 Silks
	T	
105	体能测评室(体育竞赛场地用)	Physical Fitness Test Room
106	体验区	Experience/Exploration/Discovery Area〔Zone 可代替 Area〕
107	替补席(体育竞赛场地用)	Substitutes Bench

序号	中文	英文
108	通道,过道(座位区之间)	Aisle
109	通行区;场馆公众区	Front of House〔可以缩写为FOH〕
110	团体接待	Group Reception
111	团体票	Group Ticket〔Ticket可以省略〕
112	团体入口	Group Entrance〔Entrance可以省略〕
	W	
113	文物	Cultural Relic/Relics
114	文物鉴定(古董鉴定)	Antique Authentication/Appraisals
115	文字记者席	Press Box/Seats
	X	
116	现代书画馆	Modern Painting and Calligraphy Gallery〔Gallery可以省略〕 或 Gallery of Calligraphy and Painting
117	协办单位	Co-host/Co-organizer/Co-sponsor
118	新闻办公室	Press/Media Office
119	新闻发布厅	News/Press Conference Hall
120	新闻媒体区	Media Area
121	新闻中心	Press Center
122	兴奋剂检查室(体育竞赛场地用)	Doping Control Station/Room
123	休闲区	Leisure Area
124	巡回展览	Itinerant/Roving Exhibition

序号	中文	英文
125	训练场馆	Training Venues
	Y	
126	严禁有皮肤病或其他传染性疾病者使用游泳池	People suffering from skin diseases or other infectious diseases are not allowed to swim in the pool. 或 Guests with skin diseases or other infectious diseases are not allowed in the pool.
127	医务室	Clinic 或 Medical Room
128	艺术品	Artwork
129	油画馆	Oil Paintings Gallery〔Gallery 可以省略〕
130	玉器馆	Jade Gallery〔Gallery 可以省略〕
131	原路返回	Return the Way You Came 或 Return the Same Way You Came
132	____元/半小时	____Yuan/Half Hour 或 ____Yuan/30 Minutes
133	运动员村	Athletes' Village
134	运动员席	Athletes' Seats 或 For Athletes Box
135	运动员休息室	Athletes Lounge〔Lounge 可以省略〕
136	运动员专用通道	Athletes Passage 或 Athletes Only〔用于 Passage 可以省略的场合〕
137	运营区;场馆工作区（展览场馆用）	Venue Operation Area 或 Back of House Area 或 Back of House〔可以缩写为 BOH〕
	Z	
138	赞助商	Sponsor General Sponsor〔指总赞助商〕 Leading/Lead/Chief/Main/Major/Principal/Primary Sponsor〔指主要或首席赞助商〕

序号	中文	英文
139	展板	Display Board/Panel
140	展场;展区	Exhibition/Display Area
141	展馆(厅)	Exhibition Hall/Gallery
142	展柜	Showcase
143	展架	Display Rack/Shelf
144	展品	Exhibits
145	展品不外售	Not for Sale
146	展室;陈列室	Exhibition/Display Room
147	中场休息	Halftime
148	仲裁办公室(体育竞赛场地用)	Arbitration Office 或 Jury's Office
149	主办单位(者)	Host/Organizer/Sponsor
150	主队休息室(体育竞赛场地用)	Host Team Lounge〔Lounge 可以省略〕
151	主题展览	Theme Exhibition
152	注意水深(游泳竞赛场地用)	CAUTION // Deep Water
153	综合性展览	General/Comprehensive Exhibition

注1:"〔 〕"中的内容是对英文译法的解释说明。

注2:"/"表示可选择该组词语中的一种。

注3:"//"表示书写时应当换行的断行处。需要同行书写时"//"应改为句点".",警示词后加惊叹号"!"。

注4:"_____"表示使用时应根据实际情况填入具体内容。

注5:"或"前后所列出的不同译法可任意选择一种使用。

注6:解释说明中指出某个词"可以省略"的,省略该词的译文只能用于设置在该设施上的标识中,如"瓷器馆"应译作 Porcelain Gallery,在设置于该处所的标识中可以省略 Gallery,译作 Porcelains。

C.3 体育运动项目和比赛名称英文译写示例见表C.3。表C.3按中文汉语拼音排序。

表C.3 体育运动项目名称和比赛名称英文译写示例

序号	中文	英文
	B	
1	1/8决赛;八强赛	1/8 Finals 或 Eighth Finals
2	BMX小轮车	BMX Racing
3	拔河	Tug of War
4	半决赛	Semifinals 或 Semi-Finals
5	板球	Cricket
6	棒球	Baseball
7	保龄球	Bowling
8	蹦床	Trampoline Gymnastics
9	蹦极	Bungee Jump
10	壁球	Squash 或 Racket Ball
11	冰壶	Curling
12	冰球	Ice Hockey
	C	
13	踩伞	Canopy Formation Parachuting〔Parachuting 可以省略〕
14	常规赛	Regular Season
15	场地自行车	Track Cycling 或 Cycling Track
16	超级大奖赛	Super Grand Prix

序号	中文	英文
17	超级联赛	Super League
18	超轻型飞机	Ultralight Aircraft
19	冲浪	Surfing
	D	
20	大师杯	Masters Cup
21	大师赛	Masters Tournament
22	单板滑雪	Snowboarding
23	登山	Mountaineering
24	低空伞	Low Altitude Parachuting
25	电动公路车	Electric On-Road Vehicle
26	电动越野车	Electric Off-Road Vehicle
27	电子竞技	Esports 或 e-Sports 或 Electronic Sports
28	钓鱼	Angling
29	定点跳伞	Building, Antenna, Span and Earth Jumping 或 BASE Jumping
30	定向	Orienteering
31	冬季两项	Biathlon
32	动力滑翔伞	Powered Paraglider 或 Paramotor
33	动力艇	Motor Boat
34	短道速滑	Short Track Speed Skating
35	对抗赛	Dual Meet

序号	中文	英文
	F	
36	帆板	Wind Surfing
37	帆船	Sailing 或 Yacht Racing 或 Sailboat
38	飞镖	Darts
39	风筝	Kite
	G	
40	橄榄球（英式）	Rugby
41	高尔夫球	Golf
42	高山滑雪	Alpine Skiing
43	公开赛	Open Championships
44	公开水域游泳	Open Water Swimming
45	公路自行车	Road Cycling 或 Cycling Road
46	冠军杯赛	Champions Cup
47	国际集结赛	World Rally Championships
48	国际象棋	Chess
	H	
49	花样滑冰	Figure Skating
50	花样跳伞	Artistic Events
51	花样游泳	Synchronized Swimming 或 Artistic Swimming
52	滑板	Skateboarding
53	滑冰	Skating

序号	中文	英文
54	滑草	Grass Skiing
55	滑水	Water Skiing/Ski
56	滑翔	Gliding
57	滑翔机	Glider
58	滑翔伞	Paraglider 或 Parachute Glider
59	滑雪	Skiing
60	滑雪定向	Ski Orienteering
61	混合式飞球	Hybrid Balloon
	J	
62	击剑	Fencing
63	激流回旋	Canoe and Kayak Slalom
64	GPS定向	GPS Orienteering
65	技巧	Sports Acrobatics
66	甲级联赛	League One
67	健美	Bodybuilding
68	健美操	Aerobics
69	健身气功	Health Qigong
70	毽球	Shuttlecock
71	街舞	Street Dance
72	锦标赛	Championships 或 Tournament
73	精英赛	Classic Match
74	竞技体操	Artistic Gymnastics

序号	中文	英文
75	竞速小轮车	Cycling BMX Racing
76	静水（皮划艇）	Canoe and Kayak Flatwater
77	救生	Life Saving
78	举重	Weightlifting
79	决赛	Final
	K	
80	卡巴迪	Kabaddi
81	卡丁车	Go-Karting
82	克柔术	Kurash
83	空手道	Karate
	L	
84	拉力赛	Rally Racing 或 Rallying
85	篮球	Basketball
86	垒球	Softball
87	联赛	League
88	龙舟	Dragon Boat
89	轮滑	Roller Skating 或 Roller Blading〔直排轮滑〕
90	轮椅定向	Trail Orienteering
	M	
91	马拉松游泳	Marathon Swimming
92	马术	Equestrian

序号	中文	英文
93	（盲人）五人制足球	Futsal 或 Five-a-Side Football 或 Blind Football〔盲人（五人制）足球〕
94	门球	Gate Ball 或 Croquet
95	摩托车	Motorbike 或 Motorcycling
96	摩托艇	Motorboat 或 Motorboating
	N	
97	耐力赛	Endurance Racing
98	年终总决赛	Annual Finals
	P	
99	排球	Volleyball
100	排位赛	Qualifying Tournament 或 Qualifier
101	攀岩	Rock Climbing 或 Sport Climbing
102	跑步	Running
103	皮划艇	Canoe and Kayak
104	皮划艇激流回旋	Canoe Slalom
105	皮划艇静水	Canoe Sprint
106	霹雳舞	Breaking 或 Break Dance
107	漂流	River Rafting
108	乒乓球	Table Tennis 或 Ping Pong
109	坡地滑行	Slope Sliding

序号	中文	英文
110	蹼泳	Fin Swimming
	Q	
111	骑马	Horse Riding
112	七人制橄榄球	Rugby Sevens
113	牵引伞	Parascending 或 Extraction Parachute
114	潜水	Underwater/Scuba Diving
115	潜泳	Underwater Swimming
116	桥牌	Bridge
117	青年锦标赛	Junior/Youth Championships
118	曲棍球	Hockey
119	拳击	Boxing
120	拳王争霸赛	Boxing Championship
	R	
121	热气球	Hot Air Balloon
122	柔道	Judo
123	柔术	Ju-jitsu
124	软式网球	Soft Tennis
	S	
125	赛龙舟	Dragon Boat Race
126	赛艇	Rowing〔人力〕 或 Speed Boat〔机动〕
127	三人篮球	3 × 3 Basketball
128	散打	Sanda

序号	中文	英文
129	沙壶球	Shuffleboard
130	沙滩排球	Beach Volleyball
131	山地车定向	Mountain Bike Orienteering
132	山地户外运动	Mountain Sports
133	山地自行车	Mountain Cycling 或 Cycling MTB
134	射击	Shooting
135	射箭	Archery
136	世界杯	World Cup
137	手球	Handball
138	摔跤	Wrestling
139	水球	Water Polo
140	1/4决赛;四强赛	1/4 Finals 或 Quarter Finals
141	速度滑冰	Speed Skating
	T	
142	台球	Billiards
143	跆拳道	Taekwondo
144	套路	Taolu 或 Routine
145	特技跳伞	Freefall Style Parachuting〔Parachuting 可以省略〕
146	藤球	Sepaktakraw
147	体操	Gymnastics
148	体育舞蹈	Dance Sport

序号	中文	英文
149	田径	Athletics
150	挑战赛;擂台赛	Challenge
151	跳伞	Parachuting
152	跳水	Diving
153	跳台滑雪	Ski Jumping
154	铁人三项	Triathlon
155	徒步定向	Foot Orienteering
	W	
156	网球	Tennis
157	围棋	Weiqi 或 Go
158	无线电测向	Radio Direction Finding
159	无线电通信	Radio Communication
160	无线电遥控(航空模型)	Radio-Controlled Aeromodelling
161	五子棋	Five-in-a-Row 或 Renju 或 Gobang
162	武术	Wushu 或 Martial Arts 或 Kung Fu
163	舞龙舞狮	Dragon and Lion Dance
	X	
164	现代五项	Modern Pentathlon
165	象棋	Xiangqi
166	小组赛	Group Stage

序号	中文	英文
167	信鸽	Pigeon Race
168	悬挂滑翔	Hang Gliding
169	巡回赛	Tour
170	巡回赛总决赛	Tour Finals
	Y	
171	邀请赛	Invitational Tournament
172	业余无线电	Amateur Radio
173	业余无线电台	Amateur Radio Station
174	艺术体操	Rhythmic Gymnastics
175	游泳	Swimming
176	羽毛球	Badminton
177	越野滑雪	Cross Country Skiing
178	越野锦标赛;拉力锦标赛	Rally Championships
	Z	
179	职业联赛	Professional League
180	掷球	Boules
181	中国式摔跤	Shuaijiao 或 Shuai Jiao 或 Chinese Wrestling
182	中国象棋	Xiangqi 或 Chinese Chess
183	自行车运动	Cycling
184	自由式滑雪	Freestyle Skiing

序号	中文	英文
185	足球	Football 或 Soccer

注1:"〔　〕"中的内容是对英文译法的解释说明。
注2:"或"前后所列出的不同译法可任意选择一种使用。

附录 D

（资料性）

学校和管理机构名称及学校服务信息英文译写示例

D.1 学校和管理机构名称及学校服务信息英文译写示例见表 D.1。表 D.1 按中文汉语拼音排序。

表 D.1 学校和管理机构名称及学校服务信息英文译写示例

序号	中文	英文
	B	
1	办公楼;行政楼	Administration/Office Building
2	办公室	General Affairs Office〔用于教育行政管理部门办公室〕 CPC Committee Office〔用于学校党委办公室〕 Administration Office〔用于学校行政办公室〕
3	保卫处	Division of Campus Security
4	本教室设有监控	This classroom is under video monitoring.
5	编辑部(学校校报、学报)	Editorial Office
6	不得将本食堂餐具带出	Do Not Remove Tableware
7	不得擅动实验器材	Do Not Use Any Lab Equipment Without Permission
8	不得在课桌上刻划	No Scratching or Doodling on Desk
9	不得占座	No Seat Reservation
	C	
10	财务处	Finance Division
11	采证摄像头	Photo ID Camera

序号	中文	英文
12	餐具回收处	Tray Return Station/Point〔Station/Point 可以省略〕
13	餐厅内禁止打牌	No Card Games Allowed in Canteen
14	操场	Playground
15	出版社	Press 或 Publishing House
16	出租车不得进入校园	No Taxis Allowed on Campus 或 No Taxis〔设置在校门口〕
17	出租车请从____门进入	Taxi Entrance at Gate ____
	D	
18	大礼堂;礼堂	Auditorium 或 Assembly Hall
19	大学生活动中心	Student Center
20	档案馆(室)	Archives 或 Archive Room
21	党委统战部	CPC United Front Work Department
22	党委宣传部	CPC Publicity Department
23	党委组织部	CPC Organization Department
24	德育与体育卫生艺术教育处(教育管理部门内设机构)	Division of Moral, Physical, Health and Arts Education
25	电子阅览室	Digital Reading Room
26	督导处	Supervision Division
27	读者服务	Reader Services
28	多功能教室	Multifunctional/Multifunction Classroom
29	多媒体教室	Multimedia Classroom

序号	中文	英文
30	多媒体视听室	Multimedia Audio-Visual Room 或 Multimedia Room
	F	
31	法规处（教育管理部门内设机构）	Laws and Regulations Division
32	饭票（客餐券）	Meal Voucher/Ticket
	G	
33	港澳台办公室	Office of Hong Kong, Macao and Taiwan Affairs
34	高等教育处（教育管理部门内设机构）	Higher Education Division
35	公告栏	Notice/Bulletin Board
36	公共吹风机	Hair Dryer
37	公共检索（用于图书馆）	Catalog Search
38	国际交流处（交流合作处）	Division of International Exchange and Cooperation
39	国际交流学院	School of International Exchange 或 College of International Exchange
	H	
40	还书处	Book Drop/Return
41	杭州第二中学钱江学校	Qianjiang School of Hangzhou No. 2 High School
42	杭州第四中学江东学校	Jiangdong School of Hangzhou No. 4 High School
43	杭州高级中学钱塘学校	Qiantang School of Zhejiang Hangzhou High School
44	杭州科技职业技术学院	Hangzhou Polytechnic

序号	中文	英文
45	杭州老年大学（杭州老干部大学）	Hangzhou Senior University (Hangzhou University for Retired Officials)
46	杭州师范大学	Hangzhou Normal University
47	杭州师范大学附属中学	The Affiliated High School to Hangzhou Normal University
48	杭州市财经职业学校	Hangzhou Vocational School of Finance and Economics
49	杭州市城西中学	Hangzhou Chengxi Middle School
50	杭州市电子信息职业学校	Hangzhou Vocational School of Electronics and Information
51	杭州市基础教育研究室	Hangzhou Research Institute of Elementary Education
52	杭州市交通职业高级中学	Hangzhou Vocational School of Transportation
53	杭州市教育发展服务中心	Hangzhou Education Development Service Center
54	杭州市教育考试院	Hangzhou Education Examinations Authority
55	杭州市教育科学研究院	Hangzhou Research Institute of Education Science
56	杭州市开元商贸职业学校	Hangzhou Kaiyuan Business Vocational School
57	杭州市旅游职业学校（杭州市综合中等专业学校）	Hangzhou Tourism Vocational School (Hangzhou Comprehensive Secondary Specialized School)
58	杭州市美术职业学校	Hangzhou Vocational School for Arts
59	杭州市人民职业学校	Hangzhou Renmin Vocational School
60	杭州市社会科学院	Hangzhou Academy of Social Sciences
61	杭州市源清中学	Hangzhou Yuanqing High School
62	杭州市长河高级中学	Hangzhou Changhe High School

序号	中文	英文
63	杭州市中策职业学校	Hangzhou Zhongce Vocational School
64	杭州市中策职业学校钱塘学校	Qiantang School of Hangzhou Zhongce Vocational School
65	杭州万向职业技术学院	Hangzhou Wanxiang Polytechnic
66	杭州文汇学校	Hangzhou Wenhui School
67	杭州学军中学海创园学校	Haichuangyuan School of Hangzhou Xuejun High School
68	杭州职业技术学院	Hangzhou Vocational & Technical College
69	化学实验室	Chemistry Laboratory/Lab
70	会议中心	Conference/Convention Center
	J	
71	机动车不得进入校园	No Motor Vehicles Allowed on Campus 或 No Motor Vehicles〔设置在校门口〕
72	基础教育处（教育管理部门内设机构）	Basic Education Division
73	计划财务处（教育管理部门内设机构）	Planning and Finance Division
74	计划基建财务处（教育管理部门内设机构）	Financial Division for Planned Infrastructure
75	计算机房	Computer Room
76	继续教育管理处（教育管理部门内设机构）	Division of Continuing Education Management
77	继续教育学院	School of Continuing Education 或 College of Continuing Education
78	监控摄像头	Surveillance Camera
79	健身中心	Fitness Center 或 Health Club

序号	中文	英文
80	教师窗口	Faculty Counter/Window 或 For Faculty〔用于 Counter 或 Window 可以省略的场合〕
81	教师宿舍	Faculty Dormitory/Apartments
82	教室	Classroom
83	教师食堂;教师餐厅	Faculty Canteen
84	教务处	Division of Academic Affairs 或 Division of Academic Studies
85	教学楼	Teaching/Classroom Building
86	教学秘书办公室	Academic Secretary's Office
87	阶梯教室	Lecture Theatre 或 Terrace Classroom
88	借书处	Circulation
89	仅限本校车辆(通行或停放)	Authorized Vehicles Only
90	进出校门请下车推行	Cyclists Dismount 或 Cyclists Please Dismount 或 Cyclists Dismount // Walk Bikes/Bicycles 〔设置在校门口〕
91	进入(实验室、图书馆、宿舍等)必须刷卡	Swipe Card to Enter〔刷卡式〕 或 Tap Card to Enter〔接触式〕
92	进入阅览室必须存包	Deposit Bags Before Entering the Reading Room
93	就业指导办公室	Employment Guidance Office 或 Office of Career Counseling
94	剧院;剧场	Theater〔美语〕 Theatre〔英语〕
	K	
95	科技处	Science and Technology Division
96	科研处	Academic Research Division

序号	中文	英文
97	课程表	Class Schedule 或 Timetable
	L	
98	篮球场	Basketball Court
99	离退工作处	Division of Retired Faculty and Staff Affairs
100	留学生宿舍	International Student Dormitory
	N	
101	女生宿舍,男士止步	Women Only Girls Only〔用于中小学女生宿舍〕
	Q	
102	清真餐厅	Halal Dining Hall 或 Halal Canteen
103	请爱护书籍	Please Handle Books with Care
104	请将未选中的书放回原处	Please Reshelve Unselected Books Where You Found Them
	R	
105	人民武装部	People's Armed Forces Department
106	人事处	Human Resources Division 或 Personnel Division
	S	
107	上课期间,不得使用手机	Do Not Use Cellphone in Class
108	社科处	Division of Humanities and Social Sciences
109	审计处	Audit Division
110	生物实验室	Biology Laboratory/Lab
111	声像室	Audio-Video Room 或 Multimedia Room

序号	中文	英文
112	实验楼	Laboratory Building
113	实验室	Laboratory 或 Lab
114	食堂	Dining Hall 或 Canteen
	T	
115	体育馆	Indoor Stadium 或 Gymnasium 或 Sports Hall
116	田径场	Track-and-Field Ground
117	听课证	Course Registration Card
118	图书馆	Library
119	团工委	Youth League Working Committee
120	团委	Youth League Committee 或 CCYL Committee
	W	
121	外来人员不得留宿	Guests are not allowed to stay overnight.
122	卫生所、卫生室、医务室	Clinic 或 Infirmary
123	未经同意,不得将实验器材、物品带出实验室。	Do not take out of lab any equipment or material without permission.
124	未经同意,不得私自安装、拷贝软件和资料。	Do not install or copy any software or data without permission.
125	文献检索服务	Document Retrieval Service 或 Document Search Service
126	物理实验室	Physics Laboratory/Lab

序号	中文	英文
	X	
127	西湖大学	Westlake University
128	洗衣房	Laundry
129	____系	____ Department 或 Department of ____
130	校车	School/Shuttle Bus
131	校车车站;班车点	Bus Stop〔需要时可在前面加上 School 或 Shuttle〕
132	校车路线图	Bus Route〔需要时可在前面加上 School 或 Shuttle〕
133	校车运营时间表	Bus Timetable〔需要时可在前面加 School 或 Shuttle〕
134	校广播电视台	Campus Broadcasting Station
135	校区平面图	Campus Map
136	校史馆;校史陈列室	____ History Museum/Gallery〔"____"处根据不同的学校性质填入 University 或 Collage 或 School〕
137	校医院	School Hospital
138	校园建设处	Campus Construction Division
139	校园卡	Campus Card
140	校园卡管理中心	Campus Card Center 或 Campus Card Services 或 Campus Card Office
141	校园卡自助服务中心	Campus Card Self-Service Center
142	校园内禁止鸣笛	Do Not Use Horn 或 No Honking
143	校长室	President's Office〔大学〕 Principal's Office 或 Headmaster's Office〔中小学〕

序号	中文	英文
144	心理咨询中心	Psychological Counseling Center
145	信息技术实验室	Information Technology Laboratory/Lab
146	信息中心	Information Center
147	行政审批处(教育管理部门内设机构)	Administrative Examination and Approval Division
148	宿舍内禁止豢养宠物	No Pets Allowed in Dormitory
149	宿舍内禁止使用大功率电器	Do Not Use High-Wattage Electrical Appliances
150	宣传处	Publicity Division
151	学科规划与建设办公室	Office of Academic Planning and Development
152	学生餐厅内禁止饮酒	No Alcohol Allowed in Student Canteen
153	学生窗口	Student Counter/Window 或 For Students〔用于 Counter 或 Window 可以省略的场合〕
154	学生工作处	Student Affairs Division
155	学生会	Student Union 或 Students' Union
156	学生宿舍,访客必须登记	Visitors Must Register
157	学生宿舍;学生公寓	Student Dormitory
158	学生证	Student ID Card
159	学术报告厅;报告厅	Conference/Lecture Hall 或 Lecture Theatre〔较大的或阶梯报告厅〕 〔在同一场所内应保持统一〕
160	学校安全管理处	School Safety Management Division
	Y	
161	研究生工作部	Division of Graduate Student Affairs

序号	中文	英文
162	研究生会	Graduate Student Union 或 Graduate Students' Union
163	研究生院	Graduate School
164	艺术馆	Art Museum
165	游泳池	Swimming Pool
166	游泳馆	Natatorium 或 Indoor Swimming Pool
167	语言实验室;语音室	Language Laboratory/Lab
168	语言文字管理处(教育管理部门内设机构)	Language Management Division
169	预约取书	Reserved Book Pick-up
170	远程教育学院	School of Distance Education 或 College of Distance Education
171	阅览室	Reading Room
172	运动场	Sports Ground/Playground/Field
	Z	
173	展览馆	Exhibition Center/Hall
174	招生办公室	Admissions Office
175	浙大城市学院	Hangzhou City University
176	浙江大学附属中学	The High School Attached to Zhejiang University
177	浙江省杭州第二中学	Hangzhou No. 2 High School of Zhejiang Province
178	浙江省杭州第九中学	Hangzhou No. 9 High School of Zhejiang Province
179	浙江省杭州第七中学	Hangzhou No. 7 High School of Zhejiang Province

序号	中文	英文
180	浙江省杭州第十四中学	Hangzhou No. 14 High School of Zhejiang Province
181	浙江省杭州第十一中学	Hangzhou No. 11 High School of Zhejiang Province
182	浙江省杭州第四中学	Hangzhou No. 4 High School of Zhejiang Province
183	浙江省杭州高级中学	Zhejiang Hangzhou High School
184	浙江省杭州学军中学	Hangzhou Xuejun High School of Zhejiang Province
185	浙江育英职业技术学院	Zhejiang Yuying College of Vocational Technology
186	政教处	Political Education Division
187	职业教育与成人教育处（教育管理部门内设机构）	Division for Vocational Education and Adult Education
188	注意归还日期,按时还书	Please Return Books on Time
189	专家楼	International Faculty Apartment Building
190	专用教室	Special Purpose Classroom
191	资产管理处	Assets Management Division
192	资料打印和复印	Printing and Copying
193	资料室	Resource Center
194	自习室（图书馆内）	Self-Study Room 或 Study Room
195	自助餐厅;快餐厅（学校内）	Buffet 或 Cafeteria
196	综合档案室	Archive Room
197	总务处	Division of General Services
198	足球场	Football/Soccer Field

序号	中文	英文
199	组织处	Organization Division

注1:"〔　〕"中的内容是对英文译法的解释说明。

注2:"/"表示可选择该组词语中的一种。

注3:"//"表示书写时应当换行的断行处。需要同行书写时"//"应改为句点".",警示词后加惊叹号"!"。

注4:"＿＿＿"表示使用时应根据实际情况填入具体内容。

注5:"或"前后所列出的不同译法可任意选择一种使用。

注6:解释说明中指出某个词"可以省略"的,省略该词的译文只能用于设置在该设施上的标识中。

附录E

（资料性）

医疗卫生、科研、管理、服务机构及科室名称英文译写示例

E.1 医疗卫生、科研、管理、服务机构及科室名称英文译写示例见表E.1。表E.1按中文汉语拼音排序。

表E.1　医疗卫生、科研、管理、服务机构及科室名称英文译写示例

序号	中文	英文
	B	
1	保健科	Staff Healthcare Office
2	变态反应科	Allergic Reaction Department
3	病案科	Medical Records Office
4	病理科	Pathology Department〔Department可以省略〕
	C	
5	产科	Obstetrics Department〔Department可以省略〕
6	超声科	Ultrasonography Lab〔Lab可以省略〕
7	传染病防治院	Infectious Diseases Hospital
8	传染科	Infectious Diseases Department〔Department可以省略〕
9	创伤中心	Trauma Center
	E	
10	儿科	Pediatrics Department〔Department可以省略〕
11	儿内科	Pediatric Internal Medicine Department〔Department可以省略〕
12	儿童医院	Children's Hospital

序号	中文	英文
13	儿外科	Pediatric Surgery Department〔Department 可以省略〕
14	耳鼻(咽)喉科	Otolaryngology Department 或 Ear, Nose and Throat Department 或 ENT Department〔Department 可以省略〕
15	耳鼻喉科医院	ENT Hospital
	F	
16	方舱医院	Temporary Treatment Center
17	放射介入科	Radiology Intervention Department〔Department 可以省略〕
18	放射科	Radiology Department〔Department 可以省略〕
19	放射医学研究所	Radiation Medicine Institute
20	肺科医院	Lung Hospital
21	风湿科	Rheumatology Department〔Department 可以省略〕
22	风湿免疫科	Rheumatology and Immunology Department〔Department 可以省略〕
23	妇产科医院	Women's Hospital 或 Maternity Hospital 或 Obstetrics & Gynecology Hospital
24	妇科	Gynecology Department〔Department 可以省略〕
25	妇女保健科	Women's Health Care Department〔Department 可以省略〕
26	妇女儿童医院	Women and Children Hospital 或 Women's and Children's Hospital
27	妇婴保健院;妇幼保健院	Maternal and Child Health Hospital
28	附属医院	University-Affiliated Hospital 或 Affiliated Hospital 或 Affiliate Hospital

序号	中文	英文
29	腹腔镜外科	Laparoscope Surgery Department〔Department 可以省略〕
	G	
30	肝胆科	Hepatology Department〔Department 可以省略〕
31	肝胆外科	Hepatological Surgery Department〔Department 可以省略〕
32	肝胆外科医院	Hepatobiliary Surgery Hospital
33	肝炎科	Hepatitis Department
34	肛肠科	Proctology Department
35	肛肠医院	Proctology Hospital
36	高血压科	Hypertension Department
37	高血压研究所	Hypertension Research Institute
38	公共卫生临床中心	Public Health Clinical Center
39	骨科;骨伤科	Orthopedics Department〔Department 可以省略〕
40	骨伤科医院	Orthopedics Hospital
41	国际医疗中心	International Healthcare Center
	H	
42	杭州市残疾人托管中心	Hangzhou Disability Care Center
43	杭州市残疾人综合服务中心(杭州市盲人按摩指导中心)	Hangzhou Comprehensive Service Center for Disabled Persons (Hangzhou Blind Massage Guiding Center)
44	杭州市第九人民医院	Hangzhou Ninth People's Hospital
45	杭州市第七人民医院	Hangzhou Seventh People's Hospital
46	杭州市第三人民医院	Hangzhou Third People's Hospital

序号	中文	英文
47	杭州市第一人民医院	Hangzhou First People's Hospital
48	杭州市丁桥医院	Hangzhou Dingqiao Hospital
49	杭州市儿童医院	Hangzhou Children's Hospital
50	杭州市妇产科医院（杭州市妇幼保健院）	Hangzhou Women's Hospital (Hangzhou Maternity and Child Health Care Hospital)
51	杭州市红十字会医院	Hangzhou Red Cross Hospital
52	杭州市疾病预防控制中心	Hangzhou Center for Disease Control and Prevention〔可缩写为 Hangzhou CDC〕
53	杭州市老年病医院	Hangzhou Geriatrics Hospital
54	杭州市五云山医院	Hangzhou Wuyunshan Hospital
55	杭州市西溪医院	Hangzhou Xixi Hospital
56	杭州市职业病防治院	Hangzhou Occupational Disease Prevention and Control Hospital
57	杭州市中医院	Hangzhou Hospital of Traditional Chinese Medicine
58	杭州市肿瘤医院	Hangzhou Cancer Hospital
59	核医学科	Nuclear Medicine Department〔Department 可以省略〕
60	红十字会	Red Cross Society
61	红十字会医院	Red Cross Hospital
62	呼吸内科	Respiratory Medicine Department〔Department 可以省略〕
63	护理部	Nursing Department
64	护理医院	Nursing Home〔常用于养老院〕 或 Nursing Hospital〔常用于康养医院〕

序号	中文	英文
	J	
65	疾病预防控制中心	Disease Control and Prevention Center〔可缩写为CDC〕
66	计生科	Family Planning Department
67	检验科	Clinical Lab
68	检疫所	Quarantine Office
69	健康管理中心（治未病科）	Health Management Center (Disease Prevention Department)
70	健康教育所	Health Education Center
71	介入科	Intervention Department
72	戒毒科	Drug Rehabilitation Department〔Department可以省略〕 或 Drug Rehab Department〔Department可以省略〕
73	精神科	Psychiatry Department
74	精神科（鉴定）	Psychiatry Department (Clinical Assessment)
75	精神卫生医院	Mental Health Hospital 或 Psychiatric Hospital
	K	
76	康复科	Rehabilitation Department〔Department可以省略〕 或 Rehabilitation Medicine Department〔Department可以省略〕
77	康复医学科	Rehabilitation Medicine Department〔Department可以省略〕
78	康复医院	Rehabilitation Hospital
79	口腔病防治院	Oral Diseases Prevention Clinic
80	口腔科	Stomatology Department〔Department可以省略〕

序号	中文	英文
81	口腔外科	Oral Surgery Department 〔Department 可以省略〕
82	口腔医院	Stomatological/Oral Hospital
	L	
83	老年病科	Geriatric Department 或 Geriatrics〔用于 Department 可以省略的场合〕
84	老年病医院	Geriatric/Geriatrics Hospital
85	老年友善医院	Age-Friendly Hospital
86	疗养院	Convalescent Home/Hospital
87	临床检验中心	Clinical Laboratory Center
88	临时医院	Improvised/Makeshift Hospital
	M	
89	麻醉科	Anesthesiology Department〔Department 可以省略〕
90	泌尿科	Urology Department〔Department可以省略〕
91	免疫科	Immunology Department〔Department 可以省略〕
92	免疫学研究所	Immunology Institute
93	男科;男性科	Andrology Department〔Department可以省略〕
	N	
94	脑科医院	Brain Hospital
95	内分泌科	Endocrinology Department〔Department 可以省略〕
96	内分泌研究所	Endocrinology Institute
97	内科	Internal Medicine Department〔Department可以省略〕

序号	中文	英文
	P	
98	皮肤病医院	Dermatology Hospital
99	皮肤科	Dermatology Department〔Department 可以省略〕
100	普通内科;通用内科	General Internal Medicine Department〔Department可以省略〕
101	普通外科	General Surgery Department〔Department可以省略〕
	Q	
102	气功研究所	Qigong Research Institute
103	器官移植科	Organ Transplantation Department〔Department可以省略〕
104	轻工杭州休养院	Qinggong Hangzhou Convalescent Home
	S	
105	伤骨科研究所	Orthopedic Traumatology Institute
106	伤科	Traumatology Department〔Department 可以省略〕
107	商业医疗保险机构	Commercial Medical Insurance Agency
108	烧伤科	Burns Department
109	社区卫生服务中心	Community Healthcare Center
110	社区卫生服务中心医疗服务站	Community Healthcare Clinic
111	社区诊所	Community Clinic
112	神经内科	Neurology Department〔Department可以省略〕
113	神经外科	Neurosurgery Department〔Department 可以省略〕
114	肾内科	Nephrology Department〔Department可以省略〕

序号	中文	英文
115	生物制品研究所	Research Institute of Biological Products
116	生殖健康科	Reproductive Health Care Department〔Department 可以省略〕
117	生殖科	Reproductive Medicine Department〔Department 可以省略〕
118	手外科	Hand Surgery Department〔Department 可以省略〕
119	输血科	Blood Transfusion Department〔Department 可以省略〕
	W	
120	外科	Surgery Department〔Department可以省略〕
121	微创外科	Minimally Invasive Surgery Department〔Department可以省略〕
122	卫生监督所	Public Health Inspection Office
123	卫生室、医务室	Clinic 或 Medical Room 或 Infirmary〔常用于学校、监狱等〕
	X	
124	消化内科	Gastroenterology/Gastrology Department〔Department可以省略〕
125	心理科	Psychology Department〔Department可以省略〕
126	心理咨询科	Psychological Counseling Department〔Department可以省略〕
127	心外科	Cardiac Surgery Department〔Department可以省略〕
128	心胸外科	Cardiothoracic Surgery Department〔Department可以省略〕
129	心血管内科	Cardiovascular Medicine Department〔Department可以省略〕
130	心血管研究所	Cardiovascular Medicine Institute

序号	中文	英文
131	心脏介入科	Cardiovascular Intervention Department〔Department 可以省略〕
132	心脏科	Cardiology Department〔Department 可以省略〕
133	新生儿外科	Neonatal Surgery Department〔Department 可以省略〕
134	性病科	Sexually Transmitted Diseases Department〔Department 可以省略〕 或 STD Department
135	性病医院	STD Hospital
136	胸科医院	Chest Hospital
137	胸外科	Thoracic Surgery Department〔Department 可以省略〕
138	血管介入科	Vascular Intervention Department〔Department 可以省略〕
139	血管外科	Vascular Surgery Department〔Department 可以省略〕
140	血液管理办公室	Blood Management Office
141	血液科	Hematology Department〔Department 可以省略〕
142	血液中心	Blood Center/Bank
	Y	
143	牙病防治院（所）	Dental Hospital/Clinic
144	牙科	Dental Department 或 Dentistry
145	眼病防治所	Eye Clinic
146	眼耳鼻喉科医院	Eye and ENT Hospital
147	眼科	Ophthalmology Department〔Department 可以省略〕
148	眼科医院	Eye Hospital

序号	中文	英文
149	药械科	Drug and Equipment Department〔Department 可以省略〕
150	药物研究所	Pharmacology Institute
151	医保办公室	Medical Insurance Office
152	医保定点医疗机构	Medical Insurance Designated Hospital〔用于医院〕 或 Medical Insurance Designated Clinic〔用于诊所〕
153	医护部	Medical and Nursing Department
154	医疗急救中心	Medical Emergency Center
155	医务部	Medical Affairs Department
156	医学科学技术情报研究所	Institute of Medical Science and Technology Information
157	医学心理科	Medical Psychology Department〔Department 可以省略〕
158	医院	Hospital
159	预防保健科	Preventive Medicine Department〔Department 可以省略〕
160	院感科	Hospital Infection Control Department 或 Hospital-Acquired Infection Control Department〔Department可以省略〕
	Z	
161	浙江省杭州市急救中心	Hangzhou Emergency Medical Center, Zhejiang Province
162	针灸经络研究所	Acupuncture and Meridian Research Institute
163	针灸科	Acupuncture Department〔Department 可以省略〕

序号	中文	英文
164	整形外科	Plastic Surgery and Orthodontics Department〔包括畸齿矫正〕〔Department可以省略〕 Plastic Surgery Department〔Department可以省略〕
165	正颌正畸科	Maxillofacial Surgery and Orthodontics Department〔Department可以省略〕
166	职业病防治院	Centre for the Prevention of Occupational Disease 或 Hospital for the Prevention of Occupational Disease
167	痔科	Hemorrhoid Department
168	中西医结合医院	Hospital of Integrated Traditional Chinese and Western Medicine
169	中心医院	Central Hospital
170	中医儿科	TCM Pediatrics Department〔Department可以省略〕
171	中医妇科	TCM Gynecology Department〔Department可以省略〕
172	中医骨病治疗科	TCM Orthopedics Department〔Department可以省略〕
173	中医骨伤科医院	TCM Hospital of Orthopedics
174	中医科	Traditional Chinese Medicine Department〔Department可以省略〕 或 TCM Department〔Department可以省略〕
175	中医理疗科	TCM Physiotherapy Department〔Department可以省略〕
176	中医研究所	TCM Research Institute
177	中医医院	Traditional Chinese Medicine Hospital 或 TCM Hospital
178	肿瘤科	Oncology Department〔Department可以省略〕
179	肿瘤研究所	Oncology Institute

序号	中文	英文
180	肿瘤医院	Tumor/Oncology Hospital

序号	中文	英文
181	专科医院	Specialized/Specialty Hospital
182	综合治疗科	Integrated Therapy Department〔Department 可以省略〕
183	总务室	General Affairs Office

注1:"〔 〕"中的内容是对英文译法的解释说明。
注2:"/"表示可选择该组词语中的一种。
注3:"或"前后所列出的不同译法可任意选择一种使用。
注4:解释说明中指出某个词"可以省略"的,省略该词的译文只能用于设置在该设施上的标识中。

E.2 医疗卫生服务信息英文译写示例见表 E.2。表 E.2 按中文汉语拼音排序。

表 E.2 医疗卫生服务信息英文译写示例

序号	中文	英文
	A	
1	IgM 抗体检测	IgM Antibody Testing
2	X 光摄片	X-Ray Radiography
3	艾滋病初筛实验	HIV Screening 或 HIV/AIDS Screening
4	暗室	Darkroom
	B	
5	白带化验	Leucorrhea Test
6	白带检查	Leucorrhea Examination

序号	中文	英文
7	半污染区	Buffer Area
8	B超	B-Mode Ultrasound
9	鼻拭子检测	Nasal Swab Test
10	标本登记处	Specimen Registration
11	标本接收处	Specimen Collection
12	病案室;病史室	Medical Records Room〔Room 可以省略〕
13	病毒实验室	Virus Analysis Lab
14	病房;病区	Inpatient Ward
15	病房楼	Inpatient Building
16	病理切片	Biological Section
17	病人及来访者进入医院前需接受筛查	All patients & visitors will be screened prior to hospital entry.
18	病人来院就诊时仅限一人陪同	Patients will be allowed only ONE support person during a clinic or hospital visit.
19	病人专用通道	Entrance for Patients
20	病员须知	Patient Guide
	C	
21	彩超	Color Ultrasound
22	操作室	Procedure Room
23	产房	Delivery Room
24	肠道门诊	Gastrointestinal Clinic 或 GI Clinic
25	肠镜检查	Enteroscopy
26	常规化验	Routine Test

序号	中文	英文
27	冲片室	Film Developing Room
28	抽血处	Blood Sampling
29	出入院办理处	Admission and Discharge
30	出院手续办理处	Discharge
31	处方处	Prescription
32	床边结算	Bedside Account Settlement
33	床位协调中心	Bed Allocation Center
34	此地正在医学隔离中	Notice // Isolation 或 Notice // Medical Isolation
35	刺激疗法	Stimulation Therapy
36	催眠疗法	Hypnotherapy
	D	
37	单层电梯停靠	For Odd Number Floors Only
38	当心射线	CAUTION // Radiation
39	登记处	Registry
40	DSA 导管室	DSA Catheterization Lab
41	第___诊室	Consulting Room ___
42	动态心电图	DCG 或 Dynamic Electrocardiogram 或 Holter Monitor
43	动态血压检查	Ambulatory Blood Pressure Monitoring〔可以缩写为 ABPM〕
44	毒理实验室	Toxicology Lab
45	毒性试验	Toxicity Testing
46	读片室;阅片室	Film Reading Room

序号	中文	英文
47	断层扫描（CT）	CT Scan
48	断层扫描（发射单光子计算机）	ECT 或 Emission Computed Tomography
	E	
49	儿保化验	Child Care Test
50	儿童重症监护室	Pediatric ICU 或 Pediatric Intensive Care Unit 或 PICU
	F	
51	发热门诊	Fever Clinic
52	房颤门诊	Atrial Fibrillation Clinic
53	放标本处	Specimens
54	放疗	Radiation Oncology 或 Radiotherapy
55	放射防护	Radiation Protection
56	放射免疫实验室	Radioimmunoassay Lab 或 RIA Lab
57	放射物品	Radioactive Materials
58	肥胖症门诊	Obesity Clinic
59	肺功能检查	Pulmonary Function Test
60	分子生物学实验室	Molecular Biology Lab
61	粪便化验	Excrement Test
62	负压救护车	Negative Pressure Ambulance
63	妇科化验	Gynecological Test
64	腹部B超	Abdominal Ultrasound Scan

序号	中文	英文
65	腹泻门诊	Diarrhea Clinic
	G	
66	肝功能检测	Liver Function Test
67	高压氧室;高压氧舱	Hyperbaric Oxygen Chamber
68	高压氧治疗	Hyperbaric Oxygen Therapy/Treatment
69	隔离病房	Isolation Ward
70	隔离门诊	Isolation Clinic
71	隔离区,请勿进入	Quarantine Area. Authorized Personnel Only!
72	隔离区,请勿靠近	Quarantine Area. Please Keep out!
73	隔离取血室	Isolated Blood Sampling Room
74	个人防护用品	Personal Protective Equipment 或 PPE
75	更年期保健	Menopause Health Care
76	功能检查	Function Test
77	功能训练	Functional Training
78	宫颈冷冻	Cervical Cryotherapy
79	供应保障区	Storage and Supply Area
80	供应保障组	Supply Team
81	供应室	Storage and Supply Room
82	骨密度检测	Bone Mineral Density Test
83	骨髓移植	Bone Marrow Transplantation
84	钴60治疗;同位素治疗	Cobalt-60 Treatment 或 Isotope Treatment
85	挂号、收费处	Registration and Payment

序号	中文	英文
86	挂号处	Registration
87	观察室	Observation Room
88	冠心病重症监护室	Coronary Care Unit 或 CCU
89	盥洗区	Wash Area
90	国际医疗保健中心	International Healthcare Center
	H	
91	核磁共振	MRI 或 Magnetic Resonance Imaging
92	核酸检测	Nucleic Acid Testing (NAT)
93	红外线扫描	Infrared Ray
94	候诊观察室	Waiting and Observation Room〔Room 可以省略〕
95	候诊区	Waiting Area
96	呼吸机	Ventilator 或 Respirator
97	护理门诊	Nursing Clinic
98	护士站	Nurses/Nurse Station
99	划价处;药品划价	Prescription Pricing
100	化疗	Chemotherapy
101	化验室	Laboratory 或 Lab
102	换药室	Dressing Room
103	患者入口	Patients Entrance
104	患者止步	Staff Only
105	恢复期血浆疗法	Convalescent Plasma Therapy

序号	中文	英文
106	会客区	Reception Area
107	活组织检查	Biopsy
	J	
108	急诊办公室	Emergency Department Office
109	急诊部	Emergency Department〔Department 可以省略〕
110	（急诊）分诊台	Triage
111	急诊监护病区	Emergency Intensive Care Unit 或 EICU
112	急诊须知	Emergency Patient Guide
113	集中供氧	Oxygen Supply
114	记忆紊乱门诊	Memory Disorder Clinic
115	检查、化验等候区	Lab Test Waiting Area
116	检查室	Examination Room
117	健康体检；常规体检	Health Checkup 或 Physical Examination
118	叫号台	Calling Desk
119	进入实验区,请穿好工作服	Lab Area // Lab Coats Required
120	经颅多普勒超声检查	TCD 或 Transcranial Doppler Sonography
121	静脉采血处	Venous Blood Sampling
122	救护车	Ambulance
123	就诊区	Outpatient Area
124	剧毒物品	Toxic Materials

序号	中文	英文
	K	
125	抗病毒治疗	Anti-viral Therapy
126	口腔放射	Oral Radiology
127	口腔修复	Prosthodontics
128	口腔预防	Preventive Dentistry
129	口腔正畸	Orthodontics Clinic
130	口腔种植	Oral Implantology
131	快速检测	Rapid Test
	L	
132	理疗	Physical Therapy 或 Physiotherapy
133	量血压	Blood Pressure Measurement
134	（临时）隔离区	(Temporary) Isolation Area 或 Quarantine Area
	M	
134	麻醉评估与疼痛门诊	Preoperative Anesthesia Evaluation and Pain Clinic
136	麻醉室	Anesthesia Room
137	门诊办公室	Outpatient Department Office
138	门诊部	Outpatient Department 或 Outpatients〔用于 Department 可以省略的场合〕
139	门诊煎药处	Outpatient Herbal Medicine Decoction Service 或 Outpatient TCM Decoction Service〔Service 均可以省略〕
140	门诊接待室	Reception Room〔Room 可以省略〕

序号	中文	英文
141	门诊须知	Outpatient Guide
142	门诊综合服务中心	Comprehensive Service Center for Outpatients
143	免疫检查	Immunoassay
144	免疫实验室	Immunoassay Lab
145	免疫预防接种	Vaccination and Immunization
146	免疫治疗室	Immunotherapy Room
	N	
147	男宾止步	Women Only
148	男诊室	Men's Consulting Room
149	脑、肌电图	Electroencephalography and Electromyography 或 EEG and EMG
150	内窥镜检查	Endoscopy
151	内有氧气,严禁吸烟	No Smoking // Oxygen in Use
152	尿液化验	Urine Test
153	女诊室	Women's Consulting Room
	P	
154	拍片室;摄片室	Radiography Room
155	陪护中心	Patient Caregiver Resource Center 或 Patient Caregiver Support Center
156	配餐室	Meal Preparation Room〔Room 可以省略〕
157	配液室	Infusion Preparation Room
158	皮肤风湿免疫联合门诊	Rheumatic Immunology of Dermatology Joint Clinic
159	(普通)分诊台/门诊接待室	Reception

序号	中文	英文
160	普通取血处	Routine Blood Sampling
	Q	
161	抢救室	Emergency/Resuscitation Room〔Room 可以省略〕
162	亲友等候区	Visitors Waiting Area
163	亲友告别室	Visitation Room
164	勤务中心	Service Center
165	清创室	Wound Care Room 或 Debridement Room〔Room 均可以省略〕
166	清洁区	Sterile Area 或 Cleanroom
167	请勿谈论病人隐私	Please Respect the Privacy of Our Patients 或 Please respect patients ' privacy and confidentiality.
168	请在诊室外候诊	Please Wait Outside the Consulting Room 或 Please wait outside the consulting room.
169	取报告处	Lab Report Collection
170	取报告须知	Lab Report Collection Guide
171	取检查、化验结果处	Lab Test Reports
172	取药处;收方、发药处	Dispensary
	R	
173	人工牙齿种植	Dental Implantology
174	妊高症监测	Gestational Hypertension Monitoring
175	日光疗	Heliotherapy
176	如有上述症状,请立即通知防疫人员	If you have any of the symptoms above, please alert the anti-epidemic personnel immediately.

序号	中文	英文
177	乳腺摄片	Galactophore Radiography
178	锐器！请注意	CAUTION // Sharp Objects
179	弱视治疗	Amblyopia Treatment
	S	
180	肾功能检测	Kidney Function Test
181	生化实验室	Biochemistry Lab
182	生活垃圾（存放处）（指非医用垃圾）	Non-Medical Waste
183	生物安全	Bio-Safety
184	生物危险,请勿入内	DANGER // Biohazard // No Admittance
185	实验区	Laboratory Area
186	实验室	Laboratory 或 Lab
187	示教室	Demonstration Classroom 或 Demo Room
188	市民卡登记和充值	Registration and Recharge for Citizen Card
189	试剂盒	Test Kit
190	视力维护中心	Vision Maintenance Center
191	手术病人家属谈话室	Family Consultation Room
192	手术室	Operating Room/Theater
193	手术室专用电梯	Operating Room Elevator 或 Operating Room Only〔用于 Elevator 可以省略的场合〕
194	输液室	Infusion Room
195	数字牙片	Digital Dental Film

序号	中文	英文
196	双向转诊中心	Two-Way Referral Center
197	水疗	Hydrotherapy
198	苏醒室;恢复室	Recovery Room
	T	
199	胎儿监护室	Fetus Monitoring Room〔Room 可以省略〕
200	太平间;停尸房	Mortuary 或 Morgue
201	探视入口	Visitors Entrance
202	探视时间	Visiting Hours
203	探视须知	Visitors' Guide
204	特殊病房	Special Care Unit/Ward
205	特需门诊	Special Need Clinic
206	特约门诊	Special Appointment Clinic
207	体检中心	Physical Examination Center
208	体外膜肺氧合	ECMO 或 Extracorporeal Membrane Oxygenation
209	体温测量	Temperature Taking
210	体温检测热像仪	Thermal Imaging Camera for Temperature Monitoring
211	听力测试	Audiometry
212	透视	Fluoroscopy 或 X-Ray
213	透析	Dialysis
214	团队医疗组	MDT 或 Multiple Diagnosis Team
215	推拿	Tuina 或 Manipulation

序号	中文	英文
	W	
216	危机干预	Crisis Intervention
217	微量元素实验室	Trace Element Lab
218	微生物实验室	Microbiology Lab
219	胃肠电图	Electrogastrogram 或 EGG
220	胃镜检查	Gastroscopy
221	胃十二指肠镜检查	Gastroduodenoscopy
222	污染区	Contaminated Area
223	污物间	Soiled Articles Disposal Room〔Room 可以省略〕
224	无偿献血	Voluntary Blood Donation
225	雾化室	Nebulization Room
	X	
226	细胞病理室	Cytopathology Lab
227	细胞化验室	Cell Lab
228	细菌培养室	Bacterial Culture Lab
229	细菌室	Bacteriology Lab
230	现场抢救区	On-Site Emergency Care
231	献血后休息区	Donors Rest Lounge
232	献血前等候区	Donors Waiting Lounge
233	献血前检测区	Donors Blood Test Area
234	献血体检	Blood Donor Health Check
235	献血咨询登记处	Donation Counseling and Registration

序号	中文	英文
236	消毒产品检验受理处	Sterile Items Test Registration
237	消防应急面罩	Emergency Fire Masks
238	心导管术	Cardiac Catheterization
239	心电图	ECG
240	心理测验	Psychological Test
241	心理治疗	Psychotherapy
242	心理咨询/疏导	Psychological Counseling
243	心血管介入中心	Cardiovascular Interventional Center
244	心脏超声波	Cardiac Ultrasound Scan 或 Echocardiography
245	心脏重症监护室	Cardiac Care Unit 或 CCU
246	心脏移植	Cardiac Transplantation
247	新生儿隔离病房	Neonatal Isolation Ward
248	新生儿水疗抚触	Neonatal Hydrotherapy and Massage
249	新生儿医疗中心	Neonatal Medical Center
250	新生儿重症监护室	Neonatal Intensive Care Unit 或 NICU
251	胸痛门诊	Chest Pain Clinic
252	胸痛中心	Chest Pain Center
253	宣教室	Health Education Room〔Room可以省略〕
254	血常规检查	Routine Blood Test
255	血库	Blood Bank
256	血气分析	Arterial Blood Gas Analysis

序号	中文	英文
257	血清诊断	Serodiagnosis
258	血透	Hemodialysis
259	血液采集区	Blood Collection Area
260	血液告急	Urgent! Blood Donors Needed Now!
261	血液生化检查	Blood Biochemical Test
262	血液实验室	Blood Analysis Lab
263	血液透析中心	Hemodialysis Center
	Y	
264	牙片	Dental Film
265	咽拭子检测	Throat Swab Test
266	眼科验光	Optometry
267	药房;西药房;中西药房	Pharmacy
268	夜间取血,请按门铃	Please press the bell for blood service at night.
269	一站式门诊服务	One-Stop Outpatient Service
270	医保定点药店	Medical Insurance Designated Pharmacy
271	医护人员专用通道	Entrance for Medical Staff
272	医患交流办公室	Doctor-Patient Communication Office
273	医技楼	Medical Technology Building〔Building 可以省略〕
274	医疗急救电话120	First Aid // Call 120
275	医疗急救通道	Emergency Access
276	医疗纠纷处理办公室	Complaints Office
277	医疗收费表	Medical Billing Statement

序号	中文	英文
278	医生办公室	Doctor's Office
279	医务人员不得戴手套按电梯	Medical staff shall not press the elevator buttons with a gloved hand.
280	医学美容	Medical Cosmetology
281	医用电梯	Medical Service Elevator 或 Medical Use Only〔用于 Elevator 可以省略的场合〕
282	医用垃圾(存放处)(指医用废弃物等)	Medical Waste
283	乙肝病毒携带者诊室	HBV Carriers Consulting Room
284	易燃物品	Flammable Materials
285	疫苗室	Vaccination Room〔Room 可以省略〕
286	阴超	Transvaginal Ultrasound
287	饮食疗法	Diet Therapy
288	婴儿室	Nursery
289	营养门诊	Nutrition Clinic
290	营养室	Nutrition Room
291	营养咨询	Nutrition Counseling
292	用药咨询处	Medication Consultation
293	与已确诊传染病患者曾有密切接触者,请立即通知防疫人员。	If you had close contact with infectious disease patients, please alert the anti-epidemic personnel.
294	预防保健门诊	Disease-Prevention and Healthcare Clinic〔Clinic 可以省略〕
295	预防接种	Prophylactic Vaccination
296	预检处	Inquiries

序号	中文	英文
297	预检分诊处（急诊）	Triage
298	预约处	Appointments
299	预约门诊	Advance Appointment Clinic
300	远程会诊	Telemedicine
301	院内小卖部	Store
	Z	
302	针灸	Acupuncture
303	诊室	Consulting Room
304	镇痛门诊	Aches and Pains Clinic
305	整形美容中心	Plastic and Cosmetic Center
306	支气管镜检查	Bronchoscopy
307	职业病咨询门诊	Occupational Health Consulting Clinic
308	治疗车存放处	Treatment Trolley Storage
309	治疗室	Treatment Room
310	智力测量	Intelligence Assessment
311	中草药房	TCM Pharmacy (Herbal Medicine)
312	中成药及西药房	Pharmacy (incl. Prepared Chinese Medicine)
313	中药房	TCM Pharmacy
314	中医科按摩	TCM Massage Therapy
315	中医门诊	Traditional Chinese Medicine Clinic 或 TCM Clinic
316	重症监护室	Intensive Care Unit 或 ICU
317	助听器验配	Hearing Aid Fitting

序号	中文	英文
318	住院部	Impatient Department
319	住院手续办理处;住院登记处	Admission
320	住院须知	Admission Guide
321	注射室	Injection Room
322	注射输液室	Injection and Infusion Room
323	专家门诊	Expert Clinic
324	专科门诊	Specialist Clinic
325	自助挂号;自助挂号机	Self-Service Registration Machine〔Machine 可以省略〕
326	自助预约机	Self-Service Appointment Machine〔Machine 可以省略〕
327	卒中中心	Stroke Center

注1:"〔 〕"中的内容是对英文译法的解释说明。

注2:"/"表示可选择该组词语中的一种。

注3:"//"表示书写时应当换行的断行处。需要同行书写时"//"应改为句点".",警示词后加惊叹号"!"。

注4:"____"表示使用时应根据实际情况填入具体内容。

注5:"或"前后所列出的不同译法可任意选择一种使用。

注6:解释说明中指出某个词"可以省略"的,省略该词的译文只能用于设置在该设施上的标识中,如门诊部应译作 Outpatient Department,在设置于门诊部门口的标识时可以省略 Department,译作 Outpatients。

附录F

（资料性）

商业、金融、邮电行业机构和场所名称英文译写示例

F.1 商业、金融、邮电行业机构和场所名称英文译写示例见表F.1。表F.1按中文汉语拼音排序。

表F.1 商业、金融、邮电行业机构和场所名称英文译写示例

序号	中文	英文
	A	
1	按摩店	Massage Shop〔Shop可以省略〕
	B	
2	百货商店	Department Store
3	搬家公司	Moving/Relocation Services
4	保洁公司	Cleaning Services
5	保险代理公司	Insurance Agent Company
6	保险公估公司	Insurance Assessment Company
7	保险公司	Insurance Company
8	保险经纪公司	Insurance Brokerage Company
9	保险资产管理公司	Insurance Asset Management Company
10	报刊发行站	Newspapers and Periodicals Distribution Center
11	报刊亭	Newsstand 或 News Kiosk
12	本地土特产店	Local Specialty Store Local Produce Store〔指农产品〕 或 Regional Produce Store〔指农产品〕〔Store可以省略〕

序号	中文	英文
13	便利店;方便店	Convenience Store
	C	
14	财产保险公司	Property Insurance Company
15	财务公司	Finance Company
16	仓储式商场	Warehouse Store/Supermarket
17	厂家直销店	Factory Outlet 或 Outlet Store 或品牌名+Outlet
18	超市;大卖场	Supermarket
19	成人用品商店	Adult Store
20	储蓄所	Savings Bank/Agency
21	村邮站	Postal Service Station 或 Village Mail Station
	D	
22	大型综合超市	Hypermarket
23	贷款公司	Loan Company
24	典当行	Pawnbroker 或 Pawnshop
25	电器商店;电器商城	Electronics and Home Appliances 或 Electrical and Electronics 或 Home Appliances Store
	E	
26	儿童摄影室	Children's Photo Studio
	F	
27	房产中介;房地产经纪公司	Real Estate Agency〔Agency 可以省略〕

序号	中文	英文
28	分行	Branch
29	分理处	Office
	G	
30	干洗店	Dry Cleaning Shop〔Shop 可以省略〕
31	个人贷款中心	Personal Loan Center
32	工艺品商店	Arts and Crafts Store〔Store 可以省略〕
33	购物中心;购物商城	Shopping Center/Mall
	H	
34	花店	Florist's 或 Flower Shop 或 Florist
35	会员店	Membership Store
36	婚庆公司	Wedding Services/Planner
37	婚纱店	Wedding Dress Store
38	婚纱摄影	Wedding Photo Studio
39	货币经纪公司	Money Brokerage Company
	J	
40	集邮公司	Philatelic Corporation
41	家居建材商店	Home Furnishing and Building Supplies
42	家政服务公司	Domestic Services Company 或 House-Keeping Services Company〔Company 均可省略〕
43	金店	Gold Store
44	金融控股公司	Financial Holdings Company

序号	中文	英文
45	金融资产管理公司	Asset Management Company
46	金融租赁公司	Financial Leasing Company
47	精品店(多用于服装、首饰、贵重礼品商店)	Boutique
	K	
48	快递公司	Courier Services Company〔Company可以省略〕
49	快照服务	Instant Photo Service
	L	
50	理发店	Barber's 或 Barber Shop
51	廉价小商品杂货店	Variety Store 或 Price-Point Retailer
	M	
52	贸易中心	Trade Center
53	美发厅	Hairdresser's
54	美容美发厅	Hair and Beauty Salon
55	美容院;美容美体中心	Beauty Salon/Center 或 Beauty Care
56	免税店	Duty Free Store
	P	
57	拍卖公司;拍卖行	Auction Company/House
58	批发市场	Wholesale Market
59	品牌直销购物中心(奥特莱斯购物中心)	Outlets

序号	中文	英文
	Q	
60	期货公司	Futures Company
61	期货经纪公司	Futures Brokerage Company
62	汽车金融公司	Automobile Finance Company
	R	
63	人身保险公司	Personal Insurance Company
64	人寿保险公司	Life Insurance Company
	S	
65	商场	Shopping Mall 或 Market
66	社区邮政服务站	Community Postal Service
67	食品超市	Food Supermarket
68	食品店	Food Store
69	书城	Book Mall
70	书店	Bookstore
71	熟食店	Deli 或 Delicatessen
72	数码工作室	Digital Studio
73	水疗会所;水疗生活馆	Spa
	T	
74	投资咨询公司	Investment Consulting Company
	W	
75	网上购物	Online Shopping

序号	中文	英文
76	网上商城	Online Shopping Mall
77	物流公司	Logistics Company〔Company可以省略〕
78	物业公司	Property Management Company 或 Realty Management Company〔Company 均可省略〕
	X	
79	洗衣店	Laundry
80	洗浴中心	Bath Center 或 Baths
81	小额贷款公司	Micro-Loan Company
82	信托公司	Trust Company
83	信托投资公司	Trust and Investment Company
84	信用放款合作社	Credit Loan Cooperative
85	信用合作社	Credit Cooperative
	Y	
86	眼镜店	Spectacles/Optical Store〔Store可以省略〕 或 Optician
87	医药商店;西药房	Pharmacy 或 Drug Store 或 Chemist's
88	音像制品店	Audio-Video Store
89	银行	Bank
90	邮局;邮政局;邮政所	Post Office
91	邮区中心局	Regional Mail Processing Center

序号	中文	英文
92	邮政报刊门市部	Newspapers and Periodicals
93	邮政报刊亭	Newsstand 或 News Kiosk
94	邮政代办所	Postal Agency
95	邮政公司	Post Corporation
96	邮政快递社区服务站	Community Postal Express Service
97	邮政流动服务点	Mobile Post Office
98	邮政速递物流公司	Express Mail Service 或 EMS
99	邮政支局	Branch Post Office
100	月子中心	Mom & Baby Care Center 或 Mommy and Baby Care Center 或 Mother and Baby Care Center
	Z	
101	再保险公司	Reinsurance Company
102	照相馆	Photo Studio
103	折扣店	Discount Store
104	证券公司	Securities Company/Firm
105	证券交易所	Stock Exchange
106	证券投资基金管理公司	Securities Investment Fund Management Corporation
107	支行	Sub-Branch
108	直播带货	Live-Streaming Sales/Marketing 或 Livestream Sales/Selling 或 Selling Through Livestreaming 或 Live e-Commerce

序号	中文	英文
109	中国电信	China Telecom
110	中国联通	China Unicom
111	中国移动	China Mobile
112	中国邮政集团有限公司	China Post Group Corporation Limited 或 China Post 或 China Post Group
113	中央商务区	Central Business District 或 CBD
114	中药店	TCM Pharmacy
115	珠宝商店;银楼;金店	Jewelries
116	主播带货	Anchor Sales
117	装潢公司	Interior Decoration Company〔Company 可以省略〕
118	自助摄影	Self-Service Photo Booth
119	自助银行	Self-Service Banking 或 Self-Banking
120	租车公司	Car Rental Company〔Company可以省略〕
121	租赁公司	Leasing Company
122	足疗店;足浴店	Foot Massage Shop〔Shop可以省略〕 或 Foot Care

注1:"〔 〕"中的内容是对英文译法的解释说明。

注2:"或"前后所列出的不同译法可任意选择一种使用。

注3:商店译作 Store 或 Shop,本附录在相关条目的译文中省略了后一种译法,但在特定场合中英语国家习惯使用 Shop 的除外;公司译作 Company 或 Corporation,本附录在相关条目的译文中省略了后一种译法。

F.2 商业、金融、邮电服务信息英文译写示例见表F.2。表F.2按中文汉语拼音排序。

表F.2 商业、金融、邮电服务信息英文译写示例

序号	中文	英文
	A	
1	IC卡电话	IC Card Phone
2	安全保卫部	Security Department
3	按揭贷款	Mortgage Loans
	B	
4	白金卡	Platinum Card
5	白酒	Liquor and Spirits
6	搬运服务；搬家服务	Moving/Relocation Services
7	包裹收寄电子秤	Parcel Scale 或 Electronic Scale
8	包装袋	Packing/Packaging Bag
9	包装柜台	Packing Counter
10	包装胶带；封箱带；胶带	Packaging Tape
11	包装筒	Packing/Packaging Tube
12	包装纸和薄膜	Wrapping Paper and Plastic Film
13	保管箱业务办理	Safe Box Service
14	保价邮件	Insured Mail
15	保税仓储	Bonded Warehousing
16	保温袋	Thermal Bag
17	保修及退换货服务处	Warranties and Refunds

序号	中文	英文
18	报刊发行处;报刊发行	Newspaper and Periodical Circulation
19	爆款产品	Hot/Best/Top-Selling Product/Products〔视产品数量选用〕
20	本机每笔最大存款张数:____	Maximum of ____ Bills at One Time
21	本商场设有闭路电视监控	This Area Is Under Video Surveillance
22	本网点与警方联网	This Area Is Under Police Surveillance
23	泵房	Pump House
24	必要带宽	Necessary Bandwidth
25	闭路电视	Closed Circuit Television 或 Cable TV
26	边角保护材料	Edge Protection Material
27	标签	Label
28	标签牌	Tag
29	饼干	Biscuits
30	不接受信用卡	Credit Cards Not Accepted
	C	
31	财产保险	Property Insurance
32	财务部	Accounting Department
33	裁剪熨烫	Tailoring and Ironing
34	采购部	Purchasing Department
35	彩铃服务	Color Ring Back Tone
36	彩印	Color Printing
37	餐饮服务	Food and Beverages

序号	中文	英文
38	操作维护中心	Operation Maintenance Center
39	茶	Tea
40	产地	Place of Origin 或 Made in ＿＿＿＿
41	产品销售区	Product Sales Section〔Section 可以省略〕
42	产品宣传区	Product Promotion Section〔Section 可以省略〕
43	产品展示区	Product Display Area〔Area 可以省略〕
44	车辆保险	Automobile Insurance
45	衬垫信封	Cushioned Envelope 或 Bubble Padded Envelope
46	充值卡	Refill/Recharge Card
47	宠物用品	Pet Supplies
48	宠物医院（诊所）	Pet Hospital (Clinic)
49	出口报关	Export Declaration
50	出口门到门服务	Export Door-to-Door Delivery
51	储蓄	Savings
52	储蓄存款异地托收	Non-Local Collection of Savings Deposit
53	储蓄单折挂失	Loss Report of Bank Book and Deposit Slip
54	储蓄账户开户	Savings Account Opening
55	储蓄账户销户	Savings Account Cancellation
56	传真	Fax
57	船舶移动业务	Ship Movement Service
58	床上用品	Beddings
59	炊具、餐具	Kitchenware

序号	中文	英文
60	磁卡插口	Card Slot
61	磁卡电话	Magnetic Card Phone 或 Card Phone
62	促销	Promotion
63	存包处	Locker/Lockers〔自助〕 Left Baggage〔有人服务〕
64	存款	Deposit
65	存款口	Cash In
	D	
66	打包带	Packing Strap
67	代发工资账户	Payroll Payment Account
68	代客存衣	Coat Check
69	代客送礼	Gift Delivery Service
70	代售电话卡、地图	Phone Cards and Maps
71	代售火车票	Train Tickets
72	代售民航机票	Airline Tickets
73	代售文体演出票	Tickets for Shows and Sporting Events
74	带宽	Bandwidth
75	贷记卡账户	Credit Card Account
76	贷款	Loans
77	待售	For Sale
78	待租	For Rent/Lease 或 To Let
79	蛋类（土鸡蛋、本鸡蛋）	Eggs (Free-Range Eggs)

序号	中文	英文
80	导购	Shopping Guide
81	到付件	Freight Collect Express Item
82	登记表	Registration Form
83	等候区	Waiting Area
84	等级(指商品)	Class 或 Grade
85	低保账户	Basic Living Allowance Account
86	电报	Telegram
87	电话查号台	Telephone Directory Assistance 或 Telephone Information Service 或 Directory Enquiries
88	电话号码簿(黄页)	Yellow Pages
89	电话会议	Teleconferencing
90	电话每分钟计费标准	Rate Per Minute〔可以缩写为RPM〕
91	电话区号	Area Code
92	电话区号查询	Area Code Directory
93	电话收费(标准)	Phone/Call Rates 或 Calling Rates
94	电汇	Wire Transfer
95	电控室	Power Control Room
96	电脑房	Computer Room
97	电脑耗材(配套设备)	Computer Accessories
98	电视购物	TV Shopping
99	电信服务	Telecom Service

序号	中文	英文
100	电子对账单	Electronic Account Statement
101	电子银行业务	Electronic Banking Business
102	电子邮件	Email 或 E-mail
103	订阅报刊	Newspaper and Periodical Subscription
104	动态令牌工本费	Charge for Dynamic Password
105	对方(指接听电话人)付费电话	Collect Call
106	对公跨行个人转账汇款	Inter-bank Transfer for Corporate Clients Over the Counter
107	对账单	Account Statement
108	兑换残破币	Damaged Bills Exchange
	E	
109	额度管理	Quota Management
110	恶意呼叫识别	Malicious Call Identification〔可以缩写为MCI〕
111	儿童托管	Child Care 或 Day Care
112	儿童玩具	Children's Toys
	F	
113	方便食品	Instant Foods
114	服务部	Customer Service Department〔Department 可以省略〕
115	服务承诺	Commitment to Customers
116	服务流程图	Service Flow Chart
117	服务指南	Service Guide/Information 或 Service Directory〔目录形式〕

序号	中文	英文
118	服装	Clothing
119	服装修改;改衣服务	Clothing Alterations 或 Clothing Alteration Service
120	付费电话;投币电话	Pay Phone 或 Coin Phone
	G	
121	改寄件	Express Item with Corrected Address
122	感谢惠顾	Thanks for Your Patronage
123	干洗	Dry Cleaning
124	港澳台快递	Express Service to Hong Kong, Macao and Taiwan〔发往港澳台〕 Express Service From Hong Kong, Macao and Taiwan〔寄自港澳台〕
125	糕点	Cakes and Pastries
126	个人出境游保证金证明	Security Deposit Certificate for Outbound Travelers
127	个人现金汇款	Personal Cash Transfer
128	个人养老金账户	Personal Pension Account
129	个人业务(指银行业务)	Personal Business 或 Personal Banking
130	个人业务营业时间	Personal Banking Hours〔用于银行网点〕
131	个人银行结算账户	Personal Settlement Account
132	个人资产证明	Personal Asset Certificate
133	个性化专用邮票	Personalized Postal Stamp
134	工艺礼品	Handicrafts
135	公积金贷款	Housing Provident Fund Loans

序号	中文	英文
136	公平秤	Check Scale
137	公司业务（指银行业务）	Corporate Business 或 Corporate Banking
138	公司业务营业时间	Corporate Banking Hours〔用于银行网点〕
139	公益包裹	Charity Parcel
140	公用电话亭	Telephone Booth
141	购物车	Shopping Trolley 或 Shopping Cart
142	购物车回收处	Shopping Cart Return 或 Please Return Shopping Carts Here 或 Trolley Return 或 Trolley Bay
143	购物车仅限超市购物使用,请不要将购物车推出商场停车场以外	Do Not Take Shopping Cart Beyond Parking Lot
144	购物筐	Shopping Basket
145	购物指南	Shopping Guide 或 Shopping Directory
146	购物专车;大卖场专线	Supermarket Shuttle 或 Shoppers Shuttle
147	固体饮料	Drinking Powder 或 Powder Drinks
148	顾客接待室;接待	Reception
149	挂号信;挂号邮件	Registered Mail
150	挂失	Loss Report
151	挂失手续费（每卡）（用于银行卡或购物卡）	Loss Report Fee (Per Card)
152	规格(指商品)	Specifications

序号	中文	英文
153	贵宾服务中心	VIP Service Center 或 VIP Services〔用于 Center 可以省略的场合〕
154	贵宾客户专柜	VIP Counter
155	国际保价邮件	International Insured Mail
156	国际出境快递	International Outbound Express Service
157	国际脆弱包裹	International Fragile Parcel
158	国际电话	International Call
159	国际挂号邮件	International Registered Mail
160	国际海运	International Shipping
161	国际海运大宗物品	Bulk International Shipping
162	国际航空邮件	International Airmail
163	国际进境快递	International Inbound Express Service
164	国际快递	International Express Service
165	国际漫游业务办理	International Roaming
166	国际明信片	International Postcard
167	国际平常函件	International Regular Mail 或 International Standard Mail/Letter
168	国际平常明信片	International Regular Postcard
169	国际平常印刷品	International Standard Printed Matter
170	国际普通包裹	International Surface Parcel
171	国际小包	Small Parcel (International)
172	国际邮购	International Mail Order
173	国际邮件;国际信函	International Mail
174	国际邮件袋牌	International Mail Classification Label

序号	中文	英文
175	国际邮件总包	International Postal Dispatches
176	国际直拨电话	International Direct Dial〔可以缩写为IDD〕
177	国内电话	Domestic Call
178	国内工厂提货	Domestic Factory Pick-up
179	国内快递	Domestic Express Service
180	国内漫游业务办理	Domestic Roaming
181	国内小包	Small Parcel (Domestic)
182	国内邮件	Domestic Mail
183	国内直拨电话	Domestic Direct Dial〔可以缩写为DDD〕
184	国内转运	Domestic Transshipment
185	果酒	Fruit Wine
186	过磅处;称重处	Weigh Counter
	H	
187	海外订舱	Overseas Shipment Booking
188	海外工厂提货	Overseas Factory Pick-up
189	海外清关	Overseas Customs Clearance
190	杭州通卡	Hangzhou Card
191	航空邮件	Airmail
192	号码百事通	Best Tone
193	贺卡	Greeting Card
194	贺卡信封	Greeting Card Envelope
195	黑金卡	Infinity Card

序号	中文	英文
196	呼叫等待服务	Call Waiting
197	呼叫转移服务	Call Forwarding
198	化妆品	Cosmetics
199	话费查询	Phone Bill Inquiry
200	话费充值	Prepaid Refill 或 Prepaid Recharge
201	话费套餐	Calling Plan
202	环保袋	Recycle Bag 或 Environment-Friendly Bag
203	黄金加工	Goldsmithing
204	汇款	Remittance
205	汇票	Money Order
206	会员卡办理和服务	Membership Card Service
207	货梯	Freight Elevator 或 Goods Lift
208	货物跟踪、查询服务	Cargo Tracking and Enquiry Service
	J	
209	基本话费	Basic Charge 或 Standard Charge
210	基地直发(用于水果、蔬菜等农产品生产基地)	Delivery From the Base 或 Delivery From the Planting Base
211	即时通信服务	Instant Messaging Service 或 IM Service
212	集团用户	Group Customers
213	集邮天地	Philatelic Club
214	纪念封	Commemorative Envelope

序号	中文	英文
215	纪念邮票	Commemorative Stamp
216	家电;小家电	Home Appliances
217	家居用品	Household Supplies
218	家具	Furniture
219	家庭固定电话	Home Telephone
220	家庭固定电话开户办理	Home Telephone Application
221	家庭固定电话销户办理	Home Telephone Cancellation
222	家庭固定电话移机办理	Home Telephone Relocation
223	价格	Price
224	价格标签	Price Tag
225	健身器材	Fitness Equipment 或 Gym Equipment
226	缴费业务	Bill Payment Service
227	接待问询	Information 或 Reception and Information
228	结账台;付费处;收银处	Cashier
229	借记卡	Debit Card
230	借记卡大额出账短信提醒服务	Text Message Notice for Large-Sum Expenditure of Debit Card
231	金卡	Gold Card
232	进口仓储	Import Warehouse
233	进口清关	Import Customs Clearance
234	进口全程运输	Import Door-to-Door Delivery

序号	中文	英文
235	近洋次晨达	Near-Sea Next-Business-Day Delivery by 12:00 a.m.
236	近洋次日达	Near-Sea Next-Business-Day Delivery
237	近洋当日达	Near-Sea Same-Business-Day Delivery
238	境外ATM查询	Overseas ATM Inquiry
239	酒类	Liquor and Alcoholic Beverages
	K	
240	咖啡研磨	Coffee Grinding
241	卡片工本费	Card Issuing Fee
242	空调机房	Air-Conditioning Control Room
243	空运水陆路包裹	SAL Parcel 或 Surface Air Lifted Parcel
244	库房	Warehouse
245	裤边修改	Hemming
246	跨行自助设备取现	Inter-Bank ATM Cash Withdraw
247	快递服务	Express Service 或 Courier Service
248	快递文件信封	Envelope for Express Documents
249	快递信封	Express Mail Envelope
250	捆绑式服务	Bundled Service
	L	
251	来电显示服务	Caller ID Display
252	礼宾服务	Concierge Service
253	礼品包装	Gift Wrapping 或 Gift Packing

序号	中文	英文
254	理财服务	Financial Planning Service
255	理财有风险,投资须谨慎	Financial management has risks. You must be cautious.
256	理财咨询	Financial Planning Consultation
257	理赔	Claim Settlement
258	联系远程客户经理	Contact Distant Customer Manager
259	粮食	Cereals
260	零食	Snacks
261	领取免费停车票	Parking Coupon Here
262	留学快递(速递)	Express Mail Service for Overseas Studies Applicants
	M	
263	卖场部	Sales Department
264	美甲	Manicure 或 Nails
265	密封盒	Airtight Box
266	密码单请妥善保管	Please Keep Your Password Safe
267	免费送货	Free Delivery 或 Free Home Delivery
268	面包	Bread
269	明信片	Postcard
	N	
270	奶制品	Dairy Products
271	男鞋	Men's Shoes
272	男装	Men's Wear

序号	中文	英文
273	年费	Annual Fee
274	您前面还有____人在等候,请安静等待。	There are ____ customers before you. Please wait.
275	牛皮纸封套	Brown Paper Envelope
276	牛羊肉	Beef and Mutton
277	女内衣	Women's Underwear
278	女鞋	Women's Shoes
279	女装	Women's Wear
	P	
280	派送	Delivery
281	泡沫塑料充垫物	Packing Bubble Plastics 或 Packing Foam Plastics
282	皮鞋修理	Shoe Repair
283	啤酒	Beer
284	票务服务	Ticket Service
285	拼装家具	Knock-Down Furniture 或 Ready-to-Assemble Furniture〔可缩写为 RTA Furniture〕
286	平信	Regular Mail
287	凭条	Receipt
	Q	
288	汽车用品	Car Accessories
289	钱款请当面点清	Please Count Your Cash Before You Leave
290	欠费停机	Service Suspended Due to Insufficient Balance

序号	中文	英文
291	禽肉	Poultry Meat
292	禽肉制品	Poultry Products
293	请____号(顾客)到____号柜台	No. ____, please go to Counter____.
294	请保存好购物凭证	Please Keep Your Payment Slip Safe 或 Do Not Throw Away Your Payment Slip
295	请插入您的银行卡	Please Insert Your Bank Card
296	请收好您的信用卡	Please Take Your Credit Card
297	请收好您的找零	Please Take Your Change
298	请输入您的密码	Please Enter Your PIN
299	请勿推购物车上下电动扶梯	No Shopping Cart on Escalator
300	请勿在付款前拆开商品的包装	Do Not Unwrap Any Article Before Purchase
301	请注意显示屏及语音呼叫,过号无效。	Your number will be invalid if you miss your turn.
302	驱虫用品(用于消杀蚊虫、害虫等)	Insect Repellents
303	取包处	Bag Claim
304	取车前,请先交费(在商场停车场使用)	Pay Your Parking Here 或 Scan to Pay Your Parking Here
305	取号机	Queuing Machine
306	取款	Withdrawal
307	取款口	Cash Out
308	取现手续费(每笔)	Cash Withdrawal Fee (per transaction)
309	全球移动通信系统	Global System for Mobile Communications 或 GSM

序号	中文	英文
310	全市范围免费送货	Free Citywide Delivery
	R	
311	人工服务	Manual Service
312	人工及自助挂失	Manual and Self-Service Loss Reporting
313	人工转接电话	Operator Assisted Call
314	人力资源部	Human Resources Department
315	人民币结算	RMB Settlement
316	人民币小额个人活期账户	RMB Small-Sum Personal Current Account
317	人寿保险	Life Insurance
	S	
318	散件	Loose Items
319	散装食品	Bulk Food
320	商品保养及维修	Maintenance and Repair
321	商品定制	Special Orders
322	商品名称;产品名称	Product Name
323	商品邮购	Mail Order Service
324	商业信函（直邮广告商函）	Direct Mail
325	设备故障	Out of Order
326	摄影摄像器材	Camera Products
327	省际快递	Inter-Provincial Express Service
328	省内异地快递	Intra-Provincial Express Service
329	失物招领处	Lost and Found

序号	中文	英文
330	失业保险账户	Unemployment Insurance Account
331	市内电话	Local Call
332	视听设备	Audio Visual Equipment
333	试衣室;试衣间	Fitting Room 或 Dressing Room
334	试营业	Soft Opening
335	视频会议	Videoconferencing
336	收费标准	Rates
337	收费处	Cashier 或 Payment
338	手表	Watches
339	手机充电处	Mobile Phone Recharging 或 Cell Phone Recharging
340	手机维修	Cellphone Repair
341	手机银行	Mobile Banking Service
342	手机银行注册	Mobile Banking Registration
343	手续费	Service Charge
344	手语服务	Sign Language Services
345	首日封	First Day Cover
346	首饰加工	Jewelry Smithing 或 Jeweller
347	售后服务部	After-Sales Service Department
348	售后服务热线	After-Sales Service Hotline
349	蔬菜	Vegetables
350	双币贷记卡	Dual Currency Credit Card

序号	中文	英文
351	水产品	Aquatic Products
352	水果	Fruits
353	送货服务	Delivery Service
354	送货上门	Home Delivery 或 Delivery to Your Doorstep 或 Door-to-Door Delivery
355	糖果	Candies 或 Sweets
	T	
356	特价	Special Offer
357	特卖	Special Sale
358	特种邮票	Special Stamp
359	体育用品	Sporting Goods 或 Sports Equipment
360	填表处	Fill out Forms Here
361	条码扫描口	Barcode Scanner 或 Barcode Reader 或 Scan Barcode
362	调味品	Condiments 或 Spices
363	通话时间	Call Duration
364	同城本行存款	Intra-City Intra-Bank Deposit
365	同城本行取款	Intra-City Intra-Bank Withdrawal
366	同城本行转账	Intra-City Book Transfer
367	同城快递	Intra-City Express Service
368	童车	Baby Carriages 或 Baby Strollers

序号	中文	英文
369	童装	Children's Wear
370	图卡	Art Postcard
371	图书	Books
372	吐卡口（用于自动存取款机等）	Take Back Your Card
373	团购业务	Group Purchase Service
374	团体接待	Group Reception
375	退保	Policy Cancellation 或 Insurance Cancellation
376	退换商品处	Refunds and Exchanges
377	退休金账户	Retirement Pension Account
	U	
378	USB Key 证书工本费	Charge for USB Key Certificate
	V	
379	VIP 俱乐部会员专柜	VIP Club Members
380	VIP 客户洽谈区	VIP Customer Meeting Room
	W	
381	外币兑换机	Foreign Currency Exchange Machine〔Foreign 可以省略；Machine 可以省略〕
382	外币结算	Foreign Currency Settlement
383	外汇业务	Foreign Exchange Service
384	网上银行	Online Banking Service
385	危险物品不得寄存	Hazardous Articles Prohibited
386	微波食品加热	Microwave Heating

序号	中文	英文
387	委托件(邮政业务)	Consigned Express Item
388	卫生用品	Sanitation Supplies
389	未付款商品请勿带进卫生间	Do Not Take Unpaid Items Into Toilets
390	位置服务;移动定位服务	Location-Based Service
391	文具	Stationery
392	无线充电	Wireless Charging
393	五金工具	Hardware
394	物流管理部	Logistics Management Department
395	物业行政部	Property Department
	X	
396	洗车	Car Wash 或 Auto Wash
397	洗涤用品	Detergents
398	洗漱用品	Personal Hygiene Products
399	系统故障(用于自动售票机、存取款机或售货机等)	Out of Order
400	现金存款往这里走(用于银行服务大厅)	Cash Deposits This Way 或 This Way to Cash Deposits
401	现金分期	Cash Installment
402	限时服务	Limited Hours Service
403	限时快递	Time-Definite Express
404	箱包	Bags and Suitcases

序号	中文	英文
405	消费贷款	Consumption Loans
406	小额账户	Small-Amount Account 或 Small-Sum Account
407	鞋	Shoes
408	信贷业务	Credit Service
409	信封	Envelope
410	信件	Letter
411	信箱〔收信用〕	Letter Box
412	信用卡	Credit Card
413	信用卡本行借记卡自动还款	Automatic Credit Card Repayment Using Debit Card Balance of the Same Bank
414	信用卡到期换卡	Credit Card Renewal
415	信用卡免费大额交易短信提醒服务	Text Message Notice for Large-Sum Transaction of Credit Card
416	信用卡免费账单短信提醒服务	Text Message Notice of Credit Card Bank Statement
417	休闲装	Sportswear 或 Casual Wear
	Y	
418	烟草	Cigarettes and Tobacco
419	严禁邮寄危险品、违禁品	Carriage of Contraband and Dangerous Articles Is Prohibited by Law
420	严禁在包裹中夹带现钞	Carriage of Cash in Parcels Is Prohibited
421	眼镜	Glasses
422	验光配镜	Optician Services 或 Optical Service

序号	中文	英文
423	业务受理处;业务受理	Reception
424	业务咨询处;业务咨询	Information
425	衣帽寄存处;存衣处	Cloakroom
426	医保账户	Medical Insurance Account
427	移动宽带	Mobile Broadband
428	移动通信器材	Mobile Phones and Accessories
429	易碎商品	Fragile Goods〔Goods可以省略〕
430	音像制品	Audio and Video Products
431	银行卡	Bank Card
432	婴儿用品(用于超市)	Baby's Products 或 Baby Care
433	营销策划	Marketing Planning
434	营业窗口	Service Counter/Window
435	营业时间	Business Hours 或 Opening Hours
436	营业厅	Service Hall/Center 或 Business Hall
437	营业厅导航	Service Guide
438	优惠	Discounts 或 On Sale
439	优选精品	The Best Product/Products〔视产品数量选用〕或 Well-Selected Quality Product/Products〔视产品数量选用〕
440	邮册	Stamp Album
441	邮戳	Postmark

序号	中文	英文
442	邮袋	Mailbag
443	邮袋封扎带	Mailbag Strap 或 Mailbag String
444	邮购	Mail Order
445	邮寄包裹处;邮寄包裹	Parcel Service
446	邮简	Postal Letter Sheet 或 Postal Letter Card
447	邮件(邮局传递的函件和包裹的统称)	Mail
448	邮件封面书写规范	Envelope Writing Guide
449	邮件检查	Postal Inspection
450	邮票	Stamp
451	邮筒,邮箱(寄信用)	Postbox 或 Mailbox 或 Letterbox 〔在同一场所内应保持统一〕
452	邮折	Stamp Folder
453	邮政包裹	Postal Parcel
454	邮政包裹包装箱;包装箱	Packing Box 或 Packaging Box
455	邮政编码	Postal Code 或 Zip Code〔美语〕 或 Postcode〔英语〕 〔在同一场所内应保持统一〕
456	邮政编码查询	Postal Code Inquiry 或 Postcode Inquiry
457	邮政储蓄	Postal Savings
458	邮政服务	Postal Service

序号	中文	英文
459	邮政汇款	Postal Remittance
460	邮政快件	Express Mail
461	邮政特快专递详情单	EMS Waybill
462	邮政特快专递业务单据	EMS Operational Forms
463	邮资明信片	Stamped Postcard
464	邮资票品和集邮品的分类与编码规则	Rules for Postage Classification and Coding
465	邮资信封	Stamped Envelope
466	有线电视	Cable TV
467	幼儿托管处	Child Care 或 Children's Center
468	预付费	Prepayment
469	远洋次日达	Transoceanic Next-Business-Day Delivery
470	远洋隔日达	Transoceanic Third-Business-Day Delivery
471	约投挂号信	Registered Mail Pickup
472	乐器	Musical Instruments
473	熨衣	Ironing 或 Pressing
	Z	
474	杂物室	Storage Room
475	赠品领取处	Free Gifts
476	长途电话	Long Distance Call
477	长途(电话)收费	Long Distance Rates
478	账单查询	Bill Inquiry

序号	中文	英文
479	账单分期	Bill Installment
480	账单付费	Bill Payment
481	账单还款	Bill Refund
482	账单缴费	Bill Payment
483	账户查询	Account Inquiry
484	照明用品	Lighting Products
485	＿＿＿折〔指优惠的折扣幅度〕	＿＿＿Off〔九折填入10%，八折填入20%，七折填入30%，以此类推〕
486	针棉用品	Knitwear
487	正在营业;照常营业	We Are Open 或Open
488	支票	Cheque
489	直拨电话	Direct Dial Call
490	纸箱	Cardboard 或Carton
491	智能包裹	Smart Locker Parcel
492	智能包裹箱	Smart Postal Parcel Lockers
493	智能快件箱	Smart Postal Express Lockers
494	中国邮政	China Post
495	钟表维修	Clock and Watch Repair
496	周边营业厅分布图	Map of Nearby Service/Business Halls
497	昼夜营业	Open 24 Hours
498	珠宝首饰	Jewelry
499	住房公积金账户	Housing Provident Fund Account 或Housing Accumulation Fund Account

序号	中文	英文
500	祝您购物愉快	Enjoy Your Shopping
501	专差快递	On Board Courier
502	转账	Transfer
503	转账手续费(每笔)	Transfer Fee (Per Transaction)
504	转账与缴费	Transfer and Payment
505	咨询处	Inquiry 或 Information
506	资信证明	Certificate of Financial Standing
507	自动存款机	Cash Deposit Machine 或 CDM
508	自动缴费机	Bill Payment Machine
509	自动取款机;自动存取款机	Automatic Teller Machine 或 ATM
510	自取件(邮政)	Self Pick-up Express Item
511	自由退换货	Refundable and Exchangeable
512	自助查询商品价格	Price Check
513	自助服务	Self-Service
514	自助服务区	Self-Service Area
515	自助服务终端	Self-Service Terminal
516	综合受理	General Services
517	综合业务	General Service
518	总服务台	Central Service Desk〔用于实体或虚拟〕 或 Service Desk〔用于实体或虚拟〕 或 Reception〔用于实体〕 或 Service Counter〔用于实体〕
519	总经理办公室	General Manager's Office

序号	中文	英文
520	钻石卡	Diamond Card

注1:"〔 〕"中的内容是对英文译法的解释说明。

注2:"/"表示可选择该组词语中的一种。

注3:"//"表示书写时应当换行的断行处。需要同行书写时"//"应改为句点".",警示词后加惊叹号"!"。

注4:"____"表示使用时应根据实际情况填入具体内容。

注5:"或"前后所列出的不同译法可任意选择一种使用。

注6:解释说明中指出某个词"可以省略"的,省略该词的译文只能用于设置在该设施上的标识中,如客户服务中心 Customer Service Center,在设置于该中心处的标识中可以省略 Center,译作 Customer Services。

附录 G

（资料性）

餐饮业、住宿业场所及机构和设施名称英文译写示例

G.1 餐饮业、住宿业场所及机构和设施名称英文译写示例见表 G.1。表 G.1 按中文汉语拼音排序。

表 G.1 餐饮业、住宿业场所及机构和设施名称英文译写示例

序号	中文	英文
	A	
1	按摩室	Massotherapy Room 或 Massage Room〔Room 均可省略〕
	B	
2	包间；包房	Private Room
3	保洁室；清洁间	Janitor's Closet 或 Janitor
4	报告厅（酒店内）	Conference Hall/Room
5	标准客房	Twin/Double/Standard Room
6	宾馆；酒店；旅馆	Hotel
7	布草间	Linen Room
	C	
8	擦鞋机	Shoe Shiner 或 Automatic Shoe Polisher
9	餐馆；饭店；食府	Restaurant
10	餐厅	Restaurant 或 Dining Room/Hall 或 Cafeteria〔自助式的〕
11	餐饮广场；美食城	Food Court〔建筑物内的〕 或 Food Plaza

序号	中文	英文
12	茶馆;茶楼	Teahouse
13	茶室	Tearoom
14	茶水间	Pantry Room
15	出租车候车处	Taxi Stand 或 Taxi Rank
16	存行李处	Locker〔自助〕 Left Baggage/Luggage〔有人服务〕
	D	
17	大堂	Lobby
18	大厅	Hall
19	单人房间	Single Room
20	地下车库;地下停车场	Underground Parking
21	地下室	Basement
22	点菜区	Food Ordering Area〔Area可以省略〕
23	电梯	Elevator〔美语〕 或 Lift〔英语〕
24	电子监控	Electronic Surveillance
25	订餐处	Reservation
26	多功能厅	Function Hall 或 Multi-Function Hall 或 Multi-Purpose Hall 〔在同一场所内应保持统一〕
	F	
27	风量调节	Fan Control
28	副食品商店(杂货店)	Grocer 或 Grocer's Shop 或 Grocery Store

序号	中文	英文
	G	
29	更衣室	Locker Room
30	工艺(商)品店	Crafts Shop
31	观光电梯	Sightseeing Elevator 或 Observation Elevator 或 Glass Elevator
32	贵宾餐厅	VIP Restaurant 或 VIP Dining Hall
33	过道	Passage
	H	
34	豪华套房	Deluxe Suite
35	候餐区	Waiting Area
36	会议室	Conference/Meeting Room
37	火锅店	Chinese Hot-Pot Restaurant〔Restaurant 可以省略〕
38	货梯	Freight/Cargo Elevator
	J	
39	家庭旅馆	Family Hotel/Hostel/Inn 或 B & B Family Guest House
40	坚果	Nuts
41	(坚果)过敏	____ Allergy 或 Allergic to ____
42	健身房	Gym/Gymnasium 或 Fitness Room
43	禁烟区;无烟区	Non-Smoking Area
44	经济酒店	Economy Lodge/Inn 或 Budget Hostel

序号	中文	英文
45	酒吧	Bar 或 Pub〔英式的〕
46	俱乐部	Club
	K	
47	咖啡馆;咖啡厅	Coffee Shop 或 Café
48	卡拉OK厅	Karaoke 或 KTV
49	开发票处	Invoice and Receipt
50	客房	Guest Room
51	客房部;管家部	Housekeeping Department
52	客房电梯	Guest Elevator
53	客栈	Inn
54	快餐店;快餐吧	Snack Bar 或 Snacks 或 Fast Food Restaurant〔Restaurant 可以省略〕
55	快捷酒店	Budget Hotel
	L	
56	礼宾部	Concierge Office
57	礼品商店	Gift Shop 或 Souvenirs
58	立体停车库	Mechanical Parking Lot 或 Parking Tower〔指多层的〕
59	连锁酒店	Chain Hotel
60	连锁快餐店	Fast Food Chain
61	楼梯	Stairs 或 Stairway

序号	中文	英文
62	楼梯栏杆	Handrail
	M	
63	美容护理部	Beauty Care
64	美食街	Food Street
65	门厅;前厅;大堂	Lobby 或 Foyer
66	面包房	Bakery
67	面馆	Noodle Restaurant 或 Noodles〔用于 Restaurant 省略时〕
68	民宿	Homestay
	P	
69	啤酒屋;啤酒馆	Beer House
	Q	
70	棋牌室	Chess and Cards Room〔Room 可以省略〕
71	汽车旅馆	Motel
72	前台;总台;接待迎宾	Front Desk 或 Reception
73	青年旅社	Youth Hostel
74	清真餐馆	Halal Restaurant 或 Halal Food
75	取行李处	Baggage/Luggage Claim
	S	
76	桑拿房	Sauna Room〔Room 可以省略〕
77	商务酒店	Business Hotel
78	商务中心	Business Center

序号	中文	英文
79	上楼楼梯	Stairway Up〔Stairway 可以省略〕
80	烧烤店	Grill House 或 Barbecue Restaurant〔Restaurant 可省略〕
81	失物招领处	Lost and Found
82	食品店	Food Store
83	手推车	Cart
84	双人房;双床间(两张单人床)	Twin Room
85	双人间(一张双人床)	Double Room
86	水疗美容部	Spa
	T	
87	套房;套间	Suite
	W	
88	外卖店	Take Out 或 Take Away
89	屋顶花园	Roof Garden
90	无障碍客房	Accessible Room
91	舞厅;歌舞厅	Ballroom 或 Dance Hall
	X	
92	西饼屋	Pastry Store〔Store 可以省略〕
93	西餐馆;西餐厅	Western Food Restaurant〔Restaurant 可以省略〕 或 Western Restaurant
94	下楼楼梯	Stairway Down〔Stairway 可以省略〕
95	小吃店	Snack Bar 或 Snacks

序号	中文	英文
96	小酒吧	Mini-Bar
97	小卖部	Shop
98	行李房	Baggage/Luggage Room
99	行政酒廊	Executive Lounge
100	行政套房	Executive Suite
101	休息室;休息厅	Lounge
	Y	
102	宴会厅	Banquet Hall
103	衣帽寄存处;存衣处	Cloakroom
104	饮食店;餐饮店;小饭馆	Eatery
105	(有棚的)停车库	Covered Parking Garage〔Garage可以省略〕
106	游泳池	Swimming Pool
107	员工电梯	Staff Elevator 或 Staff Only
	Z	
108	招待所	Guesthouse
109	主廊	Main Corridor
110	专属停车位	Reserved Parking
111	自动扶梯	Escalator
112	自动售货机	Vending Machine
113	自助餐厅	Cafeteria 或 Buffet 或 Buffet Restaurant〔多用于酒店等〕

序号	中文	英文
114	中餐馆;中餐厅	Chinese Food Restaurant〔Restaurant 可以省略〕 或 Chinese Restaurant
115	走廊	Corridor
116	足疗室;足浴室	Foot Massage Room〔Room可以省略〕
注1:"〔 〕"中的内容是对英文译法的解释说明。 注2:"或"前后所列出的不同译法可任意选择一种使用。		

G.2 餐饮业、住宿业服务信息英文译写示例见表G.2。表G.2按中文汉语拼音排序。

表G.2 餐饮业、住宿业服务信息英文译写示例

序号	中文	英文
	B	
1	八宝豆腐	Braised Tofu with Assorted Meat and Vegetable
2	八宝饭	Eight-Treasure Sticky Rice Pudding
3	八角;茴香	Anise 或 Chinese Anise
4	白酒	Liquor and Spirits
5	白葡萄酒	White Wine
6	板栗烧肉	Braised Pork with Chestnuts
7	保险柜	Safe Box 或 Safe
8	杯垫	Coaster
9	杯碟	Saucer

序号	中文	英文
10	被子	Quilt
11	本柜恕不接受 VIP 卡	VIP Cards Not Accepted
12	比萨	Pizza
13	宾馆修理工	Maintenance Worker
14	冰块服务	Ice Delivery
15	冰糖	Rock Sugar
16	冰箱	Refrigerator
17	不含酒精类饮料	Non-Alcoholic Beverages
18	不间断电源	Uninterruptible Power Supply 或 UPS
19	不接受信用卡结账	Credit Card Not Accepted
	C	
20	擦鞋服务	Shoe Shine Service 或 Shoe Polish
21	菜单	Menu
22	菜籽油	Rape Seed Oil
23	餐巾;餐巾纸	Napkin
24	餐具	Tableware
25	餐厅服务员	Waiter〔男〕 Waitress〔女〕
26	餐饮服务	Food and Beverages
27	叉(西餐用)	Fork
28	插卡取电	Insert Card for Power
29	茶	Tea

序号	中文	英文
30	厨师	Chef
31	厨师长	Head Chef
32	川菜(四川菜)	Chuan Cuisine 或 Sichuan Cuisine
33	窗帘	Curtains
34	吹风机	Hair Dryer
35	葱包烩	Fried Dough Sticks Wrapped in Spring Pancake
36	醋	Vinegar
	D	
37	打折;优惠	Discount 或 Reduced Rate
38	大葱	Green Chinese Onion
39	大蒜	Garlic
40	大堂副理	Assistant Lobby Manager
41	大堂经理	Lobby Manager
42	淡季	Low/Slack Season
43	蛋黄酱	Mayonnaise
44	刀	Knife
45	刀削面	Daoxiaomian Noodles 或 Knife-Pared Noodles 或 Knife-Shaved Noodles 或 Knife-Sliced Noodles
46	电话簿	Telephone Directory
47	电话服务	Telephone Service

序号	中文	英文
48	电话号码查询;信息查询	Information and Telephone Directory
49	电话机	Telephone
50	电话总机(宾馆内)	Operator
51	电热水壶;电水壶	Electric Kettle
52	电视机遥控器	TV Remote Control
53	电视节目单	TV Listings 或 TV Channel Directory
54	淀粉;芡粉	Starch
55	吊灯	Ceiling Lamp
56	碟	Plate
57	订餐;订座	Table Reservation
58	定胜糕	Victory Cake
59	东坡肉	Dongpo Pork
60	豆瓣酱	Soybean Paste
61	豆腐	Tofu 或 Doufu 或 Bean Curd
62	豆油	Soybean Oil
63	豆制品	Bean Products
64	对折;五折	50% Off
	E	
65	儿童高脚椅	Baby High Chair

序号	中文	英文
	F	
66	番茄酱	Tomato Sauce〔由番茄烹成的〕 或 Ketchup〔有包装的〕
67	方糖	Cubic Sugar
68	房间至房间（用于电话机上）	Room-to-Room
69	房卡	Room Card
70	访客请登记	All Visitors Must Register
71	非赠品	Non-Complimentary
72	风味食品	Special Delicacies
73	风味小吃	Local Snacks/Delicacies/Food
74	枫糖浆	Maple Syrup
75	蜂蜜	Honey
76	服务项目	Services Available
77	服务指南	Service Directory/Information
78	辅料	Ingredients
	G	
79	橄榄油	Olive Oil
80	干辣椒	Chili
81	干炸响铃	Fried Bean Curd Skin 或 Fried Stuffed Bean Curd Skin
82	高汤	Soup Stock
83	糕点	Cakes and Pastries
84	罐装饮料	Canned Drinks

序号	中文	英文
85	桂花	Sweet Osmanthus
86	桂皮	Cinnamon
87	国酒;国产酒	Chinese Liquors and Wines
88	果酱	Jam
89	果酒	Fruit Wine
	H	
90	海鲜	Seafood
91	杭菊鸡丝	Shredded Chicken with Hangzhou Chrysanthemum
92	杭三鲜	Hangsanxian (free-range chicken, river shrimp, pork belly, meat skin, fish ball, meat ball, Chinese cabbage, winter bamboo shoots, and more)
93	杭州酱鸭	Duck in Brown Sauce, Hangzhou Style
94	蚝油	Oyster Oil
95	荷叶粉蒸肉	Steamed Pork with Rice Flour Wrapped in Lotus Leaves
96	红葡萄酒	Red Wine
97	红烧狮子头	Braised Pork Balls in Brown Sauce
98	红糖	Brown Sugar
99	胡椒粉	Pepper
100	互联网服务	Internet Service
101	护发素	Hair Conditioner
102	花椒	Sichuan Pepper
103	花生酱	Peanut Butter

序号	中文	英文
104	花生油	Peanut Oil
105	黄酒	Yellow Rice Wine
106	黄油	Butter
107	徽菜(安徽菜)	Hui Cuisine 或 Anhui Cuisine
108	荤菜	Meat Dishes
109	馄饨	Huntun 或 Wonton
	J	
110	鸡精	Chicken Powder
111	鸡肉	Chicken
112	加床	Extra Bed 或 Extra Cot〔婴儿床、行军床〕 或 Extra Crib〔婴儿床〕〔美语〕
113	加床服务	Extra Bed Service
114	酱油	Soy Sauce
115	椒盐粉	Peppered Salt
116	叫花童子鸡	Beggar's Chicken 或 Beggar's Spring Chicken
117	叫醒服务;叫早服务	Wake-up Call 或 Morning Call
118	接待问询	Information 或 Reception and Information
119	结账(住宿);退房	Check-out
120	芥末	Mustard
121	经理	Manager

序号	中文	英文
122	镜前灯	Mirror Light
123	酒水单	Wine List〔酒类〕 Beverage Menu〔饮料类〕
	K	
124	咖啡	Coffee
125	咖啡机	Coffee Maker
126	咖喱	Curry
127	开胃菜	Appetizer
128	开胃酒	Aperitifs
129	可使用无线网络	Wi-Fi Available
130	可用信用卡结账	Credit Card Accepted
131	客房服务	Housekeeping
132	客房服务员	Room Attendant 或 Room Maid〔女性〕
133	客房价格	Room Rates 或 Tariff〔房价表〕
134	客房送餐服务	Room Service 或 In-Room Dining
135	客房钥匙	Room Key
136	空调	Air Conditioner
137	空调遥控器	Air Conditioner Remote Control
138	快餐	Fast Food
139	筷子	Chopsticks
140	宽带连接	Internet Connection

序号	中文	英文
	L	
141	拉面	Lamian Noodles 或 Hand-Pulled Noodles 或 Hand-Stretched Noodles
142	辣的	Hot 或 Spicy
143	辣酱油	Pungent Sauce
144	辣椒	Pepper
145	辣椒酱	Chili Sauce
146	冷〔用于水龙头上〕	Cold
147	理发室	Barber's 或 Barber Shop〔男士〕 Hairdresser's〔女士〕
148	栗子炒仔鸡	Fried Chicken with Chestnuts
149	鲁菜(山东菜)	Lu Cuisine 或 Shandong Cuisine
150	落地灯	Floor Lamp
151	绿茶饼	Green Tea Cake
	M	
152	麻辣的	Peppery
153	买一送一(商店促销用)	BOGOFF/BOGOF 或 Buy One Get One For Free 或 Buy One Get One Free
154	猫耳朵	Cat's Ear Noodles 或 Cat Ear Noodles 或 Cat Ear-Shaped Noodles
155	毛巾	Towel
156	毛毯袋	Blanket Bag

序号	中文	英文
157	美发厅	Beauty Salon 或 Hairdresser's〔英语〕 或 Hairdressing Salon〔美语〕 或 Hair Salon〔美语〕
158	米饭	Rice
159	米酒	Rice Wine
160	米线	Rice Noodles
161	密封盒	Airtight Box
162	免费送餐	Free Delivery
163	面包	Bread
164	面条	Noodles
165	闽菜(福建菜)	Min Cuisine 或 Fujian Cuisine
166	沐浴乳	Body Shampoo 或 Shower Lotion
	N	
167	奶酪;干酪	Cheese
168	南肉春笋	Stewed Bacon with Spring Bamboo Shoots
169	内部施工,暂停营业	Under Construction // Temporarily Closed
170	内线电话;内部电话	Internal/Inside Call
171	嫩的(指肉类等食材)	Tender
172	牛排	Steak
173	牛肉	Beef
174	暖气	Heating
	P	
175	配菜	Side Dish

序号	中文	英文
176	啤酒	Beer
177	片儿川	Pian'erchuan (Noodles with Sliced Pork, Bamboo Shoots, and Pickled Potherb Mustard)
178	票款当面点清;找零请当面点清	Please Check Your Change Before Leaving the Counter
	Q	
179	七分熟的(指牛排等)	Medium Well
180	切勿暴饮暴食	Eat Light, Eat Right
181	切勿酒后驾车	Do Not Drink and Drive
182	清淡的(指菜肴等)	Light 或 Bland
183	清汤鱼圆	Fish Balls in Light Soup
184	清真菜	Halal Food 或 Muslim Food
185	清蒸鲥鱼	Steamed Hilsa Herring Fish
186	请即打扫	Please Make Up My Room
187	请加热后食用	Heat Before Eating 或 Heat Before You Eat
188	请将您需要清洁的皮鞋放置在此。	Please place your shoes here if you would like to have them polished.
189	请将仍要使用的毛巾放在毛巾架上,感谢您帮助我们节能减排。	Thank you for helping us save water and energy. Please put the towels you will use again on the rack.
190	请留意退房时间	Our Checkout Time Is ____ O'clock 或 Check-out Time: ____ O'clock
191	请勿卧床吸烟	Do Not Smoke in Bed
192	请勿影响其他客人休息	Please Do Not Disturb Other Guests

序号	中文	英文
193	请依次取餐	Please Wait in Line
194	请在此处先刷房卡，再按目的楼层号码（电梯内）	Please Tap Your Room Card Here Before Pressing the Number of Your Floor
	R	
195	热〔用于水龙头上〕	Hot
196	热菜；热炒	Hot Dishes
197	热狗	Hot Dog
198	肉类	Meat
199	肉汁	Gravy
200	入宿登记	Check-in
	S	
201	三分熟的(指牛排等)	Rare
202	三明治	Sandwich
203	色拉	Salad
204	色拉酱	Salad Dressings
205	色拉油	Salad Oil
206	砂锅鱼头豆腐	Stewed Fish Head with Tofu in Casserole
207	商店营业员	Shop Assistant 或 Clerk
208	上网计时收费	Duration-Based Internet Access Charge
209	上网免费	Free Internet Use
210	生爆鳝片	Sautéed Eel Slices
211	生姜	Ginger

序号	中文	英文
212	十分熟的;全熟的(指牛排等)	Well Done
213	市内电话	Local Call
214	适量取食,请勿浪费	Please Take Only What You Will Eat // Do Not Waste Food 或 Do Not Waste Food
215	蔬菜	Vegetables
216	熟食	Delicatessen〔也可简作 Deli〕 或 Cooked Food
217	爽口的(指菜肴)	Smooth
218	水果	Fruits
219	宋嫂鱼羹	Sister Song's Fish Broth
220	苏菜	Su Cuisine 或 Jiangsu Cuisine
221	素菜	Vegetable Dishes
222	素鸡	Chinese Vegan Chicken 或 Chicken-Flavored Tofu
223	素食菜	Vegetarian Food
224	酸的(指菜肴味道)	Sour
225	酸辣酱	Chutney
226	笋干老鸭煲	Stewed Duck with Dried Bamboo Shoots
	T	
227	毯子	Blanket
228	碳酸饮料	Carbonate Beverages 或 Sodas
229	汤	Soup
230	汤匙	Spoon

序号	中文	英文
231	糖;白糖	Sugar
232	糖醋咕咾肉	Sweet and Sour Pork
233	糖醋排骨	Sweet and Sour Spare Ribs
234	套餐菜单	Set Menu
235	提供酒后代驾服务	Designated Driver Service Available〔Available 可省略〕
236	甜的(指菜肴味道)	Sweet
237	甜点	Dessert
238	甜面酱	Sweet Soybean Paste
239	调酒师	Bartender
240	调味品	Condiments 或 Spices
241	筒灯	Downlight 或 Can Light
242	退房时间:____点	Check-out Time:____O'clock
	W	
243	外线电话	External/Outside Call
244	碗	Bowl
245	旺季	High/Peak Season
246	味淡的(指菜肴味道)	Lightly Seasoned
247	味厚的(指菜肴味道)	Rich 或 Greasy〔特指油腻的〕
248	味精	MSG
249	味重的(指菜肴味道)	Heavily Seasoned
250	温度调节(用于宾馆客房空调)	Temperature Control

序号	中文	英文
251	文明用餐,请勿喧哗	Please Help Maintain a Quiet Atmosphere
252	五分熟的(指牛排等)	Medium
253	五香花生	Spiced Peanuts
	X	
254	西餐	Western Food/Cuisine
255	西湖莼菜汤	West Lake Water Shield Soup
256	西湖醋鱼	Steamed West Lake Fish in Vinegar Gravy
257	吸顶灯	Ceiling Light
258	洗发水	Shampoo
259	洗护发用品	Shampoo and Conditioner
260	洗衣袋	Laundry Bag
261	洗衣服务	Laundry Service〔Service 可以省略〕
262	细砂糖	Caster Sugar
263	虾类	Prawn 或 Shrimp
264	鲜奶	Milk
265	鲜肉小笼(包)	Steamed Bun Stuffed with Pork
266	鲜榨果汁	Fresh Juice
267	馅饼	Pie
268	香料	Spice
269	香油	Sesame Oil
270	香皂	Toilet Soap
271	湘菜(湖南菜)	Xiang Cuisine 或 Hunan Cuisine

序号	中文	英文
272	小葱	Chive 或 Scallion
273	谢绝外带食物;外来食品请勿入内	Outside Food Not Allowed 或 No Outside Food
274	谢谢光临	Thank You for Your Patronage
275	蟹类	Crab
276	行李服务	Baggage/Luggage Service
277	行李员	Porter
	Y	
278	鸭肉	Duck
279	烟缸	Ashtray
280	盐	Salt
281	羊排	Lamb Chop 或 Mutton Chop
282	羊肉	Mutton
283	羊肉串	Mutton Shashlik
284	洋酒	Imported Wines and Liquors
285	夜床服务	Turndown Service 或 Turn Down Service
286	夜灯	Night Light
287	一品南乳肉	Braised Pork with Fermented Tofu
288	衣柜	Closet 或 Wardrobe
289	衣架	Coat Hanger
290	已预订;预留	Reserved
291	饮料	Beverages 或 Drinks

序号	中文	英文
292	饮用水	Drinking Water
293	婴儿床	Crib/Cot
294	婴儿食品	Baby Food
295	用完餐后,请归还碗碟托盘	Please return plates and trays here. 或 Please Return Your Plates and Trays After Eating/Meal
296	油爆河虾	Sautéed Shrimps in Deep Oil 或 Stir-Fried Shrimps
297	油焖春笋	Braised Spring Bamboo Shoots
298	油焖茄子	Braised Eggplant
299	有偿使用	Not Free
300	有线电视	Cable TV
301	鱼类	Fish
302	羽绒被	Duvet
303	浴室灯	Bathroom Light
304	月饼	Moon Cake
305	阅读灯	Reading Light
306	粤菜(广东菜)	Yue Cuisine 或 Guangdong Cuisine 或 Cantonese Cuisine
	Z	
307	糟烩鞭笋	Braised Bamboo Shoots with Rice Wine Sauce
308	糟鸡	Chicken in Fermented Rice Sauce
309	赠品	Complimentary
310	斋菜	Buddhist Food

序号	中文	英文
311	长途电话	Long Distance Call
312	账单	Bill
313	招牌菜	Specialty〔美语〕/Speciality〔英语〕〔单独指某道菜时用〕 Specialties/Specialities〔作为菜单上的目录时用〕
314	照常营业	We Are Open 或 Open
315	浙菜(浙江菜)	Zhe Cuisine 或 Zhejiang Cuisine
316	枕头	Pillow
317	正在加热,当心烫伤	CAUTION // Hot Surface
318	只允许剃须刀充电〔用于插座上〕	Shavers Only
319	芝麻酱	Sesame Butter
320	中餐	Chinese Food/Cuisine
321	中式快餐	Chinese Fast Food
322	中央空调	Central Air-Conditioning
323	中央空调温控面板	Temperature Control Panel
324	猪肉	Pork
325	猪油	Lard
326	主菜	Main Dish/Course 或 Entrée〔美语〕
327	住宿登记表	Check-in Form
328	注意,不可食用	Not Edible
329	注意高温(炉灶)	CAUTION // Hot Surface 或 CAUTION // Hot

序号	中文	英文
330	注意高温(热菜)	CAUTION // Very Hot Dishes
331	孜然	Cumin
332	自助餐	Buffet
333	总开关	Master Light Switch〔电灯〕 Main Switch〔电源〕

注1:"〔　〕"中的内容是对英文译法的解释说明。
注2:"/"表示可选择该组词语中的一种。
注3:"//"表示书写时应换行的断行处。需要同行书写时"//"应改为句点".",
警示词后加惊叹号"!"。
注4:"＿＿"表示使用时应根据实际情况填入具体内容。
注5:"或"前后所列出的不同译法可任意选择一种使用。

附录H

（资料性）

通用类设施及功能信息英文译写示例

H.1 通用类设施及功能信息英文译写示例见表H.1。表H.1按中文汉语拼音排序。

表H.1 通用类设施及功能信息英文译写示例

序号	中文	英文
	B	
1	办公区域	Administration/Office Area
2	保安室;门卫室;值班岗亭	Security 或 Security Booth/Guard/Office/Room 〔在同一场所内应保持统一〕
3	备勤室	Personnel Standby Room 或 For Standby Staff/Guards
4	边门	Side Door
5	便民服务点	Handy Helper 或 Handy Help Outlet 〔在同一场所内应保持统一〕
6	玻璃门	Glass Door
7	补票处（用于车站）	Pay Upon Arrival〔用于抵达后补票〕 Stand-by Ticket 或 Stand-by Ticket Counter〔特指补候补票〕 Fare Adjustment 或 Fare Adjustment Office/Machine 或 Pay Fare Balance〔指票价补差,用于固定办公地点和机器〕
8	不可回收物（垃圾箱）	Non-Recyclables 或 Non-Recyclable〔用于垃圾箱〕
9	布告栏;公告栏;留言板	Bulletin/Notice/Message Board

序号	中文	英文
10	步行梯;楼梯	Stairs
	C	
11	残疾人厕所	Accessible Toilet/Restroom/Washroom 或 Accessible+残疾人图标 〔在同一场所内应保持统一〕
12	残疾人电梯	Accessible Elevator 或 Accessible+残疾人图标 〔在同一场所内应保持统一〕
13	残疾人专用设施	Accessible Facilities 或 Disabled Access 或 Accessible
14	残疾人专用停车位	Accessible Parking Only 或 Accessible/Reserved Parking 或 Parking for the Disabled Only 或 Parking for People with Disabilities 〔与残疾人标识一道使用〕〔在同一场所内应保持统一〕
15	插卡式公用电话;磁卡电话	Phone Card Only 或 M-Card Phone
16	出口;安全门	Exit
17	出口往前(由此出站)	Way Out
18	出门按钮	Press to Exit
19	出租车专用停车位	Taxi Parking Only 或 Taxis Only
20	厨余垃圾(垃圾箱)	Kitchen Waste
21	储物柜;存包处	Lockers
22	村级避灾安置点	Village-Level Emergency Shelter
	D	
23	大客车停车位	Bus Parking Only 或 Buses Only

序号	中文	英文
24	单号入口	Odd Numbers Entrance〔Entrance 可以省略〕
25	单价	Unit Price
26	登记处	Registration 或 Registry
27	等候区	Waiting Area/Zone
28	地下停车场	Underground Parking
29	第三卫生间	Family Restroom 或 Family 或 Inclusive 或 Whichever〔标识在男、女、残疾人图标之下〕 〔在同一场所内应保持统一〕
30	电话亭(间)	Phone Booth/Box 或 Kiosk 〔在同一场所内应保持统一〕
31	电话预订	Telephone Reservation
32	电梯	Elevator〔美语〕 或 Lift〔英语〕 〔在同一场所内应保持统一〕
33	订票热线;票务热线	Booking Hotline
34	东(南、西、北)出口	East (South, West, North) Exit
35	东(南、西、北)进口	East (South, West, North) Entrance
	F	
36	非机动车专用停车位	Non-Motor Vehicle Parking Only 或 Non-Motor Vehicles Only
37	非水冲座便器(无需冲水)	No-Flush Toilet
38	非饮用水	Not for Drinking 或 Non-Potable Water 〔在同一场所内应保持统一〕
39	扶梯;自动扶梯	Escalator

序号	中文	英文
40	服务处;服务中心	Service Center
41	服务监督电话	Service and Complaints Hotline
42	服务区	Service Area/Zone
43	服务热线	Service Hotline 或 Hotline
44	服务台	Service Desk
45	复印室	Copy Room
	G	
46	干手机	Hand Dryer
47	婴儿更衣处; 更换尿布处	Baby Change 或 Baby Changing Station 或 Diaper Change 〔在同一场所内应保持统一〕
48	更衣室	Locker Room
49	公共停车场	Public Parking
50	公共自行车	Public Bike/Bicycle
51	公用IC卡电话	IC Card Phone
52	公用电话	Telephone 或 Pay Phone 〔在同一场所内应保持统一〕
53	顾客服务中心(客服中心)	Customer Service Center
54	广播室;广播站	Broadcasting Room〔规模较大〕 Broadcast Room〔规模较小〕
55	贵宾电梯	VIP Elevator 或 VIP Only
56	贵宾休息室	VIP Only 或 VIP Lounge

序号	中文	英文
	H	
57	货梯(运货使用的电梯)	Freight/Cargo Elevator 或 Service Elevator 〔在同一场所内应保持统一〕
58	会议室	Conference Room〔中型的〕 Convention Room〔大型的〕 Meeting Room〔通用型的〕
59	火警出口	Fire Exit
60	火情警报;火情警报器	Fire Alarm
61	火灾疏散示意图	Emergency Exit Route 或 Fire Escape Route
	J	
62	急救室;急救中心	Emergency 或 First Aid〔可加 Center〕
63	急救站;医疗急救室	First Aid Station〔Station 可以省略〕
64	急停开关(用于电梯)	Stop Button
65	价目表	Price List 或 Tariff〔主要用于旅馆、餐厅等〕
66	检票处	Ticket Check-in〔Ticket 可省略〕
67	缴费窗口;缴费处	Pay Here 或 Cashier
68	接待室	Reception Room
69	紧急报警器	Emergency Alarm
70	紧急出口	Emergency Exit
71	紧急呼叫点	Emergency Call
72	紧急救护电话:120	Ambulance: 120
73	紧急求助电话:110	Emergency: 110

序号	中文	英文
74	紧急疏散地	Evacuation Area
75	紧急疏散集合地	Evacuation Assembly Area
76	紧急疏散示意图	Emergency Exit Route
77	紧急停车道	Shoulder〔美语〕 或 Hard Shoulder〔英语〕 或 Emergency Lane
78	进口(入口)往前(由此进站)	Way In
79	进口;入口	Entrance
80	禁烟区;无烟区	Non-Smoking Area
81	警务室	Police Office 或 Police
82	救生衣	Life Vest 或 Life Jacket
	K	
83	开水间;开水房	Boiler Room 或 Hot Water Room〔Room 可以省略〕
84	可回收物(垃圾箱)	Recyclables 或 Recyclable〔用于垃圾箱〕
85	客服台	Service Desk
86	客服中心	Customer Service Center
87	客户服务电话;客户服务热线	Customer Service Hotline
88	客户服务中心	Customer Service Center 或 Customer Services〔用于 Center 可以省略的场合〕
	L	
89	垃圾车	Garbage Truck
90	垃圾房	Garbage Room

序号	中文	英文
91	垃圾桶;废物箱	Dustbin 或 Rubbish 或 Rubbish Bin 或 Waste 或 Waste Bin 〔在同一场所内应保持统一〕
92	拉(门)	Pull
93	老弱病残孕专座;老弱病残孕优先(席)	Priority Seating 或 Priority Seats〔用指多个座位〕 或 Courtesy Seats〔用指多个座位〕
94	冷冻机房	Refrigeration/Refrigerating Room
95	临时出口	Temporary Exit
96	临时入口	Temporary Entrance
97	临时停车场	Temporary Parking
98	留言栏	Bulletin/Message Board
99	楼层	Floor 或 Level
100	楼层示意图	Floor Layout/Plan
101	楼梯	Stairs 或 Stairway
102	轮椅通道	Wheelchair Access
	M	
103	免费存包处	Free Lockers
104	免费停车场	Free Parking
105	免费项目	Free Items〔用于公示牌标题,后列出免费项目〕 Complimentary〔指本项目免费〕
106	灭火器	Fire Extinguisher

序号	中文	英文
107	母婴(哺乳)室	Baby Care Room 或 Baby Care 或 Nursing Room 〔在同一场所内应保持统一〕
	N	
108	男厕所	Men 或 Gents 〔在同一场所内应保持统一〕
109	男更衣室	Men's Locker Room 或 Men's
110	内部停车场;员工专用停车场	Reserved Parking 或 Private Parking〔私人用〕 Staff Parking〔员工用〕或 Staff Only〔员工用〕
111	女厕所	Women 或 Ladies 〔在同一场所内应保持统一〕
112	女更衣室	Women's Locker Room 或 Women's
113	您所在的位置(用于导向指示图)	You Are Here 或 Your Location
	P	
114	配电间	Switch Room/House 或 Switching Room 或 Electrical Room 或 Power Distribution Room 或 Distribution Room 〔在同一场所内应保持统一〕
115	票价 ——老人票价 ——成人票价 ——儿童票价 ——学生票价 ——半票	Ticket Rates 或 Fares ——Senior ——Adult ——Child ——Student ——Half Price/Fare

序号	中文	英文
116	票务服务(售、退、补票等综合服务)	Ticket Service
117	票务服务;售票处 ——团体票 ——退票 ——取票 ——散客票 ——补票	Ticket Service ——Group ——Refund ——Collection ——FIT ——Fare Adjustment〔特指收费增减〕或Stand-by〔特指候补票〕
118	票务热线	Booking Hotline
	Q	
119	其他垃圾(垃圾箱)	Other Waste 或Residual Waste
120	前台;接待;总服务台	Reception 或Front Desk
121	强电间	High Voltage Room 或HV Room 〔在同一场所内应保持统一〕
122	清洁车	Street Sweeper/Cleaner 或Road Sweeper/Cleaner
123	求助按钮	Press for Help
124	全日停车场(昼夜服务)	24-Hour Parking
	R	
125	弱电间	Low Voltage Room 或LV Room 〔在同一场所内应保持统一〕
	S	
126	扫码支付	Scan QR Code to Pay 或Scan to Pay 或Pay by Scanning QR Code 或QR Code Payment

序号	中文	英文
127	上楼楼梯	Stairway Up〔Stairway可以省略〕
128	设备间	Equipment Room
129	伸手出水;感应出水	Automatic Faucet/Tap 或 Sensor Faucet/Tap 或 Touch Sensor Faucet/Tap 〔在同一场所内应保持统一〕
130	失物招领(处)	Lost and Found 或 Lost Property Office
131	时刻表	Timetable 或 Schedule
132	示意图	Diagram 或 Sketch Map 或 Sketch
133	收费处	Cashier 或 Payment
134	收银台;结账处	Cashier
135	手机充电处	Mobile Phone Recharging
136	售完(售罄)	Sold Out
137	书报亭	Kiosk 或 Newsstand/News Stand 或 News Kiosk
138	疏散示意图;紧急疏散指示图	Evacuation Chart/Plan/Guide 或 Evacuation Flow Chart
139	疏散通道	Evacuation Route
140	刷脸支付	Pay with Your Face 或 Pay with Face Recognition 或 Pay by Face Scanning 或 Facial (Recognition) Payment 或 Face-Scan Payment
141	双号入口	Even Numbers Entrance〔Entrance可以省略〕

序号	中文	英文
	T	
142	踏板放水	Pedal to Operate 或 Foot Operated Tap 或 Pedal Operated Tap 〔在同一场所内应保持统一〕
143	天气预报(用于告示牌等)	Weather Forecast
144	停车场	Parking 或 Parking Lot 或 Park〔英语〕
145	停车场入口	Parking Entrance
146	停车收费系统	Parking Payment System
147	停车位	Parking Space
148	投币口	Insert Coin Here 或 Coin Slot
149	推(门)	Push
150	退票处	Refund 或 Ticket Refund 或 Refund Office/Counter〔用于柜台处〕 或 Ticket Refund Office/Counter〔用于柜台处〕 〔在同一场所内应保持统一〕
	W	
151	外币兑换处	Currency Exchange 或 Foreign Currency Exchange 或 Money Exchange/Changer 或 Foreign Exchange Office 〔在同一场所内应保持统一〕
152	网上订票取票处	Online Ticket Reservation 或 Online-Reserved Ticket Collection 〔在同一场所内应保持统一〕
153	维修服务中心	Maintenance Service Center 或 Service Station/Center

序号	中文	英文
154	问讯处	Enquiry 或 Information
155	无接触电梯按钮	Virtual Elevator Buttons
156	无障碍（设施）	Wheelchair Accessible
157	无障碍观众席区	Wheelchair Accessible Area
158	无障碍坡道	Wheelchair Accessible Ramp〔Ramp 可以省略〕
159	无障碍售票口	Wheelchair Ticketing 或 Wheelchair Accessible Ticketing〔Ticketing 可以省略〕
160	无障碍通道	Wheelchair Accessible Passage〔Passage 可以省略〕
161	无障碍座位	Accessible Seats 或 Accessible Seating 或 Wheelchair Access Seats
	X	
162	吸烟区	Smoking Area
163	吸烟室	Smoking Room
164	洗车	Car Wash 或 Vehicle Cleaning
165	洗手间；卫生间；厕所；盥洗室	Toilet；Toilets〔导览图中用于标示男女厕所时用复数〕 或 Restroom；Restrooms〔导览图中用于标示男女厕所时用复数〕 或 Washroom；Washrooms〔导览图中用于标示男女厕所时用复数〕 〔在同一场所内应保持统一〕
166	下楼楼梯	Stairway Down〔Stairway 可以省略〕
167	现金支付	Pay in Cash 或 Cash Only
168	消防车	Fire Engine

序号	中文	英文
169	消防软管卷盘	Fire Hose Reel
170	消防逃生通道	Fire Escape
171	消防通道	Fire Lane
172	消防应急面罩	Fire Mask
173	消防应急照明灯	Emergency Light
174	消防员专用开关	Fireman's Switch
175	消火栓	Fire Hydrant
176	消火栓箱	Fire Hydrant Box
177	新风机房	Ventilation Room
178	信用卡支付	Credit Cards Accepted
179	行李寄存处;行李存放处	Luggage/Baggage Deposit 或 Left Luggage/Baggage 或 Luggage/Baggage Depository 或 Bag Storage
180	行李手推车	Luggage/Baggage Cart 或 Luggage Trolley〔英语〕
181	行李提取	Luggage/Baggage Claim
182	行人专用道	Pedestrians Only
183	休息室	Lounge
184	休闲区	Leisure Area/Zone 或 CRD〔用于城市功能分区及建成区〕 或 RBD〔用于休闲商务〕 或 Recreational Area〔用于室外向公众开放〕 或 Recreation Area〔用于餐厅、健身房、书吧、影视厅等〕 或 Lounge〔用于室内功能布局〕 或 Relax/Relaxation Zone〔用法较宽泛,如用于前厅、工作区等〕

序号	中文	英文
185	旋转门	Revolving Door
	Y	
186	烟感探头	Smoke Detector/Sensor/Alert
187	业务受理	In Service
188	一、二、三、四、五层（地上）	1F, 2F, 3F, 4F, 5F 或 L1, L2, L3, L4, L5 〔在同一场所内应保持统一〕
189	一、二、三、四、五层（地下）	B1, B2, B3, B4, B5
190	一站式窗口;"最多跑一次"窗口	One-Stop Service Counter/Window〔Counter 或 Window 可以省略〕
191	衣帽间;存衣处	Cloakroom
192	医务室	Clinic
193	易腐垃圾(垃圾箱)	Perishable Waste
194	意见箱	Suggestions & Complaints Box〔Box 可以省略〕
195	音控室	Audio Control Room
196	饮用水	Drinking Water 或 Potable Water 〔在同一场所内应保持统一〕
197	应急避难场所;避灾安置点	Emergency Shelter
198	应急避难设施	Emergency Facilities
199	应急电话	Emergency Call
200	应急电话;紧急呼救电话	Emergency Telephone
201	应急启动把手;紧急手柄	Emergency Handle

序号	中文	英文
202	应急疏散图	Emergency Exit Route
203	应急照明	Emergency Lighting
204	优惠价格	Discount Price 或 Favorable Rates
205	优惠票窗口	Discount Ticket
206	优先通道	Priority Lane
207	有害垃圾(垃圾箱)	Hazardous Waste
208	有人;使用中(用于厕所等)	Occupied
209	余额不足	Insufficient Balance
210	雨伞架	Umbrella Rack/Stand
211	预订处	Reservation
212	预订票取票处	Ticket Collection 或 Ticket Collection Counter/Point〔用于柜台处〕 〔在同一场所内应保持统一〕
213	员工电梯	Staff Elevator 或 Staff Only
214	员工更衣室	Staff Locker Room 或 Staff Lockers
215	员工通道	Staff Passage 或 Staff Only〔用于 Passage 可以省略的场合〕
216	员工休息室	Staff Room
	Z	
217	在此刷卡	Swipe Here 或 Swipe Card Here 或 Swipe Your Card Here〔卡槽刷卡〕 Tap Here 或 Tap Card Here 或 Tap Your Card Here〔非接触式〕
218	赠品	Complimentary

序号	中文	英文
219	正门	Main Gate/Entrance 或 Front Door
220	执勤岗	Duty Post
221	值班室	Duty Room
222	志愿服务微笑亭	Volunteer Service
223	志愿者服务中心	Volunteer Service Center
224	专属停车位	Reserved Parking
225	咨询服务中心	Information Center〔Center 可以省略〕
226	咨询室	Counseling/Consulting Room
227	自动冲洗（厕所马桶）	Automatic Flush 或 Auto Flush 〔在同一场所内应保持统一〕
228	自动充值机	Add Value Machine 或 Top-up Machine 〔在同一场所内应保持统一〕
229	自动检票机	Self-Service Check-in 或 Automatic Check-in Machine 或 Automatic Ticket Checker 或 Automatic Gate〔需要缩写时用 AG〕 〔在同一场所内应保持统一〕
230	自动门	Automatic Door
231	自动取款机	Automatic Teller Machine〔需要缩写时用 ATM〕
232	自动人行道;电动步道	Travelator 或 Moving Sideway/Walkway 〔在同一场所内应保持统一〕
233	自动售货机	Vending Machine 或 Automatic Vending Machine〔需要缩写时用 AVM〕 〔在同一场所内应保持统一〕

序号	中文	英文
234	自动售票机	Ticket Vending Machine〔需要缩写时用TVM〕
235	自行车停放架	Bike Racks 或 Bicycle Racks
236	自行车租车处	Bike/Bicycle Rental
237	自助查询机	Self-Service Information
238	自助寄存柜	Self-Service Lockers
239	租车处	Car Rental

注1:"〔 〕"中的内容是对英文译法的解释说明。
注2:"/"表示可选择该组词语中的一种。
注3:" ____ "表示使用时应根据实际情况填入具体内容。
注4:"或"前后所列出的不同译法可任意选择一种使用。
注5:解释说明中指出某个词"可以省略"的,省略该词的译文只能用于设置在该设施上的标识中,如"应急车道"应译作Emergency Lane,在设置于该车道上的标识中可以省略Lane,译作Emergency。

H.2　通用类公共服务信息英文译写示例见表H.2。表H.2按中文汉语拼音排序。

表H.2　通用类公共服务信息英文译写示例

序号	中文	英文
	A	
1	爱护消防设施,如遇火灾请正确使用。	Take care of fire-fighting facilities and use them correctly in case of fire.
2	安全检查	Security Check
3	安全须知	Safety Instructions
4	按下按钮报警(救助)	Press for Help in Emergency
5	按下红色按钮,绿灯亮时对准话筒报警。	To call police, press red button and speak into microphone when green light is on.

序号	中文	英文
	B	
6	办公时间	Office Hours
7	保持畅通	Keep Clear
8	保持环境卫生	Please Keep This Area Clean
9	报警及急救电话	Alarm and Emergency Call
10	报警请拨打110	Call 110 in Case of Emergency 或 Emergency Call 110
11	本柜(台)暂停服务，请至其他台席办理	Out of Service Temporarily. To Other Counters Please.
12	本柜(台)只接受VIP卡	VIP Cards Only
13	本柜(台)只接受现金缴费	Cash Only at This Counter
14	必须穿救生衣	Life Vest Required
15	必须戴安全帽	Head Protection Must Be Worn 或 All Personnel Must Wear a Hard Hat
16	必须戴防护眼镜	Wear Protective Goggles
17	必须下车推行	Cyclists Must Dismount 或 Cyclists Dismount
18	闭店时间;关门时间	Closing Time
19	闭馆整修	Closed for Renovation
20	便后请冲洗(用于厕所内)	Flush After Use
21	别让您的烟头留下火患	Dispose of Cigarette Butts Properly
22	不得带入食物	No Food Allowed Inside
23	不得带入饮料	No Beverages Allowed Inside
24	不得乱扔垃圾	No Littering

序号	中文	英文
25	不得随地吐痰	No Spitting
26	不得躺卧	No Lying Down Here
27	不得携带宠物;宠物不得入内	No Pets
28	不要随地扔垃圾	No Trash on Floor 或 No Littering
29	不准泊车	No Parking
30	不准穿越(指行人)	No Pedestrian Crossing
31	不准带入食品和饮料	No Food or Beverages Inside
32	不准遛狗	No Dogs
33	不准停车或候客,只可上下旅客	Pick-up and Drop-off Only // No Parking
34	不准停放自行车	No Bike Parking 或 No Bicycle Parking
	C	
35	残疾人优先(用于商场内)	Priority for Customers with Disabilities 或 Priority for Disabled
36	操作指南	Instructions
37	车位已满	Full
38	充电	Recharge 或 Charge
39	宠物便后请打扫干净	Please Clean up After Your Pet
40	出门请按钮	Press to Exit 或 Press Button to Exit
41	出租车候车处	Taxi Stand
42	此处施工,带来不便请谅解	Under Construction // Sorry for the Inconvenience
43	此电梯至地下停车场	Elevator to Underground Parking

序号	中文	英文
44	错时共享（用于停车位）	Staggered Sharing 或 Time Staggered Sharing Parking
	D	
45	打开安全杆（用于安全设施）	Lift Safety Bar
46	代客泊车	Valet Parking
47	代客存衣	Coat Check
48	代售电话卡、地图	Phone Cards and Maps
49	待消毒	To Be Sterilized
50	单层电梯停靠	For Odd Number Floors Only 或 Odd Floors Only
51	当日有效（指车票、公园门票等）	Valid Only on Day of Issue 或 Valid on Issuing Day Only
52	当心绊倒	Mind Your Step 或 Watch Your Step
53	当心爆炸	Danger // Explosion Risk
54	当心触电	DANGER // High Voltage 或 DANGER! // Electric Shock
55	当心电缆	Caution // Cable Here
56	当心高空坠物	CAUTION // Falling Objects
57	当心滑跌	CAUTION! // Slippery Surface
58	当心火险	CAUTION // Fire Hazard 或 Fire Hazard
59	当心夹脚	Mind Your Feet
60	当心夹手；小心夹手	Mind Your Hand/Hands 或 Pinch Point Hazard // Keep Hands Clear 或 Pinch Point Hazard // Watch Your Hands
61	当心剧毒	DANGER // Highly Toxic 或 DANGER // Toxic Hazard

序号	中文	英文
62	当心碰头	Mind Your Head
63	当心碰撞	Beware of Collisions
64	当心台阶;当心踏空;注意脚下	Mind/Watch Your Step
65	当心中毒	Danger // Toxic Hazard
66	当心坠落	WARNING // Be Careful Near the Edge 或 Pay Attention to the Risk of Falling 或 DANGER // Risk of Falling 或 Beware of the Risk of Falling
	E	
67	24小时服务热线	24-Hour Hotline
68	24小时营业	24-Hour Service 或 Open 24 Hours
69	24小时自助服务	24-Hour Self-Service
70	儿童车借用	Strollers Available 或 Baby Carriages Available
71	儿童须由成人陪同	Children must be accompanied by an adult.
	F	
72	防洪通道,请勿占用	Flood Control Channel // Keep Clear
73	防止坠落(用于电梯内外)	Be Careful Not to Fall
74	非火警时请勿挪用	Fire Emergency Only
75	非紧急情况不得停留	Emergency Stop Only
76	非请莫入	No Entry Unless Authorized
	G	
77	高血压、心脏病患者以及晕车、晕船、醉酒者请勿乘坐	Visitors with hypertension, heart condition, motion sickness or excessive drinking are advised not to ride.

序号	中文	英文
78	工作时间	Office/Business Hours
79	顾客止步;乘客止步;员工通道;闲人免进;闲人莫入;员工专用	Staff Only 或 Authorized Personnel Only
80	关注安全,有你有我	Safety is everybody's responsibility. 或 Safety is the responsibility of everyone, everywhere.
81	广播寻人启事	Paging Service
82	广播寻人寻物	Paging Service 或 Lost and Found Broadcast Service
83	贵重物品请自行妥善保管	Please Keep Your Valuables with You
	H	
84	欢迎多提宝贵意见	Your Comments Are Welcome
85	欢迎光临	Welcome
86	火警请拨打119	Call 119 in Case of Fire
87	火警时按下,严禁非法使用	Press Button in Case of Fire // Penalty for Improper Use
88	火警压下;火警时压下	Press in Case of Fire
	J	
89	计时停车	Hour/Hourly/Metered Parking
90	急救请拨打120	Call 120 in Case of Medical Emergency
91	节假日不办理(不营业)	Closed on Weekends and Public Holidays
92	节假日照常营业	Open on Weekends and Public Holidays
93	仅作火警安全出口	Fire Exit Only

序号	中文	英文
94	紧急出口,保持通畅	Emergency Exit 或 Keep Clear
95	紧急情况时,轻按压此杆开门	Push the Bar to Open in Emergency
96	紧急情况下,旋转把手开启	Turn the Handle in Emergency
97	紧急时击碎玻璃	Break (the) Glass in Emergency
98	紧急时请按(此)按钮	Press (the) Button in Emergency
99	进门请按钮	Press to Enter 或 Press Button to Enter
100	进门请上锁	Please Lock the Door Behind You
101	进门请刷卡	Swipe Card to Enter〔刷卡式〕 或 Tap Card to Enter〔接触式〕
102	禁带宠物	No Pets Allowed
103	禁推婴儿车(电梯侧板标识)	No Pushchair 或 No Pram〔英语〕 或 No Baby Strollers 或 No Baby Carriage/Buggy〔美语〕
104	禁用手机	No Mobile Phones 或 No Cellphones
105	禁运大件物品(电梯侧板标识)	No bulky baggage is allowed.
106	禁止摆卖	No Vending Allowed
107	禁止泊车	No Parking 或 No Parking at Any Time
108	禁止车辆停留	No Stopping No Standing〔短暂停车也不准许〕
109	禁止宠物入内	No Pets Allowed
110	禁止出入	No Passage 或 No Entry // No Exit

序号	中文	英文
111	禁止电动车进入电梯	No e-Scooters Inside the Elevator 或No e-scooters are allowed inside (the elevator). 或 No Entry of e-Bicycles Into the Elevator
112	禁止堆放物品	Keep Clear
113	禁止翻越;禁止攀爬; 禁止攀登	No Climbing
114	禁止行乞	No Begging
115	禁止滑板	No Skateboarding
116	禁止黄、赌、毒	Pornography, Gambling and Drugs Prohibited
117	禁止机动车通行	No Motor Vehicles
118	禁止进入	No Admittance
119	禁止开窗	Keep Windows Closed
120	禁止刻画(涂鸦)	No Graffiti
121	禁止跨越	No Crossing
122	禁止跨越护栏	Do Not Climb Over Fence 或No Climbing Over Fence
123	禁止浏览黄色网站	Do Not Visit Pornographic Websites
124	禁止录音	No Recording
125	禁止乱扔废物	No Littering
126	禁止轮滑	No Roller Skating
127	禁止明火;严禁明火	Open Flame Prohibited 或 No Open Flame
128	禁止逆行(自动扶梯 旁使用)	No Riding the Wrong Way 或 The Wrong Way
129	禁止拍照	No Photos/Pictures/Photography/Cameras
130	禁止攀爬、翻越围栏	No Climbing Over Railings

序号	中文	英文
131	禁止抛物;禁止高空抛物	Do Not Toss Objects From Height 或 Do Not Throw Objects From Height
132	禁止骑车带人	No Cycling Double
133	禁止燃放烟花爆竹	No Fireworks 或 Fireworks Prohibited
134	禁止入内	No Admittance/Entry
135	禁止摄像	No Videoing
136	禁止摄影	No Photography/Photos/Pictures
137	禁止使用闪光灯	No Flash
138	禁止驶入	Do Not Enter 或 No Entry
139	禁止手扶	No Holding
140	禁止躺卧(用于车厢内)	No Lying Down
141	禁止通过	No Admittance 或 No Entry
142	禁止通过;严禁通行	No Through Traffic
143	禁止吐痰	No Spitting
144	禁止外来车辆停放;专用车位;访客禁停	Reserved Parking 或 Permit Parking Only
145	禁止未成年人进入	Adults Only
146	禁止吸食毒品	No Drugs
147	禁止吸烟	No Smoking
148	禁止吸烟、饮食、逗留	No Smoking, Eating, Drinking or Loitering
149	禁止携带宠物	No Pets 或 No Pets Allowed

序号	中文	英文
150	禁止携带剧毒物品及有害液体	Poisonous Materials and Harmful Liquids Prohibited 或 No Poisonous Materials or Harmful Liquids
151	禁止携带托运放射性及磁性物品	Radioactive and Magnetic Materials Prohibited 或 No Radioactive or Magnetic Materials
152	禁止携带托运易燃及易爆物品	Flammable and Explosive Materials Prohibited 或 No Flammables or Explosives
153	禁止携带武器及仿真武器	Weapons and Simulated Weapons Prohibited 或 No Weapons or Simulated/Imitation Weapons
154	禁止悬吊(用于车厢内)	No Swinging
155	禁止倚靠	No Leaning
156	禁止倚靠车门(用于车厢内)	Stand Clear of the Door
157	禁止饮食(用于车厢内)	No Eating or Drinking
158	禁止饮用	Not for Drinking
159	禁止游泳	No Swimming
160	禁止张贴	Do Not Post Bills 或 Do Not Post Notices
161	禁止张贴广告	No Posters
162	禁坐栏杆	Do Not Sit on Handrail/Railing 或 No Sitting on Handrail/Railing
163	警告! 防止坠落	WARNING! Fall From Height
164	警告! 靠门危险(用于电梯内)	WARNING! No Leaning
165	警告! 请勿扒门(用于电梯内)	WARNING! Do Not Force the Door Open
166	警告! 请勿推门(用于电梯内)	WARNING! Do Not Push the Door
167	敬告;通知	Notice

序号	中文	英文
168	敬请谅解(因维修、施工等带来不便)	Sorry for the Inconvenience (Caused by Maintenance/Construction)
169	军人优先	Priority for Servicemen
	K	
170	开放时间	Opening Hours
171	靠门危险(用于电梯内外)	Do Not Lean on Door 或 No Leaning on Door
172	咳嗽或打喷嚏时请用纸巾遮掩口鼻	Please use tissues to cover your mouth and nose when you cough or sneeze.
173	咳嗽或打喷嚏时请遮掩口鼻	Please Cover Your Cough or Sneeze 或 Please cover your cough or sneeze.
	L	
174	老弱幼病残及不适者乘梯时,需有人陪同。(电梯侧板标识)	Look after the elderly, infirm, infant, sick, physically challenged and any other one in need.
175	老幼乘梯需家人陪同	Seniors and Children Must Be Accompanied
176	雷雨天禁止拨打手机	Do Not Use Cellphone During Thunderstorm
177	留意场所内疏散通道和安全出口的位置。	Beware of exits and fire escapes.
178	轮椅勿入(电梯侧板标识)	No Wheelchairs
179	轮椅租用;轮椅租借;轮椅借用	Wheelchair Hire/Rentals/Rental
	M	
180	每分钟计费标准	Per Minute Charge
181	免费(进入);免费开放	Free Admission
182	免费泊车	Free Parking
183	免费使用	Free

序号	中文	英文
184	免费使用(用于宾馆客房内免费饮料、食品等)	Complimentary
185	免费饮水	Free Drinking Water
	N	
186	内部施工,暂停开放	Under Construction // Temporarily Closed
187	您所在的位置	You Are Here 或 Your Position
188	您已进入人员密集场所,注意预防火灾。	You have entered a public assembly venue. Beware of fire hazards.
	P	
189	凭票入场	Admission by Ticket Only
	Q	
190	钱款当面点清,离柜概不负责	Please Count Your Change Before Leaving
191	切勿站在马桶上	Do Not Stand on Toilet 或 No Standing on Toilet
192	清洁中	Cleaning in Progress
193	请爱护公共设施	Please Show Respect for Public Property 或 Please Protect the Property 或 Please Help to Protect Public Property
194	请爱护古迹;请保护古迹	Please Show Respect for the Historic Site 或 Please Protect Our Historic Site 或 Please Preserve the Value of the Historic Site
195	请爱护林木	Please Show Respect for Trees 或 Please Protect Our Trees
196	请按顺序排队	Please Line Up 或 Please Proceed in Order
197	请把女士卫生用品放入墙上的收纳盒	Please put lady items (napkins, tampons) into the wall container.

序号	中文	英文
198	请保持(至少)两米的社交距离	Please maintain a minimum distance of 2 meters between yourself and others. 或 Please Keep Two Meters Distance
199	请保持安静,禁止喧哗	Please Keep Quiet
200	请保持场内清洁	Please Keep This Area Clean
201	请保持马桶清洁	Please Flush Clean All the Time 或 Please Flush After Use and Keep the Toilet Clean
202	请保持社交距离	Please Maintain Social Distancing 或 Keep Safe // Use Social Distancing 或 Practise Social Distancing 或 Practice Social Distance
203	请保持整洁	Please Keep Clean 或 Please Keep This Area Clean
204	请保管好个人(自己的)物品;请保管好您的贵重物品(财物)	Please Do Not Leave Your Valuables/Personal Belongings Unattended 或 Please Look After Your Belongings 或 Please Keep Your Valuables With You 或 Please Keep Your Belongings Safe
205	请不要把卫生巾、卫生纸扔进马桶	Please do not dispose sanitary napkins and toilet paper down the toilet.
206	请不要堵住入口	Keep Clear of Entrance
207	请不要将异物随意投入马桶	Toilet Paper Only
208	请不要乱扔垃圾;请勿乱扔废弃物	No Littering
209	请不要随意移动隔离墩	Do Not Move Isolation Piers 或 Do Not Move Any Barrier
210	请不要遗忘个人物品	Please Do Not Leave Your Belongings Behind
211	请出示您的身份证	Please Show Your ID

序号	中文	英文
212	请出示您的护照	Please Show Your Passport
213	请戴口罩	Please Wear Your Face Mask 或 Please Wear a Face Mask 或 Please Wear a Mask
214	请戴口罩,以防止细菌(病毒)扩散到空气中	Please wear a mask to prevent germs (viruses) from spreading to the air.
215	请对着自己衣袖咳嗽或打喷嚏	Please cough or sneeze into your arm.
216	请扶稳坐好	Please Be Seated
217	请给有需要的人让座	Please offer your seat if someone is in need.
218	请关闭手机	Please Switch off Your Mobile Phone〔英语〕/Cell Phone〔美语〕
219	请关闭通信设备	Please Turn off Your Devic Communication
220	请将您的自行车锁好	Please Lock Your Bicycle
221	请将手机设置为静音	Please Mute/Silence Your Mobile Phone/Cell Phone
222	请将用过的厕纸扔进马桶纸篓	Please put/dispose the used toilet paper into the toilet basket.
223	请节约用水	Please Conserve Water 或 Please Save Water
224	请节约用纸(用于厕所)	Please Save Toilet Paper
225	请紧握扶手	Please Hold Handrail
226	请紧握扶手,注意安全!	For your safety, please hold the handrail.
227	请紧握扶手、站稳	Hold the Handrail and Stand Still 或 Hold the Handrail and Steady Yourself
228	请看管好/照看好您的小孩	Please Do Not Leave Your Child/Children Unattended

序号	中文	英文
229	请靠右站立	Keep Right
230	请排队（上车或入场）	Please Line up (for Boarding/Bus/Admission)
231	请排队等候叫号	Please Wait for Your Number to Be Called
232	请排队等候入场	Please Line Up to Proceed 或 Please Wait in Line
233	请绕行	Detour
234	请稍候	Please Wait
235	请随手关灯	Turn off Lights Before You Leave 或 Turn off the Light When You Leave
236	请锁好您的自行车	Please Lock Up Your Bike
237	请停车入位	Park in Bays Only
238	请握好扶手	Please Hold the Handrail
239	请勿扒门（用于电梯内外）	Do Not Force the Door Open
240	请勿踩踏	Do Not Step Here 或 Do Not Trample 或 No Trampling 或 Keep Off
241	请勿触碰	Please Do Not Touch
242	请勿打扰	Please Do Not Disturb
243	请勿带宠物入内	No Pets Allowed 或 No Pets
244	请勿堵塞	Keep the Passageway/Entrance Clear 或 Do Not Block the Passageway/Entrance
245	请勿践踏草坪	Please Keep off the Grass
246	请勿将身体伸出扶梯外（电梯侧板标识）	Do Not Lean Over Handrail
247	请勿将头手伸出（车）窗外	Keep Head and Hands Inside

序号	中文	英文
248	请勿将外来食品、饮料带入	No Outside Food or Drinks/Beverages Allowed
249	请勿开(车)窗	Please Do Not Open Window
250	请勿留弃食品或食品包装	Do Not Leave Behind Food or Food Wrappings
251	请勿乱扔垃圾	Do Not Litter 或 No Littering
252	请勿拍打玻璃	Do Not Tap on Glass
253	请勿拍照	No Photography 或 No Photos/Pictures
254	请勿让孩子独自搭乘电梯	Children Must Be Accompanied by an Adult
255	请勿入内	No Entry
256	请勿使用闪光灯	No Flash 或 No Flash Photography
257	请勿使用手机	Please Keep Your Cellphone Switched off 或 Please Keep Your Mobile Phone Switched off
258	请勿探身(电梯侧板标识)	Do not lean over the escalator.
259	请勿停留(用于电梯口、车站出入口等处)	Please Keep Clear
260	请勿推门(用于电梯内外)	Do Not Push Door
261	请勿外带食品	No Outside Food Allowed
262	请勿吸烟	Thank You for Not Smoking
263	请勿嬉戏打闹	Do Not Disturb Other Visitors
264	请勿戏水	No Wading
265	请勿向(车)窗外扔东西	Do Not Throw Anything out of Window

序号	中文	英文
266	请勿携带宠物	No Pets Allowed 或 No Pets
267	请勿携带易燃易爆等危险物品进入商场。	Don't carry flammable, explosive and other dangerous articles into the mall.
268	请勿喧哗;保持安静	Please Keep Quiet
269	请勿遗忘随身物品	Please Do Not Leave Your Belongings Behind
270	请勿倚靠车门	Please Do Not Lean on Door 或 No Leaning on Door
271	请勿在出入口逗留（电梯侧板标识）	Keep away from the entry and exit areas.
272	请勿在热水炉上置物	Please do not leave anything on the hot water oven.
273	请勿坐卧	No Sitting or Lying Down
274	请勿坐在护栏上	Do Not Sit on Guardrail 或 No Sitting on Guardrail
275	请系好安全带	Fasten Your Seat Belt
276	请下车推行(指自行车)	Please Walk Your Bicycle
277	请寻求工作人员帮助	Please Ask Our Staff for Assistance
278	请在此等候	Please Wait Here
279	请在此开票	Invoices/*Fapiaos* Here 或 Invoice/*Fapiao* Claims/Claim
280	请在此排队	Line Forms Here 或 Please Queue (up) Here 或 Please Line Up Here 或 Please Form a Line Here
281	请在黄线外等候	Please Wait Behind the Yellow Line
282	请在一米线外等候	Please Wait Behind the One-Meter Line 或 Please Wait Behind the/This Line 或 Please Wait One Meter Away

序号	中文	英文
283	请找工作人员协助	Please See Staff for Assistance
284	请照看好个人行李和物品	Please do not leave your luggage and other personal belongings unattended.
285	请走旋转门	Please Use the Revolving Door
286	请走其他门	Please Use Other Doors
287	请遵守场内秩序	Please Keep Order
288	区域平面示意图	Floor Map
	R	
289	如需帮助,请按键	Press Button for Assistance
290	如需帮助,请对讲	Lift the Handset for Assistance
291	如需帮助,请与工作人员联系。	For assistance, please contact our staff.
292	如有上述症状,请立即通知前台。	If you have any of the above-mentioned symptoms, please alert the front desk immediately.
293	如遇火警,请勿使用电梯	Do Not Use Elevator in Case of Fire
294	如遇紧急情况,请按此按钮关闭电梯。	Press this button in an emergency. 或Emergency Stop Button Here
295	入室请刷卡	Swipe Your Card to Enter
	S	
296	上面施工,请注意安全	Warning! Men Working Above.
297	上下楼梯请靠右	Keep Right on the Stairs
298	失物招领	Lost and Found
299	施工期间,恕不开放	Construction in Progress // Temporarily Closed

序号	中文	英文
300	食品饮料谢绝入内	No Food or Beverages Inside
301	视频监控区域	This area is under video surveillance. 或 Video Surveillance Area
302	收费标准	Rates/Fees 或 Charging Standard 或 Fee Scale/Schedule
303	收费项目;有偿服务项目	Pay Items; Paid Services 或 Paid Service Items
304	手语服务	Sign Language Services
305	手杖借用	Walking Sticks Available
306	手杖租借	Walking Canes Hire/Rental
307	双层电梯停靠	For Even Number Floors Only 或 Even Floors Only
308	随手关门	Close the Door Behind You
	T	
309	提供轮椅	Wheelchairs Available
310	提供手杖;提供拐杖	Walking Canes/Sticks Available 或 Crutches Available
311	停车场须知	Parking Notice
312	停车时限:____分钟	Parking Time Limit: XX Minutes 或 ____-Minute Parking
313	停车收费标准	Parking Rates
314	投入硬币	Insert Coin
315	投诉电话;投诉热线	Complaints Hotline
316	投诉与建议箱	Complaints and Suggestions
	W	
317	外部车辆请勿入内	Authorized Vehicles Only

序号	中文	英文
318	外来食品和饮料不得入内	No Outside Food or Beverages 或 No Outside Food or Beverages Allowed
319	危险物品	Hazardous Materials
320	未成年人不得入内	Adults Only
321	未经授权 禁止入内	Authorized Entry Only 或 No Entry Without Authorization
322	未经授权 禁止使用	Unauthorized Use Is Prohibited
323	文明乘梯,先出后进 （设置在电梯旁）	Manner Matters. Exit First. 或 Please Stand Aside for Exiting Passengers 或 Please Let Passengers off First
324	文明如厕	Don't forget toilet etiquette. 或 Make sure you know toilet etiquette. 或 Practice Good Toilet Etiquette
325	无人;未使用(用于厕所内)	Vacant
236	勿将头探出(电梯侧板标识)	Do not stick your head out.
327	勿靠侧板 （电梯侧板标识）	Do not lean on the sides.
328	勿运货物(电梯侧板标识)	No Freight
329	勿追跑打闹(电梯侧板标识)	Do not run or play. 或 No Horseplay
X		
330	先出后进	Exit First
331	限紧急情况下使用	Emergency Use Only
332	向前一小步 文明一大步(用于男厕所小便池上方)	We aim to please. You aim too, please. 或 Please kindly keep close to the urinal. 或 Please Stand Closer
333	消毒中	Sterilizing

序号	中文	英文
334	消防通道,不得占用	Fire Lane // Do Not Block 或 Fire Lane // Keep Clear
335	消防通道,禁止停车	Do Not Block Fire Engine Access
336	消防通道,请勿占用	Fire Lane. Keep Clear.
337	消防通道应处于常闭状态	Keep the Fire Door Closed
338	小心玻璃(指玻璃门)	CAUTION // Glass Door
339	小心地滑(地面有水)	Caution. Wet Floor. 或 Caution. Slippery Floor.
340	小心滑倒	CAUTION // Slippery Surface 或 CAUTION // Wet Floor
341	小心滑倒(地面建筑材质本身较光滑)	CAUTION // Slippery
342	小心火灾	Caution. Fire Hazard.
343	小心夹手	Mind Your Hands
344	小心脚下;注意台阶;小心台阶;当心踏空;下台阶时请您小心	Mind the Step 或 Mind Your Step 或 Watch Your Step
345	小心落水	WARNING // Deep Water 或 Be Careful Not to Fall into Water
346	小心碰头	Mind Your Head
347	小心碰撞;小心磕碰	Beware of Collisions
348	小心烫伤(开水)	CAUTION // Hot Water 或 Caution. Hot.
349	小心障碍	Beware of Obstruction/Obstructions
350	小心坠落	WARNING // Be Careful Near the Edge
351	小心灼伤	CAUTION // Hot Surface
352	谢谢合作	Thank You for Your Cooperation

序号	中文	英文
	Y	
353	严禁触摸	Do Not Touch
354	严禁存放易燃、易爆、枪支弹药、毒品等违禁品	No Flammable, Explosive, Poisonous or Other Illegal Articles 或 Flammable, Explosive, Poisonous and Other Illegal Articles (Strictly) Prohibited
355	严禁赌博	Gambling Is Forbidden by Law
356	严禁明火	No Open Flame
357	严禁携带、燃放、存放烟花爆竹	No Fireworks or Firecrackers
358	严禁携带爆炸物	Explosives Prohibited
359	严禁携带危险品	Dangerous Articles Prohibited
360	严禁烟火	Smoking or Open Flames Prohibited
361	严禁自行车或滑板在便道上行驶	No Biking or Skateboarding on Sidewalk
362	衣冠不整者谢绝入内	Proper Attire Required
363	已消毒	Sterilized
364	易碎物品,请轻拿轻放	FRAGILE // Handle with Care
365	婴儿车服务(租用)	Baby Carriages 或 Pushchair Hire 或 Stroller/Baby Buggy Rental
366	营业时间	Open Hours 或 Business Hours
367	用完餐后,请把餐具送到指定地方。	After meal, please return your food tray to the designated place.
368	油漆未干	Wet Paint
369	有害气体,注意安全	CAUTION // Noxious Gas

序号	中文	英文
370	逾期交费	Overdue Payment
371	雨伞借用	Umbrellas Available
372	雨伞租借;雨具租用	Umbrella Hire/Rental
373	遇有火灾不得使用电梯	Do Not Use the Elevator in Case of Fire
374	员工返岗前必须洗手	Employees Must Wash Hands Before Returning to Work
375	允许导盲犬进入	Guide Dogs Are Allowed to Enter 或 Guide Dogs Welcome
	Z	
376	暂停服务;暂停开放;临时关闭	Temporarily Closed 或 Temporarily out of Service
377	照顾儿童(电梯侧板标识)	Children must be supervised/attended.
378	正常开放	Open
379	正在检修,请您稍候	Maintenance in Progress // Please Wait
380	正在施工 敬请谅解	Construction in progress. Sorry for the inconvenience.
381	正在维修	Under Repair
382	正在维修 敬请谅解	Maintenance in progress. Sorry for the inconvenience.
383	正在维修 注意安全	CAUTION // Maintenance in progress.
384	至(某场所)	To (...)
385	注意,此处设有视频监控	This Area Is Under Video Surveillance
386	注意安全,请勿靠近	CAUTION // Keep Away
387	注意安全,请勿入内	DANGER // Do Not Enter
388	注意保护个人隐私	Please Guard Your Personal Information

序号	中文	英文
389	注意防火;小心火灾	CAUTION // Fire Risk/Danger 或 CAUTION // Fire Hazard
390	注意门后有人	Beware of People Behind the Door
391	自行车租赁点	Bike Hire/Rentals 或 Bicycle Rental
392	租车服务	Car Rental/Hire

注1:"〔 〕"中的内容是对英文译法的解释说明。

注2:"/"表示可选择该组词语中的一种。

注3:"//"表示书写时应当换行的断行处。需要同行书写时"//"应改为句点".",警示词后加惊叹号"!"。

注4:"＿＿"表示使用时应根据实际情况填入具体内容。

注5:"或"前后所列出的不同译法可任意选择一种使用。

注6:解释说明中指出某个词"可以省略"的,省略该词的译文只能用于设置在该设施上的标识中,如"应急车道"应译作 Emergency Lane,在设置于该车道上的标识中可以省略 Lane,译作 Emergency。

附录 I

（资料性）

旅游景区景点日文译写示例

I.1 旅游景区景点名称日文译写示例见表I.1。表I.1按分类条目中文汉语拼音排序。

表I.1 旅游景区景点名称日文译写示例

序号	中文	日文
	（自然景观）	
1	池	池
2	岛	島
3	洞	洞
4	洞窟	洞窟
5	峰	峰
6	谷	谷
7	海滩	砂浜
8	河	川
9	湖	湖
10	涧	谷
11	江	江
12	岭	嶺
13	瀑布	滝
14	泉	泉
15	溶洞	鐘乳洞

序号	中文	日文
16	山	山
17	山脉	山脈
18	湿地	湿地
19	石	石
20	石林	石林
21	潭	淵
22	湾	湾
23	温泉	温泉
24	溪	渓
25	峡谷	峡谷
	（人文景观）	
26	庵	庵
27	碑	碑
28	碑记	碑文
29	碑林	碑林
30	别墅	別荘
31	博物馆	博物館
32	草堂	草堂
33	陈列馆	陳列館
34	祠	祠
35	道观	道場
36	堤	堤
37	殿	殿堂

序号	中文	日文
38	雕塑	彫刻
39	坊	坊
40	阁	閣
41	公墓	共同墓地
42	宫	宮
43	古道	古道
44	鼓楼	鼓楼
45	故里	故郷
46	馆	館
47	广场	広場
48	花圃	花畑
49	会址	会議旧跡
50	纪念碑	記念碑
51	纪念馆	記念館
52	假山	築山
53	教堂	礼拝堂
54	精舍	精舎
55	井	井
56	酒坊	酒造
57	旧居	旧居
58	旧址	旧跡
59	居	居
60	廊	廊

序号	中文	日文
61	历史馆	歴史館
62	烈士陵园	烈士霊園
63	楼	楼
64	庐	廬
65	门	門
66	庙	廟
67	墓	墓
68	牌坊;牌楼	記念アーチ;メモリアルアーチ
69	桥	橋
70	清真寺	モスク
71	石碑	石碑
72	石刻	石刻
73	世界文化遗产	世界文化遺産
74	书房	書斎
75	书院	書院
76	寺	寺
77	塔	塔
78	台	台
79	堂	堂
80	题记	題記(名高い文章)
81	题刻	文字彫刻
82	厅	庁
83	亭	亭

序号	中文	日文
84	轩	軒
85	遗址	遺跡
86	园	園
87	苑	苑
88	院	院
89	造像	塑像
90	斋	斎
91	宅	宅
92	照壁	照壁
93	钟楼	鐘楼
94	庄	荘
95	宗祠	祠
	（综合景观）	
96	爱国主义教育基地	愛国主義教育基地
97	宾馆	ホテル
98	步行街	歩行者天国
99	动物园	動物園
100	度假村	リゾート
101	饭店	飯店
102	公园	公園
103	国家级景区	国家級観光地
104	国家级文物保护单位	国家級文化財保護機構
105	海滨浴场	海水浴場

序号	中文	日文
106	海洋公园	シーパラダイス
107	历史街区	歴史街区
108	疗养院	老人ホーム
109	旅游度假区	リゾートエリア
110	旅游景区	観光地
111	民宿	民宿
112	民族文化街	民族文化街
113	农家乐	アグリツーリズム
114	商店街	商店街
115	水上乐园	マリンリゾート
116	水族馆	水族館
117	游乐场	遊園地
118	植物园	植物園

注1:条目中文"( )"中的内容是对中文内涵的补充说明。
注2:条目日文"( )"中的内容是对日文译写的解释或补充说明。

I.2 旅游服务设施日文译写示例见表I.2。表I.2按分类条目中文汉语拼音排序。

表I.2 旅游服务设施日文译写示例

序号	中文	日文
	（通用基础设施设备）	
1	安全出口	非常口
2	安全检查站	セキュリティーチェック； 保安検査所

序号	中文	日文
3	办公区	オフィス街
4	保安室	警備室
5	报刊亭	雑誌新聞売り場
6	便民服务站	サービスセンター
7	表演区； 表演时间	ステージ； ショータイム
8	布告栏	掲示板
9	厕所;公共厕所;卫生间;洗手间;厕所;盥洗室 ——男厕所、卫生间等 ——女厕所、卫生间等 ——收费厕所 ——残疾人厕所(一般用于该设施所处方位的指示和导引)	トイレ/お手洗い/化粧室 ——男性トイレ ——女性トイレ ——有料トイレ ——障がい者専用トイレ
10	茶室	喫茶室
11	撤离路线;疏散通道	緊急通路
12	出口	出口
13	储物柜;存包处	ロッカー
14	地下室	地下室
15	地下通道	地下通路
16	地下一层/二层/三层	地下一階/二階/三階
17	电话 ——公用电话 ——公用IC卡电话	電話 ——公衆電話 ——ICカード電話
18	电话查号台	電話番号案内サービス
19	电话间	電話コーナー

序号	中文	日文
20	电梯 ——扶梯/自动扶梯 ——贵宾电梯 ——货梯 ——残疾人电梯(一般用于该设施所处方位的指示和导引) ——上行扶梯 ——下行扶梯 ——工作人员专用梯	エレベーター ——エスカレーター ——VIP専用エレベーター ——貨物(荷物)専用エレベーター ——障がい者用エレベーター ——上りエスカレーター ——下りエスカレーター ——スタッフ専用エレベーター
21	废物箱;垃圾桶	ゴミ箱
22	服务处	サービスセンター
23	服务窗口	サービス窓口
24	咨询电话	お問い合わせ電話
25	服务区	サービスセンター
26	服务台	サービスカウンター
27	更换尿布处	オムツ替え台
28	更衣室 ——男更衣室 ——女更衣室	更衣室 ——男性更衣室 ——女性更衣室
29	广播室	アナウンス室
30	行李寄存(处);小件寄存(处)	荷物お預かり所
31	火警119	火災119番
32	火警出口	火災時非常口
33	火警通讯电话	火災通報電話
34	火情警报设施	火災警報設備
35	急救室	救護室

序号	中文	日文
36	急救中心	救護センター
37	缴费处	お支払い
38	接待室;会客室	応接室
39	接待中心	接客センター
40	紧急报警器	非常警報機
41	紧急电话	非常電話
42	紧急呼叫点	緊急呼出
43	紧急呼救电话	緊急呼出電話
44	紧急呼救设施	緊急呼出設備
45	紧急救护电话120	救急ダイヤル120番
46	紧急疏散地	緊急避難所
47	紧急疏散指示图	緊急避難経路
48	禁烟席	禁煙席
49	可回收垃圾箱	リサイクルゴミ箱
50	快餐	ファーストフード
51	垃圾车;清洁车	ゴミ収集車;清掃車
52	垃圾房	ゴミ捨て場
53	垃圾桶	ゴミ箱
54	老弱病残专席	優先席
55	临时出口	臨時出口
56	留言板	伝言板
57	留言簿	メッセージ帳
58	楼层	フロア

序号	中文	日文
59	楼梯 ——上行楼梯 ——下行楼梯	階段 ——上り階段 ——下り階段
60	轮椅通道	車椅子用通路
61	灭火器	消火器
62	灭火器箱	消火器格納箱
63	母婴(哺乳)室	授乳室
64	派出所	交番
65	热线;服务热线	サービスホットライン
66	人员、物品安检通道	セキュリティーチェック
67	入口	入口
68	设备间 ——强电间 ——弱电间 ——配电柜 ——配电室/开关室 ——配电箱 ——开关房/室/间 ——水泵房 ——水阀间 ——新风机房 ——冷冻机房	設備室 ——高電圧室 ——低電圧室 ——配電盤 ——配電室 ——配電ボックス ——スイッチルーム ——ポンプ室 ——バルブ室 ——新送風室 ——冷凍機室
69	声讯服务	音声サービス
70	失物招领	遺失物センター
71	收费标准	料金プラン
72	收银台;收款台;结帐;收费处	レジ;お会計
73	手机充电处	携帯電話充電スポット

序号	中文	日文
74	疏散示意图	避難経路図
75	疏散通道	非常通路
76	刷卡处	カード支払
77	投诉电话	苦情ホットライン
78	投诉热线;监督电话	ご意見専用ダイヤル
79	问询处	案内カウンター
80	吸烟区;吸烟室	喫煙コーナー;喫煙室
81	消防车	消防車
82	消防器材	消防器
83	消防软管卷盘	消防ホース格納箱
84	消防设施	消防施設
85	消防栓;消火栓	消火栓
86	消防逃生通道	火災時避難通路
87	消防通道	避難径路
88	消防应急面罩	消防用マスク
89	消防应急照明灯	火災時用非常灯
90	消防员专用开关	消防隊員専用スイッチ
91	休息区	休憩所
92	休息厅;休息处;休息区;顾客休息室	休憩室
93	一/二/三/四/五层	一/二/三/四/五階
94	医疗点;医疗室	医務室

序号	中文	日文
95	意见簿;意见箱;举报信箱 ——评议箱	ご意見ノート;ご意見箱
96	音控室	音響室
97	饮水处;饮用水 非饮用水	給水スポット;飲用水 非飲料水
98	应急开启把手	緊急レバー
99	有偿手机充电装置	有料携帯電話充電器
100	志愿者工作站	ボランティアセンター
101	咨询室	問い合せ窓口
102	咨询台	受付
103	自动充值机	自動チャージ機
104	自动出水;伸手出水	自動水栓
105	自动门	自動ドア
106	自动取款机	ATM
107	自动售货机	自動販売機
108	自助查询机	自動案内機
109	自助寄存柜	コインロッカー
	(机场火车站相关设施)	
110	____号站台	～番ホーム
111	补票处	乗り越し精算所
112	残疾人候车室	障がい者用待合室
113	改签窗口	チケット変更窓口
114	贵宾厅	VIP専用ホール
115	贵宾通道	VIP通路

序号	中文	日文
116	贵宾休息室	VIPルーム
117	国际到达	国際便到着
118	国际换乘	国際便乗り換え
119	国内到达	国内便到着
120	国内换乘	国内便乗り換え
121	行李检查台	荷物検査台
122	行李手推车	カート
123	航站楼	ターミナル
124	候车室	(駅の)待合室
125	候机大厅	(空港の)待合室
126	火车站	駅
127	货币兑换;外币兑换处	両替;外貨両替
128	机场	空港
129	检票口	改札口
130	开水间	給湯室
131	免税店	免税店
132	时刻表	時刻表
133	售票处	チケット売り場
134	售票窗口	チケット販売窓口
135	售票大厅	チケット売り場
136	退票窗口	チケット払い戻し窓口
137	自动检票口	自動改札口

序号	中文	日文
138	自动售票机	自動券売機
	（宾馆相关设施设备）	
139	报告厅	多目的ホール
140	残疾人客房	障がい者向けルーム
141	茶馆	茶房
142	大厅	ロビー
143	多功能厅	多目的ホール
144	风量调节 ——温度调节	風量調節 ——温度調節
145	复印室	コピー室
146	干手机	ハンドドライヤー
147	干洗店	クリーニング店
148	会议室	会議室
149	会议影视厅	視聴覚会議室
150	会议中心	会議センター
151	纪念品店	記念品店
152	价格表 标示价格 优惠价格	価格表 表示価格 割引価格
153	健身房	ジム
154	健身中心	スポーツセンター
155	酒吧	バー
156	咖啡吧	喫茶店
157	开发票处	領収書発行所

序号	中文	日文
158	客房部	客室部門
159	理发店	美容室
160	美容院	エステ
161	品牌专卖店	ブランドジョップ
162	棋牌室	麻雀室
163	前台	フロント
164	清洁车	清掃用カート
165	清洁中	清掃中
166	商务中心	サービスコーナー
167	摄像室	撮影室
168	玩具店	玩具屋
169	网吧	ネットカフェ
170	西饼屋	洋菓子店
171	西餐厅	レストラン
172	小卖店	売店
173	烟感探头	煙感知機
174	音乐厅	コンサートホール
175	饮水机	ウォーターサーバー
176	游泳池	プール
177	有线电视	ケーブルテレビ
178	雨伞架	傘立て
179	浴室	風呂場

序号	中文	日文
180	员工通道	スタッフ専用通路
181	折扣店	ディスカウントショップ
182	中餐厅	中国料理店
183	足浴店	フットマッサージ店
	（交通及停车场相关设施）	
184	出租车	タクシー
185	出租车计价器	タクシーメーター
186	出租车扬招点	タクシー乗り場
187	出租汽车专用发票	タクシー専用領収書
188	道路交通信息	道路交通情報
189	地铁	地下鉄
190	地铁车站	地下鉄の駅
191	地铁乘车点	地下鉄乗り場
192	地下停车场	地下駐車場
193	公共汽车站	バス停
194	机场巴士	空港リムジンバス
195	计时停车场	有料駐車場
196	紧急停车道	緊急停車エリア
197	禁烟车	禁煙車
198	旅游车	観光バス
199	旅游大巴停车场	観光バス駐車場
200	免费停车场	無料駐車場

序号	中文	日文
201	内部停车场;员工专用停车场	職員専用駐車場
202	汽车专用道	自動車専用道路
203	天桥	歩道橋
204	停车场 ——收费停车场 ——全日(昼夜)停车场	駐車場 ——有料駐車場 ——24時間営業駐車場
205	停车场入口	駐車場入口
206	停车场须知	駐車場注意事項
207	停车车位	駐車スペース
208	停车费	駐車料金
209	停车时限	駐車時限
210	停车收费系统	駐車料金精算システム
211	洗车店	洗車店
212	游客停车场	観光客専用駐車場
213	长途汽车站	遠距離バスターミナル
214	专用车位	専用駐車スペース
215	自行车停放处	駐輪場
	(景区相关设施)	
216	采摘区	(果樹園・菜園)摘み取るエリア
217	参观路线	見学コース
218	参观通道(设于该通道入口处)	見学コース
219	陈列室	陳列室
220	宠物乐园	ペットふれあい広場

序号	中文	日文
221	垂钓	釣り
222	大型水滑梯;戏水滑道	ウォータースライダー
223	大型游乐场	大型遊園地
224	带索救生圈	救命浮き輪
225	单行线	一方通行
226	导览册	ガイドブック
227	导览机	案内機
228	导游处	ガイド紹介所
229	导游服务中心	ガイドサービスセンター
230	导游手册	ガイドブック
231	导游亭	案内所
232	登记处	登録窓口
233	登山避难处	登山避難所
234	登山步道	登山歩道
235	等候区;登山避难处	待合区域;登山避難所
236	电动游览车	観光遊覧車
237	陡坡滑雪牵引索	リフト
238	儿童游乐场;儿童乐园	子供の遊び場
239	服装出租处	衣装レンタル
240	公园管理处	公園管理事務所
241	购物区	ショピングエリア
242	顾客服务中心;客服中心	お客様サービスセンター

序号	中文	日文
243	观光车	観光遊覧車
244	观光电瓶车	観光遊覧車
245	观光梯	観光エレベーター
246	观光休闲厅	観光休憩所
247	观景台	展望台
248	观赏区	観賞エリア
249	过山车	ジェットコースター
250	行人专用道	歩行者専用道路
251	杭州特产店	杭州物産店
252	划船	ボート
253	缓跑小径	ジョギングコース
254	集体票	団体チケット
255	景区简介	概要
256	缆车(封闭式)	ロープウェイ
257	缆车(椅式)	リフト
258	缆车入口	ロープウェイ乗り場
259	礼品店	ギフトショップ
260	礼品兑换处	景品引き替え所
261	礼堂	ホール
262	露营地	キャンプ場
263	旅游度假区	リゾート地
264	旅游服务中心	観光サービスセンター

序号	中文	日文
265	旅游纪念品商店	観光ギフトショップ
266	旅游投诉电话	ご意見専用ダイヤル
267	门票价格;票价	チケット価格;料金
268	年票	年間パスポート
269	您所在的位置(用于导向指示图)	現在地
270	票价 ——老人票价 ——成人票价 ——儿童票价 ——学生票价	チケット価格 ——お年寄り価格 ——大人価格 ——子ども価格 ——学生価格
271	票务服务;售票(处) ——团体票 ——退票 ——取票	チケット売り場 ——団体チケット ——チケット払い戻し ——予約チケット受け取り
272	票务热线	チケット専用ダイヤル
273	亲子区	ファミリーエリア
274	洒水车	散水車
275	三轮车接待站	輪タク乗り場
276	扫地车	清掃車
277	示意图(导游图)	案内図
278	试衣间	試着室
279	室外观光廊	室外観光用通路
280	收费项目	料金表
281	手工艺展示	手工芸品展
282	狩猎区	狩猟区

序号	中文	日文
283	索道	ロープウェー
284	徒步旅行	ハイキング
285	团队入口	団体客入口
286	团体检票	団体客改札口
287	团体接待	団体客受け付け
288	团体票	団体チケット
289	退货处理处	返品受付
290	退押金处	デポジット払戻し所
291	拓展区(公园里)	アクティビティーエリア
292	外卖店	テイクアウト販売店
293	网上订票取票处	ネット予約チケット受け取り窓口
294	维修服务中心	修理サービスセンター
295	无烟区	禁煙エリア
296	无障碍售票口;无障碍（设施）	バリアフリーチケット販売窓口;バリアフリー施設
297	无障碍通道	バリアフリー通路
298	休闲区	レジャーセンター
299	宣传资料	パンフレット
300	学生票	学生割引チケット
301	养殖场	養殖場
302	饮食区	飲食エリア
303	婴儿车租赁	ベビーカー貸出中
304	营火	キャンプファイヤー

序号	中文	日文
305	优惠办法	割引方法
306	优先通道	優先通路
307	游步道	遊歩道
308	游程信息	観光情報
309	游船	遊覧船
310	游船码头	遊覧船乗り場
311	游客报警电话(110)	観光客通報ダイヤル(110番)
312	游客服务中心	観光客サービスセンター
313	游客投诉电话	観光客苦情ホットライン
314	游客须知/游园须知	観光の注意事項
315	游客咨询电话	観光客お問合せ電話
316	游览车车站	観光バス乗り場
317	游览车发车时间	観光バス発車時間
318	游览观光车	観光バス
319	游览图	遊覧マップ
320	游览栈道	遊覧桟道
321	娱乐中心	娯楽センター
322	语音讲解	音声解説サービス
323	园长接待处	園長応接室
324	员工通道	スタッフ通路
325	月票	定期券
326	赠票	招待券
327	展板	掲示板

序号	中文	日文
328	展览馆;陈列馆	展示館
329	展区	展示エリア
330	展厅	展示ホール
331	展厅入口	展示ホール入口
332	值班岗亭	警備室
333	值班室	当直室
334	治安值班室	警備員当直室
335	中央展厅	中央展示ホール
336	主廊	メインアーケード
337	主入口	メインエントランス
338	主入口浮雕	メインエントランスレリーフ(浮き彫り)
339	住宿区	宿泊エリア
340	专题展区	テーマ展示エリア
341	自行车租赁	レンタルサイクル
342	自然保护区	自然保護区
343	字画店	書画店
344	综合服务区	総合サービスエリア
345	综合艺术厅	総合芸術ホール
346	走失儿童认领	迷子センター
347	租车处	レンタカー
348	租船处	レンタルボート

注1:条目中文"( )"中的内容是对中文内涵的补充说明。
注2:条目日文"( )"中的内容是对日文译写的解释或者补充说明。

I.3 告知、提示和警示信息日文译写示例见表I.3。表I.3按分类条目中文汉语拼音排序。

表I.3 告知、提示和警示信息日文译写示例

序号	中文	日文
	（通用告知类信息）	
1	安全保卫	セキュリティー
2	安全检查	セキュリティーチェック
3	安全提示;安全须知	安全のための注意事項
4	残疾人服务	障がい者向けサービス
5	残障人士使用(专用)(直接用于相关设施处,标示该设施为残障人士使用或专用)	障がい者専用
6	电话每分钟计费标准	電話料金案内
7	电话区号	市外局番
8	电话收费	電話料金
9	电话停机	この電話はご利用になれません
10	电话预订	電話予約
11	电讯服务	通信サービス
12	二十四小时营业	24時間営業
13	工作时间 ——营业时间 ——闭店时间	営業時間;勤務時間 ——営業時間 ——閉店時間
14	故障	故障中
15	故障停用;机器故障;电梯维修,暂停使用	現在、ご利用になれません
16	广播服务	アナウンスサービス
17	广播寻人寻物	迷子・落し物のお知らせ

序号	中文	日文
18	检修中	点検中
19	开放时间	利用時間
20	可以信用卡支付	クレジットカード可
21	临时关闭;暂停服务;暂停收款	一時閉鎖中;サービス一時停止中; レジ一時休止中
22	免费	無料
23	免费寄存	荷物お預かり所(無料)
24	免费使用	無料
25	免费送货;免费送餐	お食事の配達(無料)
26	免费项目	無料品一覧
27	免费饮水	ご自由にお飲みください
28	清洁中	清掃中
29	扫码付费	QRコード支払い
30	施工期间,恕不开放	工事中につき、休業させていただきます
31	特色餐饮	名物料理
32	通知	お知らせ
33	危险物品	危険物
34	允许拍照留念	記念撮影可
35	正常开放	通常営業
36	正在维修	修理中
37	自助买单	セルフレジ
	(通用提示及警示类信息)	
38	保持安静;请勿大声喧哗	お静かに

序号	中文	日文
39	别让您的烟头留下火患	吸い殻は灰皿に
40	别遗忘随身物品（用于提醒乘客、顾客）	身の回り品をお忘れにならないようお気をつけください
41	食品及饮料请勿带入	飲食物の持ち込み禁止
42	不准擅入	立ち入り禁止
43	不准擅自带出	無断持ち出し禁止
44	不准擅自带入	無断持ち込み禁止
45	场内严禁吸烟	場内禁煙
46	出门按钮	出る時はここを押してください
47	当心绊倒	足元注意
48	当心触电	感電注意
49	当心电缆	コードに注意
50	地面湿滑，小心滑倒	滑りやすいので、足元にご注意ください
51	贵重物品请您自己妥善保管	貴重品にご注意ください
52	火警压下；火警时压下	火災の際には強く押してください
53	紧急情况请拨打XXX	緊急時×××におかけください
54	紧急情况下，旋转把手开启	緊急時ハンドルを回して開けてください
55	紧急时击碎玻璃	緊急時ガラスを割って避難してください
56	紧急时请按按钮；发生紧急情况时，请按按钮报警	緊急時ボタンを押すと警察につながります
57	紧握扶手	手すりにしっかりとつかまってください
58	禁用手机；请勿使用手机	携帯電話のご使用はご遠慮ください

序号	中文	日文
59	老幼乘梯需家人陪同	ご年輩の方と小さなお子様は家族の同伴が必要です
60	雷雨天禁止拨打手机	雷雨の時は、携帯電話のご使用はお控えください
61	钱款当面点清,离柜概不负责	金額やおつりはその場でご確認ください
62	请保持场内清洁	ゴミはゴミ箱に
63	请保持整洁	きれいにしてください
64	请保管好私人物品;请保管好自己的财物(常用于更衣室)	貴重品にご注意ください; 貴重品は身から離さず保管するようご注意ください
65	请不要乱扔垃圾;请勿乱扔废弃物	ゴミはゴミ箱に
66	请不要随地吐痰	みだりに痰を吐かないでください
67	请出示证件	身分証明書をご提示ください
68	请关闭通信设备	電子機器の電源をお切りください
69	请将手机静音	携帯電話をマナーモードにしてください
70	请节约用水	節水にご協力ください
71	请节约用纸	紙の節約にご協力ください
72	请勿触摸;请勿抚摸;请勿手扶	触らないでください
73	请勿打电话	通話はご遠慮ください
74	请勿打扰	邪魔しないでください
75	请勿堵塞	立ち止まらずにそのままお進みください
76	请勿将烟头扔进容器	容器にタバコの吸殻を捨ててください
77	请勿将杂物扔进容器	容器にゴミを捨ててください

序号	中文	日文
78	请勿跨踏边缘（自动扶梯入口处）	黄色の線の内側にお立ちください
79	请勿留弃食品或食品包装	ゴミをお持ち帰りください
80	请勿录音	録音禁止
81	请勿录影录像;请勿摄像	録画禁止;撮影禁止
82	请勿拍打玻璃	ガラスを叩かないでください
83	请勿拍照;请勿摄影	撮影禁止
84	请勿让孩子独自搭乘电梯;小孩乘电梯须有大人陪伴	お子様がご利用の場合は、保護者の同伴が必要です
85	请勿入内	立ち入り禁止
86	请勿使用扩音器	スピーカー使用禁止
87	请勿使用闪光灯	フラッシュ撮影禁止
88	请勿使用手机	携帯電話のご使用はご遠慮ください
89	请勿躺卧	ここで横にならないでください
90	请勿吸烟	禁煙
91	请勿遗忘物品	身の回り品をお忘れにならないようお気をつけください
92	请勿倚靠;严禁倚靠	よりかからないでください
93	请勿坐卧	座ったり横になったりしないでください
94	请在此等候	こちらでお待ちください
95	请在黄线外排队;请站在黄线后	黄色い線の内側にお並びください
96	请在台阶下等候	階段の下でお待ちください。
97	请找工作人员协助	スタッフにご相談ください
98	请照看好您的小孩	お子様から目を離さないようお願いします

序号	中文	日文
99	请照看好您的行李和物品（常用于候车、船、机大厅等）	身の回り品にはご注意ください
100	请注意上方	頭上注意
101	请走转门	回転ドアをご利用ください
102	请遵守场内秩序	マナーをお守りください
103	危急时请速报110	緊急時110番へ通報してください
104	危险,请勿靠近	危険ですから、近寄らないでください
105	未成年人严禁入内	未成年者立ち入り禁止
106	闲人免进	関係者以外立ち入り禁止
107	小心玻璃	ガラスにご注意ください
108	小心触电/有电危险 ——高压危险	感電注意 ——高圧危険
109	小心地滑	足元にご注意ください
110	小心火灾	火の元にご注意ください
111	小心夹手	手を挟まないようにご注意ください
112	小心脚下;注意台阶;小心台阶;当心踏空;下台阶时请您小心	段差にご注意ください
113	小心流氓	痴漢に注意
114	小心碰撞	衝突注意
115	小心台阶	段差注意
116	小心烫伤	やけどに注意
117	小心障碍	障害物にご注意ください
118	谢绝参观	見学はご遠慮ください

序号	中文	日文
119	须紧扶小孩	お子様の手を離さないでください
120	这里请不要拍照	撮影禁止
121	正在检修,请您稍候	点検中につき、少々お待ちください
122	注意安全,请勿靠近	危険ですので、近寄らないでください
123	注意防火	火の用心
124	注意上方;小心碰头	頭上注意
	(机场、火车站告知类信息)	
125	本柜(台)只接受现金缴费	現金のみ;カード不可
126	本柜恕不接受VIP卡	VIPカードはご利用いただけません
127	出口往前(由此出站)	出口はこちら
128	行李安全检查	荷物検査;手荷物検査
129	行李提取	荷物受け取り
130	检票	改札
131	快递	宅配便
	(机场、火车站提示及警示类信息)	
132	保持平放(指货物、行李的摆放)	天地無用
133	本柜暂停服务,请至其他台席办理	ただ今サービスを停止しております。ほかの窓口をご利用ください
134	乘此梯至地下停车场	地下駐車場行きエレベーター
135	打开安全杠	安全レバーを引いてください

序号	中文	日文
136	打开过顶安全杠	頭上の安全レバーを引いてください
137	关上安全杠	安全レバーを閉めてください
138	关上过顶安全杠	頭上の安全レバーバーを閉めてください
139	留神行李	手荷物にご注意くだい
140	切勿倒置（指货物、行李的摆放）	天地無用
141	切勿挤压（指货物、行李的摆放）	荷物のとり扱い注意
142	切勿倾倒（指货物、行李的摆放）	斜め放置禁止
143	请补足差额	差額の支払いをお願いします
144	易碎物品请轻拿轻放（指货物、行李的摆放）	割れ物注意
	（宾馆告知类信息）	
145	欢迎光临;欢迎惠顾	いらっしゃいませ
146	谢谢光临	ご来店ありがとうございます
147	自助餐	放題
	（宾馆提示及警示类信息）	
148	欢迎多提宝贵意见	ご意見・ご感想聞かせてください
149	遇有火灾请勿用电梯	火災の際、エレベーターはご使用になれません
150	只用于紧急出口。推动此门,警号即响	非常時以外は利用しないでください。このドアを開けると、非常ベルが鳴ります
	（交通、停车场告知类信息）	
151	车位已满	満車

序号	中文	日文
152	此路不通	前方行き止まり
153	此路封闭	前方道路閉鎖中
154	道路施工	道路工事中
155	行人专用道	歩行者専用道路
156	换乘地铁	地下鉄への乗り換え
157	计时停车	有料駐車
158	临时停车	一時停車
159	现金支付	現金払い
160	限乘15人	15人乗り
161	限乘人数	乗車人数制限
162	限制重量	重量制限
（交通、停车场提示及警示类信息）		
163	不准穿越	横断禁止
164	不准乱停自行车	自転車は指定場所に駐輪してください
165	不准停车或候客，只可上下旅客	乗客の乗り降り以外、駐停車禁止
166	车内请勿吸烟	車内禁煙
167	防洪通道，请勿占用	非常用通路につき、駐車禁止
168	访客禁停	お客様の駐車はご遠慮ください
169	非机动车禁止入内	自動車以外進入禁止
170	行人不准穿越	歩行者横断禁止
171	禁鸣喇叭；禁止鸣笛	クラクション禁止

序号	中文	日文
172	禁止非机动车通行	自転車通行禁止
173	机动车道	自動車専用道路
174	禁止机动车通行	車両通行禁止
175	禁止开窗	窓を開けないでください
176	禁止旅游车辆进入	観光バス進入禁止
177	禁止驶入	車両進入禁止
178	禁止停车	駐車禁止 ; 車進入禁止
179	禁止停留	駐停車禁止
180	禁止通过;严禁通行	通行禁止
181	禁止头手伸出窗外	窓から顔や手を出さないでください
182	禁止外来车辆停放	関係者以外駐車禁止
183	禁止携带宠物	ペットの同伴お断り
184	禁止携带易燃易爆物品	危険物持込禁止
185	禁止中途下车	途中下車はできません
186	旅游车辆禁止入内	観光バス進入禁止
187	前方弯路慢行	前方カーブ注意
188	请将您的车辆锁好	車をしっかりロックしてください
189	请排队上车	並んでご乗車ください
190	请维护好车厢的清洁卫生,谢谢	車内マナーを守りましょう
191	请勿将手臂伸出车外	車の窓から手を出さないでください
192	请勿向窗外扔东西	窓からものを捨てないでください
193	请勿倚靠车门	ドアに寄りかからないでください

序号	中文	日文
194	请系好安全带	シートベルトをしっかりとお締めください
195	请依规定整齐停放	規定に従って、駐車してください
196	外部车辆请勿进入	外部車両の出入りはできません
197	为了您和他人的安全请自觉遵守乘车秩序	順番にお乗りください
198	勿放潮湿处(指货物、行李的摆放)	湿気の多いところを避けて置きましょう
199	勿放顶上(指货物、行李的摆放)	上に載せないでください
200	勿将头探出	危険ですので、頭を外に出さないでください
201	先下后上	降車のお客様に続いてご乗車ください
202	限紧急情况下使用	緊急時以外は使用しないでください
203	消防通道,禁止停车	避難通路につき、駐車禁止
204	消防通道,请勿占用	避難通路につき、物を置かないでください
205	消防通道应处于常闭状态	非常時以外は避難通路は使用しないでくだあい
206	注意缓行	徐行
207	注意转弯车辆	右左折車両に注意
	(景区告知类信息)	
208	闭馆整修	休館中
209	闭园时间	閉園時間
210	撤离路线;疏散通道	緊急通路
211	导游服务;讲解服务	ガイドサービス

序号	中文	日文
212	电动船租赁	電動ボートレンタル
213	返回验印	再入場チェック
214	非吸烟区	禁煙エリア
215	进口(入口)往前(由此进站)	入口はここからです
216	开园时间	オープン時間
217	免票	チケット不要
218	内部施工,暂停开放	工事中につき、一時閉館中
219	您所在的位置(用于导向指示图)	現在地
220	票价 ——老人票价 ——成人票价 ——儿童票价 ——学生票价	チケット価格 ——お年寄り価格 ——大人価格 ——子ども価格 ——学生価格
221	票务服务;售票(处) ——团体票 ——退票 ——取票	チケット売り場 ——団体チケット ——チケット払い戻し ——予約チケット受け取り
222	票务热线	チケット専用ダイヤル
223	票已售出,概不退换	チケットの払戻しはできません
224	票已售完	売り切れ
225	售完	売り切れ
226	提供拐杖	杖の貸出あり
227	提供轮椅	車椅子の貸出あり
228	提供婴儿车	ベビーカー貸出あり
229	优惠价格	割引価格
230	暂停售票(收款、服务);临时关闭	一時休止中

序号	中文	日文
231	照相服务	フォトサービス;撮影サービス（有料）
	（景区提示及警示类信息）	
232	爱护一草一木	草木を大切に
233	爱护一草一木,珍惜绿色空间	草木を大切に
234	必须戴安全帽	必ずヘルメットをご着用ください
235	步行游客请在此下车	歩いていく方はここでおりてください
236	宠犬便后请打扫干净	ペットのフンは飼い主が責任を持って片付けましょう
237	此处不准遛狗	犬の散歩お断り
238	当日使用,逾期作废	当日限り有効
239	当心动物伤人	動物出没注意
240	当心高空坠物	落下物注意
241	当心划船区域	周りのボートに注意
242	当心滑跌	スリップ注意
243	当心火车	列車に注意
244	当心机械伤人	機械に触れないでください;ケガする恐れがあります
245	当心落水	落水注意
246	当心伤手	怪我をする恐れがあります
247	殿内请勿燃香	屋内で線香に火をつけないでください
248	对不起,此票不能使用(检票机上提示信息)	このチケットはご利用できません
249	（队伍)排成单列/两列/三列	お並びください

序号	中文	日文
250	(队伍)在此排队	こちらに並んでください
251	非工作人员禁止入内	スタッフ以外立ち入り禁止
252	非火警时请勿挪用	火災の時以外は触れないでください
253	非紧急情况不得停留	緊急時以外は立ち止まらないでください
254	非游览区,请勿进入	スタッフ以外立ち入り禁止
255	风力较大勿燃香,请敬香	風が強い時は、線香に火をつけないでください
256	改为步行的游客请在此下车	歩いていく場合はここでお降りください
257	高血压、心脏病患者以及晕车、晕船、酗酒请勿乘坐	高血圧、心臓病患者の方、車や船に酔いやすい方、酒に酔う方は、ご遠慮ください
258	购票后,恕不退票	チケットの払い戻しはできません
259	顾客止步;乘客止步;员工通道;闲人免进;闲人莫入;员工专用	スタッフ以外立入り禁止
260	禁区;谢绝入内	立ち入り禁止
261	禁止摆卖	路上販売禁止
262	禁止采摘	無断で取らないでください
263	禁止踩踏	踏み入らないでください
264	禁止车辆入内	車両進入禁止
265	禁止车辆通行	車両通行禁止
266	禁止大声喧哗	大声で騒がないでください
267	禁止带火种;禁止放易燃物	火気厳禁;危険物の持込禁止
268	禁止带入易燃物品	危険物持ち込み禁止
269	禁止钓鱼	釣り禁止

序号	中文	日文
270	禁止丢弃杂物;勿扔垃圾;勿乱扔杂物	ゴミはゴミ箱に;ポイ捨て禁止
271	禁止放置易燃品	燃えやすい物をここに置かないでください
272	禁止风筝放飞	凧揚げ禁止
273	禁止滑冰	スケート禁止
274	禁止跨越护栏;禁止攀爬	立ち入り禁止;登らないでください;柵を乗り越えないでください
275	禁止露营	キャンプ禁止
276	禁止乱画	落書き禁止
277	禁止轮滑	ローラースケート禁止
278	禁止排放污水	廃水を流さないでください
279	禁止攀登	登らないでください
280	禁止攀折	花や木を大切に;花を取ったり、木の枝を折ったりしないでください
281	禁止骑自行车下坡	下り坂では自転車を降りてください
282	禁止燃放鞭炮	爆竹禁止
283	禁止燃放烟花爆竹	花火禁止
284	禁止入内;禁止驶入;请勿入内;严禁入内;谢绝参观;游客止步	立入禁止
285	禁止狩猎	狩猟禁止
286	禁止调头	ユータン禁止
287	禁止跳下	(ここから)飛び降りないでください
288	禁止停留	立ち止まらないでください

序号	中文	日文
289	禁止喂食	動物に餌を与えないでください
290	禁止无照经营	無許可営業禁止
291	禁止戏弄	(動物に)いたずらをしないでください
292	禁止戏水	水遊びをしないでください
293	禁止携入	持ち込み禁止
294	禁止烟火	火気厳禁
295	禁止游泳	水泳禁止
296	敬请谅解(因维修、施工等带来不便)	ご迷惑をおかけしています
297	酒后不能上船	飲酒後のご乗船はご遠慮ください
298	临时施工,观众止步	工事中につき、立入禁止
299	凭票入场	チケットをお買い求めのうえ、ご入場ください
300	请爱护洞内景观	洞窟内ではマナーを守りましょう
301	请爱护公共财产	公共施設を大切にしましょう
302	请爱护公共设施	公共施設を大切にしましょう
303	请爱护景区设施	施設を大切にしましょう
304	请爱护林木	緑を大切にしましょう
305	请爱护文物/保护文物	文化財を大切にしましょう
306	请按顺序排队;请按顺序出入——请排队等候入场	順番にお並びください;順番に出入りください——順番にご入場ください
307	请保护古迹	古跡を守ってください
308	请保护古树	古樹を大切に

序号	中文	日文
309	请不要随意移动隔离墩	設置物をみだりに移動しないでください
310	请不要坐在护栏上	柵の上に座らないでください
311	请穿好救生衣	救命胴衣を着用してください
312	请靠右站立	右側にお立ちください
313	请您购票	チケットのご購入をお願いします
314	请绕行 ——前面施工,请绕行	迂回してください ——前方工事中につき、迂回してください
315	请抬起护栏	柵を持ちあげてください
316	请勿踩踏	踏み入らないでください
317	请勿践踏草坪	芝生に入らないでください
318	请勿进行球类活动	ボール使用禁止
319	请勿惊吓动物	動物を驚かせるような行為はお控えください
320	请勿跨越	乗り越えないでください
321	请勿投食	餌を与えないでください
322	请勿携带宠物	ペット同伴禁止
323	请下车推行	ここから先は自転車を降りてください
324	请沿此路上山	この道に沿って登山してください
325	请原路返回	ここでユータンしてください
326	请自觉维护场内卫生环境	きれいな環境づくりにご協力をお願いします
327	请尊重少数民族习俗	少数民族の風習に従いましょう
328	善待自然,保护生态	自然を大切に

序号	中文	日文
329	上面施工,请注意安全	工事中につき、頭上にご注意ください
330	上坡路请不要使用自行车	登り坂では自転車を降りてください
331	施工给您带来很多不便,感谢您的理解和支持	工事中につき、ご迷惑をおかけします。ご理解とご協力をお願いします
332	食品饮料谢绝入内	飲食物の持ち込み禁止
333	水深危险,禁止靠前	あぶないから、近寄らないでください
334	小草在成长,请勿来打扰	草花を大切に
335	小心落水	落水注意
336	沿此路返回	お帰りはこちらの道をご利用ください
337	易碎物品,轻拿轻放	割れ物注意
338	1.2米以下儿童免票	身長1.2メートル以下のお子様は無料
339	1米以下儿童须家长陪同乘坐	身長1メートル以下のお子様は必ず保護者の同伴が必要です
340	游人止步	立ち入り禁止
341	有佛事活动,请绕行	法要中につき、迂回してください
342	在此刷卡;请刷卡 ——请重新刷卡	カードをタッチしてください ——もう一度カードをタッチしてください
343	注意落石	落石注意

注1:条目中文"( )"中的内容是对中文内涵的补充说明。
注2:条目日文"( )"中的内容是对日文译写的解释或补充说明。

附录 J

（资料性）

旅游景区景点韩文译写示例

J.1 旅游景区景点名称韩文译写示例见表 J.1。表 J.1 按分类条目中文汉语拼音排序。

表 J.1 旅游景区景点名称韩文译写示例

序号	中文	韩文
	（自然景观）	
1	池	지（연못）
2	岛	도
3	洞	동
4	洞窟	동굴
5	峰	봉
6	谷	곡
7	河	하
8	湖	호
9	涧	간（산골 물）
10	江	강
11	岭	령
12	瀑布	폭포
13	泉	천
14	溶洞	종유동
15	山	산

序号	中文	韩文
16	山脉	산맥
17	湿地	습지
18	石	석
19	石林	석림
20	潭	담
21	湾	만
22	温泉	온천
23	溪	계
24	峡谷	협곡
	（人文景观）	
25	庵	암（암자）
26	碑	비
27	碑记	비문
28	碑林	비림
29	别墅	별장
30	博物馆	박물관
31	草堂	초당
32	陈列馆	전시관
33	祠	사（사당）
34	道观	도교 사원
35	堤	제（둑）
36	殿	전

序号	中文	韩文
37	雕塑	조각
38	阁	각
39	公墓	공동 묘지
40	宫	궁
41	古道	고도
42	鼓楼	고루
43	故里	고향
44	古桥	고교
45	古塔	고탑
46	故居	옛집(생가)
47	馆	관
48	广场	광장
49	花圃	화포
50	纪念碑	기념비
51	纪念馆	기념관
52	假山	가산(조형물)
53	教堂	교회(예배당)
54	精舍	정사
55	井	정(우물)
56	运河	운하
57	酒坊	주방(술 양조장)
58	旧居	옛집

序号	中文	韩文
59	旧址	옛터
60	居	거
61	廊	랑
62	历史馆	역사관
63	烈士陵园	열사 묘역
64	楼	루
65	庐	려
66	门	문
67	庙	묘(사당)
68	墓	묘(무덤)
69	牌坊	패방
70	牌楼	패루
71	桥	교
72	清真寺	이슬람교 사원
73	石碑	석비
74	石刻	석각
75	世界文化遗产	세계문화유산
76	书房	서재
77	书院	서원
78	寺	사
79	塔	탑
80	台	대

序号	中文	韩文
81	堂	당
82	题记	제기(명승지에 남긴 글귀)
83	题刻	제각(새긴 글귀)
84	亭	정
85	轩	헌
86	遗址	유적지
87	园	원
88	苑	원
89	院	원
90	造像	조각상
91	斋	재
92	宅	택
93	照壁	조벽
94	钟楼	종루
95	庄	장
96	宗祠	사당
97	码头	부두
98	仓	창(창고)
99	坊	방
100	坡	파
101	洲	주
102	埠	부(나루)

序号	中文	韩文
	（综合景观）	
103	爱国主义教育基地	애국주의 교육기지
104	宾馆	호텔
105	步行街	보행자 거리
106	动物园	동물원
107	度假村	리조트
108	饭店	식당/호텔
109	公园	공원
110	国家级景区	국가급 관광지
111	国家级文物保护单位	국가급 문화재
112	海滨浴场	해수욕장
113	海洋公园	해양공원
114	历史街区	역사거리
115	疗养院	요양원
116	旅游度假区	관광 리조트
117	旅游景区	관광지
118	民宿	민박
119	民族文化街	민족문화거리
120	农家乐	농가 맛집
121	商店街	상가
122	水上乐园	워터파크
123	水族馆	수족관

序号	中文	韩文
124	游乐场	놀이터
125	植物园	식물원
126	天地	천지
127	水上公交	수상 버스
128	运河岸	운하 기슭
129	集散中心	집산 센터
130	茶馆	찻집
131	茶室	다도실

注1:条目中文"（　）"中的内容是对中文内涵的补充说明。
注2:条目韩文"（　）"中的内容是对韩文译写的解释或补充说明。

J.2　旅游服务设施韩文译写示例见表J.2。表J.2按分类条目中文汉语拼音排序。

表J.2　旅游服务设施韩文译写示例

序号	中文	韩文
	（通用基础设施设备）	
1	安全出口	비상구
2	安全检查站	안전 검문소
3	办公区	사무 구역/오피스존
4	保安室	경비실
5	报刊亭	신문 잡지 판매소
6	便民服务站	서비스 센터
7	标本室	표본실

序号	中文	韩文
8	表演区	공연 구역
9	表演时间	공연 시간
10	布告栏	게시판
11	厕所;公共厕所;卫生间;洗手间;厕所;盥洗室 ——男厕所、卫生间等 ——女厕所、卫生间等 ——收费厕所 ——残疾人厕所(一般用于该设施所处方位的指示和导引)	화장실/공중화장실 ——남자 화장실 ——여자 화장실 ——유료 화장실 ——장애인 전용 화장실
12	撤离路线;撤离通道	대피 통로
13	出口	출구
14	储物柜;存包处	물품 보관함/가방 보관소
15	地下通道	지하 통로
16	地下室	지하실
17	地下一层/二层/三层	지하1층/2층/3층
18	电话 ——公用电话 ——公用IC卡电话	전화 ——공중전화 ——공중IC카드전화
19	电话查号台	전화번호 안내 센터
20	电话亭(间)	전화 부스

序号	中文	韩文
21	电梯 ——扶梯/自动扶梯 ——贵宾电梯 ——货梯 ——残疾人电梯(一般用于该设施所处方位的指示和导引) ——上行扶梯 ——下行扶梯 ——工作人员专用梯	엘리베이터 ——에스컬레이터 ——VIP 엘리베이터 ——화물용 엘리베이터 ——장애인 전용 엘리베이터 ——상행 에스컬레이터 ——하행 에스컬레이터 ——직원용 엘리베이터
22	废物箱;垃圾桶	쓰레기함/쓰레기통
23	服务处	서비스 센터
24	服务监督电话	서비스 신고 전화
25	服务区域	서비스 구역
26	服务台	안내 데스크/프런트
27	更换尿布处	기저귀 교환소
28	更衣室 ——男更衣室 ——女更衣室	탈의실 ——탈의실(남) ——탈의실(여)
29	广播室	방송실
30	行李寄存处;小件寄存处	물품(짐) 보관소
31	火警 119	화재 신고 전화 119
32	火警出口	화재 비상구
33	火警电话请拨	화재 신고 전화
34	火警通讯电话	화재 긴급 전화
35	火情警报设施	화재 경보 설비
36	急救室	응급실

序号	中文	韩文
37	急救中心	응급센터
38	缴费处	비용 납부하는 곳
39	接待室;会客室	응접실
40	接待中心	리셉션 센터
41	紧急报警器	긴급 비상벨
42	紧急电话号码	긴급 전화 번호
43	紧急呼叫点	긴급 호출 지점
44	紧急呼救电话	긴급 호출 전화
45	紧急呼救设施	긴급 호출 장치
46	紧急救护电话120	긴급 구조 전화 120
47	紧急疏散地	긴급 대피소
48	紧急疏散指示图	긴급 대피 안내도
49	禁烟席	금연석
50	可回收垃圾箱	재활용 쓰레기통
51	快餐	패스트푸드
52	垃圾车;清洁车	쓰레기 수거 차량/청소 차량
53	垃圾房	쓰레기 수거실
54	老弱病残专席	노약자, 장애인 전용 좌석
55	临时出口	임시 출구
56	留言板;留言栏	게시판
57	(观众)留言簿;意见簿	방명록/의견부
58	楼层	층수

序号	中文	韩文
59	楼梯 ——上行楼梯 ——下行楼梯	계단 ——상행 계단 ——하행 계단
60	轮椅通道	휠체어 통로
61	灭火器	소화기
62	灭火器箱	소화전함
63	母婴(哺乳)室	수유실
64	派出所	파출소
65	热线;服务热线	핫라인/서비스 전화
66	人员、物品安检通道	안전 검사 통로
67	入口	입구
68	设备间 ——强电间 ——弱电间 ——配电柜 ——配电室/开关室 ——配电箱 ——开关房/室/间 ——水泵房 ——水阀间 ——新风机房 ——冷冻机房	설비실 ——강전실 ——약전실 ——배전캐비닛 ——배전실/스위치실 ——배전함 ——스위치실/칸 ——펌프장 ——벨브실 ——송풍기실 ——냉동기계실
69	声讯服务	음성안내서비스
70	失物招领	분실물 센터
71	收费标准	요금표
72	收银台;收款台;结帐;收费处	카운터/계산대/계산하는 곳
73	手机充电处	휴대폰 충전소

序号	中文	韩文
74	疏散示意图	대피 안내도
75	刷卡处	카드 지불
76	投诉电话;投诉热线;监督电话	소비자 고발 직통 전화/민원 신고 전화
77	问讯处;咨询处	안내소/안내데스크
78	吸烟区;吸烟室	흡연구역/흡연실
79	消防车	소방차
80	消防器材	소방기구
81	消防软管卷盘	소방호스릴
82	消防设施	소방시설
83	消防栓;消火栓	소화전/소방전
84	消防通道	소방통로
85	消防应急面罩	소방 응급 마스크
86	消防应急照明灯	소방 응급 라이트
87	消防员专用开关	소방관 전용 스위치
88	行李提取	짐 찾는 곳
89	休息厅;休息处;休息区;顾客休息室	휴게실/라운지/고객 휴게실
90	休闲区	레저 공간
91	医疗点;医疗室	의무실
92	意见簿;意见箱;举报信箱——评议箱	의견부/건의함/신고편지함——합평함
93	音控室	오디오 조절실
94	——处;饮用水——水	——식수대/식수——음용 금지

序号	中文	韩文
95	应急开启把手/紧急手柄	비상 손잡이, 비상 핸들
96	有偿手机充电装置	휴대폰 유료 충전하는 곳
97	咨询室	문의실
98	自动充值机	카드 충전기
99	自动出水;伸手出水	센서 수도꼭지/감지기 수도꼭지/손을 대면 물이 나옵니다
100	自动门	자동문
101	自动取款机	현금자동인출기
102	自动售货机	자동판매기
103	志愿者工作站	자원봉사자센터
104	自助查询机	셀프 검색기
105	自助寄存柜	셀프 보관함
	（机场火车站相关设施）	
106	~号站台	~번 플랫폼
107	补票处	탑승 후 요금 결제/재발권처
108	残疾人候车室	장애인 대합실
109	改签窗口	티켓 변경 창구
110	贵宾厅	VIP룸
111	贵宾通道	VIP통로
112	贵宾休息室	VIP휴게실
113	国际到达	국제 도착
114	国际换乘	국제 환승
115	国内到达	국내 도착

序号	中文	韩文
116	国内换乘	국내 환승
117	行李检查台	수하물 검사대
118	行李手推车	수하물 카트
119	行李提取	짐 찾는 곳
120	航站楼	공항터미널
121	候车室	대합실
122	候机大厅	공항 대합실
123	火车站	기차역
124	货币兑换;外币兑换处	환전
125	机场	공항
126	检票口	개표구
127	开水间	뜨거운 물 받는 곳
128	免税店	면세점
129	时刻表	시간표
130	售票处	매표소
131	售票窗口	매표창구
132	售票大厅	티켓팅홀
133	退票窗口	티켓 환불 창구
134	自动检票口	자동개표구
135	自动售票机	자동매표기/승차권 자동발매기
	（宾馆相关设施设备）	
136	报告厅	컨벤션홀

序号	中文	韩文
137	残疾人客房	장애인 객실
138	茶馆	찻집
139	大厅	로비
140	多功能厅	다기능 홀
141	风量调节 ——温度调节	풍량 조절 ——온도 조절
142	复印室	복사실
143	干手机	핸드 드라이어
144	干洗店	세탁소
145	会议室	회의실
146	会议影视厅	시청각 회의실
147	会议中心	회의센터
148	纪念品店	기념품 가게
149	价格表 标示价格 优惠价格	가격표 정가 할인 가격
150	健身房	헬스장
151	健身中心	헬스클럽
152	酒吧	바
153	咖啡吧	커피숍
154	开发票处	영수증 받는 곳
155	客房部	객실부
156	理发店	이발소
157	美容院	미용실

序号	中文	韩文
158	品牌专卖店	브랜드 전문매장
159	棋牌室	오락실
160	前台	프런트
161	清洁车	청소차
162	清洁中	청소중
163	商务中心	비즈니스센터
164	摄像室	영상실
165	玩具店	완구점
166	网吧	PC방
167	西饼屋	베이커리 카페
168	西餐厅	레스토랑
169	小卖店	소매점
170	烟感探头	화재탐지기
171	音乐厅	콘서트홀
172	饮水机	음수기
173	游泳池	수영장
174	有线电视	케이블 티비
175	雨伞架	우산 거치대
176	浴室	욕실
177	员工通道	직원 통로
178	折扣店	할인점
179	中餐厅	중식당

序号	中文	韩文
180	足浴店	발 마사지
	（交通及停车场相关设施）	
181	出租车	택시
182	出租车计价器	택시 미터기
183	出租车扬招点	택시 승차장
184	出租汽车专用发票	택시 영수증
185	道路交通信息	교통 정보
186	地铁	지하철
187	地铁车站	지하철역
188	地铁乘车点	지하철 승차장
189	地下停车场	지하주차장
190	公共汽车站	버스터미널
191	机场巴士	공항버스
192	计时停车场	시간제 유료주차장
193	紧急停车道	긴급 주차지역
194	禁烟车	금연 차량
195	旅游车	관광차
196	旅游大巴停车场	관광버스 주차장
197	免费停车场	무료 주차장
198	内部停车场;员工专用停车场	내부 주차장/직원 전용 주차장
199	汽车专用道	자동차 전용 도로
200	天桥	육교

序号	中文	韩文
201	停车场 ——收费停车场 ——全日(昼夜)停车场	주차장 ——유료 주차장 ——24시간 영업 주차장
202	停车场入口	주차장 입구
203	停车场须知	주차장 주의사항
204	停车车位	주차 자리
205	停车费	주차료
206	停车时限	주차 시한
207	停车收费系统	주차요금정산시스템
208	洗车店	세차장
209	游客停车场	관광객 주차장
210	长途汽车站	시외버스터미널
211	专用车位	전용 주차 자리
212	自行车停放处	자전거 거치소
	(景区相关设施)	
213	采摘区	과일따기 체험 구역
214	参观路线	관람 루트
215	参观通道(设于该通道入口处)	관람 입구
216	陈列室	진열실
217	宠物乐园	애완동물 놀이터
218	垂钓	낚시
219	大桥模型	대교 모형
220	大型水滑梯;戏水滑道	대형 물놀이용 미끄럼틀

序号	中文	韩文
221	大型游乐场	대형 놀이공원
222	带索救生圈	끈 달린 구명 튜브
223	单行线	일방 통로
224	导览册	가이드북
225	导览机	음성안내기
226	导游处	안내센터
227	导游亭	안내소
228	登记处	등록처
229	登山避难处	등산 대피소
230	等候区	대기구역
231	登山步道	등산로
232	陡坡滑雪牵引索	스키 리프트
233	服装出租处	의상 대여소
234	服务台	안내 데스크/프런트
235	公园管理处	공원관리처
236	购物区	쇼핑 구역
237	顾客服务中心;客服中心	고객서비스센터/관광서비스센터
238	观光车	관광버스
239	观光休闲厅	관광 라운지
240	观光梯	관광 엘리베이터
241	观赏区	관람 구역
242	观景台	전망대

序号	中文	韩文
243	过山车	롤러 코스터
244	行人专用道	보행자 전용 도로
245	杭州特产店	항주 특산물 가게
246	划船	보트
247	缓跑小径	조깅로
248	禁烟车	금연 차량
249	景区简介	관광지 소개
250	缆车(封闭式)	케이블카(밀폐식)
251	缆车(椅式)	케이블카(의자형)
252	缆车入口	케이블카 탑승구
253	礼品店	기념품 가게
254	礼品兑换处	경품 수령처
255	礼堂	강당
256	露营地	야영지
257	旅游度假区	관광휴양단지
258	旅游服务中心	관광서비스센터
259	旅游纪念品商店	관광기념품 가게
260	旅游投诉电话	관광 신고전화
261	门票价格;票价	입장권 가격
262	年票	1년 정기권
263	您所在的位置	지금 계신 곳/현위치
264	集体票	단체표

序号	中文	韩文
265	纪念碑	기념비
266	纪念品店	기념품 가게
267	计时停车	시간제 유료 주차장
268	票务热线	티켓 예매 전화
269	亲子区	키즈존
270	洒水车	살수차
271	三轮车接待站	삼륜차 대기소
272	扫地车	청소차
273	示意图(导游图)	안내도
274	室外观光廊	실외 관광 통로
275	收费项目	유료 서비스
276	手工艺展示	수공예품 전시
277	狩猎区	사냥 구역
278	售票处	매표소
279	索道	삭도
280	徒步旅行	도보 여행
281	团队入口	단체객 입구
282	团体检票	단체객 개표구
283	团体接待	단체객 안내소
284	团体票	단체권
285	退货处理处	반품 처리소
286	退押金处	보증금 환불소

序号	中文	韩文
287	拓展区	야외훈련장/아웃워드 바운드
288	问讯处;咨询处	안내소/안내데스크
289	外卖店	테이크 아웃 업소, 배달 업소
290	网上订票取票处	인터넷주문 티켓 수령처
291	无烟景区	금연 관광지
292	无障碍售票口;无障碍（设施）	장애인 전용 매표소/무장애(시설)
293	吸烟区;吸烟室	흡연구역/흡연실
294	洗车	세차
295	休息厅;休息处;休息区;顾客休息室	휴게실/라운지/고객 휴게실
296	休闲区	레저 공간
297	序厅	로비
298	学生票	학생표
299	宣传资料	홍보자료
300	学术交流厅	콘퍼런스홀
302	婴儿车租赁	유모차 대여
303	应急开启把手;紧急手柄	비상 손잡이/비상 핸들
304	营火	캠프파이어
305	优先通道	우대 통로
306	游程信息	여행 스케쥴
307	优惠办法	할인 방법
308	游步道	산책로
309	游船	유람선

序号	中文	韩文
310	游船码头	유람선 선착장
311	游客报警电话(110)	경찰 신고 전화(110)
312	游客服务中心	고객서비스센터
313	游客投诉电话	관광객 신고 전화
314	游客须知;游园须知	유람객 주의사항/관광지 주의사항
315	游客止步	관객 통행 금지
316	游客咨询电话	고객 문의 전화
317	游览车车站	관광버스 정거장
318	游览车发车时间	관광버스 발차 시간
319	游览观光车	관광버스
320	游览图	관광 안내도
321	游览栈道	관광 잔도
322	游乐场;游乐园	놀이공원/유원지
323	游泳池	수영장
324	语音讲解	음성 해설
325	预定	예약
326	员工通道	직원 전용 통로
327	园长接待处	원장 접견실
328	月票	월 정기권
329	赠票	초대권
330	展板	전시판
331	展览馆;陈列馆	전시관/진열관
332	展区	전시 구역

序号	中文	韩文
333	展厅	전시장
334	展厅入口	전시장 입구
335	值班岗亭	당직 카운터
336	值班室	숙직실/당직실
337	治安值班室	치안 당직실
338	中央展厅	중앙 전시홀
339	主廊	메인 복도
340	主入口	메인 입구
341	主入口浮雕	메인 입구의 부조
342	专题展区	테마 전시 구역
343	住宿区	숙박 구역
344	字画店	서예 및 그림 가게
345	自然保护区	자연보호구역
346	自行车租赁	자전거 대여소
347	综合服务区	종합 서비스 구역
348	综合艺术厅	종합예술홀
349	走失儿童认领	미아 보호소
350	租车处	차량 대여소
351	租船处	배 대여소
注1:条目中文"( )"中的内容是对中文内涵的补充说明。 注2:条目韩文"( )"中的内容是对韩文译写的解释或补充说明。		

J.3 告知、提示和警示信息韩文译写示例见表J.3。表J.3按分类条目中文汉语拼音排序。

表J.3 告知、提示和警示信息韩文译写示例

序号	中文	韩文
	（通用告知类信息）	
1	安全保卫	경비
2	安全检查	안전 검사
3	安全提示；安全须知	안전 주의사항
4	残疾人服务	장애인 서비스
5	残障人士使用（专用）（直接用于相关设施处，标示该设施为残障人士使用或专用）	장애인 전용
6	电话每分钟计费标准	전화요금 안내
7	电话区号	전화 지역번호
8	电话收费	유료 전화
9	电话停机	전화 이용 불가
10	电话预订	전화 예약
11	电讯服务	텔레콤 서비스
12	二十四小时营业	24시간 영업
13	工作时间 ——营业时间 ——闭店时间	영업 시간/근무 시간 ——영업 시간 ——폐점 시간
14	故障	수리 중
15	故障停用；机器故障；电梯维修，暂停使用	수리 중이니 이용할 수 없습니다.
16	广播服务	방송 서비스
17	广播寻人寻物	사람, 유실물 찾는 방송 안내

序号	中文	韩文
18	检修中	검수 중
19	开放时间	이용 가능 시간
20	可以信用卡支付	신용카드 사용 가능
21	临时关闭;暂停服务;暂停收款	임시 폐업/임시 폐관/서비스 일시 중지
22	免费	무료
23	免费寄存	무료 보관해 드립니다.
24	免费使用	무료 사용 가능합니다.
25	免费送货;免费送餐	무료 배송해 드립니다.
26	免费项目	무료 서비스
27	免费饮水	무료 제공 음용수
28	清洁中	청소 중
29	扫码付费	QR코드로 지불 가능
30	施工期间,恕不开放	공사 중이니 잠시 영업하지 않습니다.
31	特色餐饮	특색 요리
32	通知	공지
33	危险物品	위험 물품
34	允许拍照留念	기념 사진 촬용 가능합니다.
35	正常开放	정상 개방
36	正在维修	수리 중
37	自助买单	셀프 결제
	(通用提示及警示类信息)	
38	保持安静;请勿大声喧哗	조용히 하세요/떠들지 마세요.

序号	中文	韩文
39	保持平放(指货物、行李的摆放)	눕혀 놓으세요.
40	别让您的烟头留下火患	담뱃불 조심하세요.
41	别遗忘随身物品(用于提醒乘客、顾客)	소지품을 잊지 마세요.
42	不准带入食品、饮料或口香糖 ——食品及饮料请勿带入	음식, 음료수, 껌 반입금지 ——외부 음식물 반입금지
43	不准擅入	무단 진입 금지
44	不准擅自带出	무단 반출 금지
45	不准擅自带入	무단 반입 금지
46	场内严禁吸烟	장내 금연
47	出门按钮	버튼을 누르면 문이 열립니다.
48	当心绊倒	넘어지지 않도록 조심하세요.
49	当心触电	감전 조심하세요.
50	当心电缆	케이블 조심하세요.
51	地面湿滑,小心滑倒	바닥이 미끄러우니 넘어지지 않도록 조심하세요.
52	贵重物品请您自己妥善保管	귀중품은 스스로 잘 보관하세요.
53	火警压下;火警时压下	화재 발생시 누르세요.
54	紧急情况请拨打XXX	긴급 상황 시XXX로 전화하세요.
55	紧急情况下,旋转把手开启	긴급 상황 시, 핸들을 돌려 주세요.
56	紧急时击碎玻璃	긴급 상황 시, 유리를 깨세요.
57	紧急时请按按钮;发生紧急情况时,请按按钮报警	긴급 상황 시, 버튼을 누르세요. 긴급 상황 시, 버튼을 눌러 경찰에 신고하세요.

序号	中文	韩文
58	紧握扶手	손잡이를 꼭 잡으세요.
59	禁用手机;请勿使用手机	휴대폰 사용 금지
60	老幼乘梯需家人陪同	노인과 어린이는 보호자와 동승하세요.
61	雷雨天禁止拨打手机	뇌우 시, 휴대폰 사용하지 마세요.
62	钱款当面点清,离柜概不负责	거스름돈은 받은 즉시 확인하세요.
63	请保持场内清洁	장내 청결 유지
64	请保持整洁	청결을 유지해 주세요.
65	请保管好私人物品;请保管好自己财物(常用于更衣室)	개인 소지품을 잘 보관하세요.
66	请不要乱扔垃圾;请勿乱扔废弃物	쓰레기를 함부로 버리지 마세요.
67	请不要随地吐痰	침을 함부로 뱉지 마세요.
68	请出示证件	신분증을 제시해 주세요.
69	请关闭通信设备	휴대폰을 꺼 주세요.
70	请将手机静音	휴대폰은 무음으로 설정하세요.
71	请节约用水	물을 아껴 씁시다.
72	请节约用纸	휴지를 아껴 씁시다.
73	请勿触摸;请勿抚摸;请勿手扶	손대지 마세요/만지지 마세요/손으로 잡지 마세요.
74	请勿打电话	통화하지 마세요.
75	请勿打扰	방해하지 마세요.
76	请勿堵塞	가로막지 마세요.
77	请勿将烟头扔进容器	담배꽁초를 용기에 버리지 마세요.

序号	中文	韩文
78	请勿将杂物扔进容器	쓰레기를 용기에 버리지 마세요.
79	请勿跨踏边缘(自动扶梯入口处)	탑승시 에스컬레이터 가장자리를 밟지 마세요.
80	请勿留弃食品或食品包装	음식이나 포장지를 함부로 버리지 마세요.
81	请勿录音	녹음하지 마세요.
82	请勿录影录像;请勿摄像	녹화하지 마세요/촬영하지 마세요.
83	请勿拍照;请勿摄影	사진 촬영하지 마세요/촬영하지 마세요.
84	请勿拍打玻璃	유리를 두드리지 마세요.
85	请勿拍照	사진 촬영하지 마세요.
86	请勿让孩子独自搭乘电梯;小孩乘电梯须有大人陪伴	어린이는 보호자와 함께 엘리베이터에 탑승하세요.
87	请勿入内	진입 금지
88	请勿使用扩音器	확성기 사용 금지
89	请勿使用闪光灯	플래시 사용 금지
90	请勿使用手机	휴대폰 사용 금지
91	请勿躺卧	눕지 마세요.
92	请勿吸烟	흡연 금지 구역
93	请勿遗忘物品	소지품을 확인하세요.
94	请勿倚靠;严禁倚靠	기대지 마세요.
95	请勿坐卧	앉거나 눕지 마세요.
96	请在此等候	여기에서 대기하세요.
97	请在黄线外排队;请站在黄线后	노란선 밖에서 줄 서세요/노란선 밖에서 대기하세요.

序号	中文	韩文
98	请在台阶下等候	계단 아래에서 대기하세요.
99	请找工作人员协助	스태프에게 협조를 구하세요.
100	请照看好您的小孩	아이를 잘 돌보세요.
101	请照看好您的行李和物品（常用于候车、船、机大厅等）	소지품을 잘 보관하세요.
102	请注意上方	위쪽을 주의하세요.
103	请自觉维护场内卫生环境	장내 환경위생을 유지하세요.
104	请走转门	회전문을 이용하세요.
105	请尊重少数民族习俗	소수민족 풍속을 존중해 주세요.
106	请遵守场内秩序	장내 질서를 지켜 주세요.
107	危急时请速报110	긴급 상황 시 110으로 전화하세요.
108	危险,请勿靠近	위험하니 가까이 하지 마세요.
109	未成年人严禁入内	미성년자 출입 금지
110	闲人免进	관계자외 출입 금지
111	小心玻璃	유리 조심
112	小心触电;有电危险 ——高压危险	감전 조심/감전 위험, ——고압선 위험/고압 주의
113	小心地滑	미끄러우니 조심하세요.
114	小心火灾	화재 주의
115	小心夹手	손이 끼이지 않도록 조심하세요.
116	小心脚下;注意台阶;小心台阶;当心踏空;下台阶时请您小心	발밑 조심하세요/계단 조심하세요.
117	小心落水	물에 빠지지 않도록 조심하세요.

序号	中文	韩文
118	小心碰撞	충돌하지 않도록 조심하세요.
119	小心烫伤	뜨거우니 조심하세요.
120	小心台阶	계단 조심하세요.
121	小心障碍	장애물 조심하세요.
122	谢绝参观	방문을 사절합니다.
123	须紧扶小孩	어린이를 꽉 잡으세요.
124	这里请不要拍照	촬영 금지/이곳은 촬영 금지 구역입니다.
125	正在检修,请您稍候	점검 중이니 잠시만 기다려 주세요.
126	注意安全,请勿靠近	안전에 주의하세요, 가까이 가지 마세요.
127	注意防火	불 조심하세요.
128	注意上方;小心碰头	위쪽을 조심하세요/머리 조심하세요.
	(机场、火车站告知类信息)	
129	本柜(台)只接受现金缴费	본 카운터는 현금만 수납합니다.
130	本柜恕不接受VIP卡	본 카운터는 VIP카드 사용 불가합니다.
131	出口往前(由此出站)	출구 방향(출구로 가는 길)
132	行李安全检查	수하물 안전 검사
133	行李提取	수하물 수령
134	检票	개표
135	快递	택배
	(机场、火车站提示及警示类信息)	

序号	中文	韩文
136	保持平放（指货物、行李的摆放）	눕혀 놓으세요.
137	本柜暂停服务，请至其他台席办理	잠시 업무 중단이오니 다른 카운터를 사용해 주세요.
138	乘此梯至地下停车场	지하주차장 연결 엘리베이트
139	打开安全杠	안전 빗장을 열어 주세요.
140	打开过顶安全杠	머리 위 안전 빗장을 열어 주세요.
141	关上安全杠	안전 빗장을 닫아 주세요.
142	关上过顶安全杠	머리 위 안전 빗장을 닫아 주세요.
143	留神行李	수하물 주의
144	切勿倒置（指货物、行李的摆放）	거꾸로 놓지 마세요.
145	切勿挤压（指货物、行李的摆放）	내리 누르지 마세요.
146	切勿倾倒（指货物、行李的摆放）	수직으로 놓으세요.
147	请补足差额	차액을 보충하세요.
148	易碎物品请轻拿轻放（指货物、行李的摆放）	부서지기 쉬운 물품이므로 취급 주의 요망
	（宾馆告知类信息）	
149	欢迎光临；欢迎惠顾	어서 오세요.
150	谢谢光临	찾아 주셔서 감사합니다.
151	自助餐	뷔페식
	（宾馆提示及警示类信息）	
152	欢迎多提宝贵意见	소중한 의견 제시를 적극 환영합니다.

序号	中文	韩文
153	遇有火灾请勿用电梯	화재 발생시 엘리베이터 사용 금지
154	只用于紧急出口。推动此门,警号即响	비상시 사용하는 출구입니다. 이 문을 열면 사이렌이 울립니다.
	(交通、停车场告知类信息)	
155	车位已满	만차
156	此路不通	통행 금지
157	此路封闭	도로 폐쇄
158	道路施工	도로 공사 중
159	行人专用道	보행자 전용 도로
160	换乘地铁	지하철 환승
161	计时停车	시간제 유료 주차
162	临时停车	임시 주차
163	现金支付	현금 지불
164	限乘15人	최대 15인 탑승 가능
165	限乘人	최대 탑승 인원수
166	限制重量	중량 제한
	(交通、停车场提示及警示类信息)	
167	不准穿越	횡단 금지
168	不准乱停自行车	자전거 함부로 주차하지 마세요.
169	不准停车或候客,只可上下旅客	주차 또는 대기 금지, 상하차만 가능
170	车内请勿吸烟	차내 흡연 금지
171	防洪通道,请勿占用	비상용 통로이니, 주차 금지

序号	中文	韩文
172	访客禁停	방문 차량 주차 금지
173	非机动车禁止入内	비동력차량 구내 진입 금지
174	非紧急情况不得停留	긴급상황 외, 정류 금지
175	行人不准穿越	보행자 횡단 금지
176	禁鸣喇叭;禁止鸣笛	경적 금지
177	禁止非机动车通行	비동력차량 통행 금지
178	禁止机动车通行	자동차 통행 금지
179	禁止开窗	창문을 열지 마세요.
180	禁止跨越护栏;禁止攀爬	가드레일 횡단 금지/등반 금지
181	禁止骑自行车上坡	오르막길에서 자전거를 타지 마세요.
182	禁止骑自行车下坡	내리막길에서 자전거를 타지 마세요.
183	禁止入内;禁止驶入;请勿入内;严禁入内;谢绝参观;游客止步	출입 금지/방문 사절/관광객 출입 금지
184	禁止驶入	차량 통행 금지
185	禁止停车	주차 금지
186	禁止停留	정류 금지
187	禁止通过;严禁通行	통행 금지
188	禁止头手伸出窗外	머리나 손을 창밖으로 내밀지 마세요.
189	禁止喂食	먹이주기 금지
190	禁止外来车辆停放	외래 차량 주차 금지
191	禁止携带宠物	반려동물 출입 금지
192	禁止携带易燃易爆物品	위험 물품 반입 금지

序号	中文	韩文
193	禁止中途下车	중도 하차 금지
194	旅游车辆禁止入内	관광 버스 출입 금지
195	前方弯路慢行	전방 우회 도로 주의하세요.
196	请将您的车辆锁好	차를 잘 잠그세요.
197	请排队上车	순서대로 승차하세요.
198	请维护好车厢的清洁卫生，谢谢	차 내 위생을 잘 유지하세요 감사합니다.
199	请勿手扶；严禁手扶	손 대지 마세요.
200	请勿向窗外扔东西	창밖으로 물건을 던지지 마세요.
201	请勿倚靠；严禁倚靠	기대지 마세요.
202	请勿倚靠车门	차문에 기대지 마세요.
203	请下车推行	자전거에서 내려 끌고 가세요.
204	请勿将手臂伸出车外	손을 차밖으로 내밀지 마세요.
205	请系好安全带	안전벨트를 착용하세요.
206	请依规定整齐停放	규정대로 질서있게 주차하세요.
207	外部车辆请勿进入	외부 차량 출입 금지
208	为了您和他人的安全请自觉遵守乘车秩序。	안전을 위해 순서대로 승차하세요.
209	勿放潮湿处(指货物、行李的摆放)	습도 높은 곳에 보관하지 마세요.
210	勿放顶上(指货物、行李的摆放)	위에 놓지 마세요.
211	勿将头探出	머리를 밖으로 내밀지 마세요.
212	先下后上	승객이 내린 후에 승차하세요.
213	限紧急情况下使用	긴급 상황시 사용하세요.

序号	中文	韩文
214	消防通道,禁止停车	소방 통로, 주차 금지
215	消防通道,请勿占用	소방 통로, 물건을 놓지 마세요.
216	消防通道应处于常闭状态	비상시 외 소방 통로 사용 금지
217	注意缓行	서행하세요.
218	注意转弯车辆	회전 차량을 주의하세요.
	(景区告知类信息)	
219	闭馆整修	휴관
220	闭园时间	폐원 시간
221	撤离路线;疏散通道	대피 노선/대피 통로
222	导游服务;讲解服务	가이드 서비스/해설 서비스
223	电动船租赁	전기보트 임대
224	返回验印	재입장 체크
225	非吸烟区	금연 구역
226	进口(入口)往前(由此进站)	입구 방향(입구로 가는 길)
227	开园时间	개원 시간
228	免票	티켓 면제
229	内部施工,暂停开放	공사 중, 잠시 영업 중지
230	您所在的位置(用于导向指示图)	지금 계신 곳/현위치
231	票价 ——老人票价 ——成人票价 ——儿童票价 ——学生票价	표값 ——경로 요금 ——성인 요금 ——어린이 요금 ——학생 요금

序号	中文	韩文
232	票务服务;售票(处) ——团体票 ——退票 ——取票	매표소 ——단체표, 단체권 ——티켓 환불 ——티켓 수령
233	票务热线	티켓 예매 직통 전화
234	票已售出,概不退换	티켓 환불 불가
235	票已售完	티켓 매진
236	售完	매진
237	提供拐杖	지팡이 대여 서비스
238	提供轮椅	휠체어 대여 서비스
239	提供婴儿车	유모차 대여 서비스
240	优惠价格	가격 할인
241	暂停售票(收款、服务);临时关闭	티켓 판매 일시 중지/임시 폐업
242	照相服务	사진 촬영 서비스(유료)
(景区提示及警示类信息)		
243	爱护一草一木	나무와 풀을 보호합시다.
244	爱护一草一木,珍惜绿色空间。	나무와 풀을 소중히 합시다.
245	必须戴安全帽	안전모를 반드시 착용하세요.
246	步行游客请在此下车	보행자는 여기서 하차하세요.
247	宠犬便后请打扫干净	애완견 배설물을 깨끗이 청소하세요.
248	此处不准遛狗	애완견 산책 금지 구역입니다.
249	当日使用,逾期作废	당일만 사용 가능합니다.
250	当心动物伤人	동물 공격을 조심하세요.

序号	中文	韩文
251	当心高空坠物	고공 추락물을 조심하세요.
252	当心划船区域	뱃놀이 구역엔 진입 금지입니다.
253	当心滑跌	미끄러우니 조심하세요.
254	当心机械伤人	기계 조심
255	当心落水	익수주의
256	当心伤手	손을 다치지 않게 조심하세요.
257	殿内请勿燃香	전당 내 분향 금지
258	对不起,此票不能使用(检票机上提示信息)	사용할 수 없는 티켓입니다.
259	(队伍)排成单列/两列/三列	일렬/이열/삼열로 서 주세요.
260	(队伍)在此排队	줄 서는 곳
261	非工作人员禁止入内	관계자 외 출입 금지
262	非火警时请勿挪用	화재사고 외 사용 금지
263	非紧急情况不得停留	긴급상황 외 정류 금지
264	非游览区,请勿进入	관광구역이 아니오니 들어오지 마세요.
265	风力较大勿燃香,请敬香	바람이 세니, 향을 피우지 마세요.
266	改为步行的游客请在此下车	산책 코스를 택하신 분은 여기서 하차하세요.
267	高血压、心脏病患者以及晕车、晕船、酗酒请勿乘坐	고혈압, 심장병 환자, 멀미하는 자, 과음자 탑승 금지
268	购票后,恕不退票。	티켓 구매 후, 환불 불가
269	顾客止步;乘客止步;员工通道;闲人免进;闲人莫入;员工专用	고객 출입금지 구역/직원 전용 통로/외부인 출입금지/직원 전용
270	禁区,谢绝入内	금지 구역이오니 출입 금지

序号	中文	韩文
271	禁止摆卖	노점판매 금지
272	禁止采摘	과일 채취 금지
273	禁止踩踏	밟지 마세요
274	禁止车辆入内	차량 진입 금지
275	禁止车辆通行	차량 통행 금지
276	禁止大声喧哗	떠들지 마세요
277	禁止带火种;禁止放易燃物	불 조심/인화물 금지
278	禁止带入易燃物品	인화물 반입 금지
279	禁止钓鱼	낚시 금지
280	禁止丢弃杂物;勿扔垃圾;勿乱扔杂物	쓰레기를 함부로 버리지 마세요.
281	禁止放置易燃品	인화물 놓지 마세요
282	禁止风筝放飞	연 날리기 금지 구역
283	禁止滑冰	스케이팅 금지 구역
284	禁止跨越护栏;禁止攀爬	가드레일 횡단 금지/등반 금지
285	禁止露营	야영 금지 구역
286	禁止乱画	낙서 금지
287	禁止轮滑	롤스케이팅 금지 구역
288	禁止排放污水	오수 방류 금지
289	禁止攀登	등반 금지
290	禁止攀折	오르거나 꺾지 마세요.
291	禁止燃放鞭炮	폭죽 금지

序号	中文	韩文
292	禁止燃放烟花爆竹	폭죽 금지
293	禁止入内;禁止驶入;请勿入内;严禁入内;谢绝参观;游客止步	출입 금지/방문 사절/관광객 출입 금지
294	禁止狩猎	사냥 금지 구역
295	禁止调头	유턴 금지
296	禁止跳下	뛰어내리지 마세요.
297	禁止停留	정류 금지
298	禁止喂食	먹이를 함부로 투식하지 마세요.
299	禁止无照经营	무허가 영업 금지
300	禁止戏弄	장난 금지/(동물을) 놀래지 마세요.
301	禁止戏水	물놀이 금지
302	禁止携入	반입 금지
303	禁止烟火	화기 금지
304	禁止游泳	수영 금지
305	敬请谅解(因维修、施工等带来不便)	양해를 구합니다.
306	酒后不能上船	음주 후, 승선 불가
307	临时施工,观众止步	공사중이니 관객 출입 금지합니다.
308	凭票入场	입장시 티켓 보여 주세요.
309	请爱护洞内景观	동굴 내 경물을 보호합시다.
310	请爱护公共财产	공공물을 보호합시다.
311	请爱护公共设施	공공시설을 보호합시다.
312	请爱护景区设施	관광지를 보호합시다.

序号	中文	韩文
313	请爱护林木	삼림자원을 보호합시다.
314	请爱护文物;保护文物	문화재를 보호합시다.
315	请按顺序排队;请按顺序 出入 ——请排队等候入场	선착순으로 입장하세요. ——선착순으로 대기 입장하세요. ——차례대로 승차하세요.
316	请保护古迹	유적지를 보호합시다.
317	请保护古树	고목을 보호합시다.
318	请不要随意移动隔离墩	교통분리대를 함부로 움직이지 마세요.
319	请不要坐在护栏上	난간 위에 앉지 마세요.
320	请穿好救生衣	구명조끼를 착용하세요.
321	请靠右站立	우측으로 서 주세요.
322	请您购票	티켓 구매하세요.
323	请绕行 ——前面施工,请绕行	우회하세요. ——전방 공사중이니 우회하세요.
324	请抬起护栏	난간을 올리세요.
325	请勿踩踏	밟지 마세요.
326	请勿践踏草坪	잔디를 밟지 마세요.
327	请勿进行球类活动	구기 운동 금지 구역
328	请勿惊吓动物	동물을 놀래지 마세요.
329	请勿跨越	뛰어넘지 마세요.
330	请勿投食	투식하지 마세요.
331	请勿携带宠物	애완동물 출입 금지
332	请下车推行	자전거에서 내려 끌고 가세요.
333	请沿此路上山	이 길이 등산길입니다.

序号	中文	韩文
334	请原路返回	오신 길로 돌아가세요.
335	请自觉维护场内卫生环境	장내 청결 유지
336	请尊重少数民族习俗	소수민족 풍속을 존중해 주세요.
337	善待自然,保护生态。	대자연을 보호합시다.
338	上面施工,请注意安全	위에서 공사 중이니 안전 조심하세요.
339	上坡路请不要使用自行车	오르막길에서 자전거를 타지 마세요.
340	施工给您带来很多不便,感谢您的理解和支持	공사 중 불편을 드려 죄송합니다. 감사합니다.
341	食品饮料谢绝入内	음식 음료수 반입 금지
342	水深危险,禁止靠前。	물이 깊으니 가까이 가지 마세요.
343	小草在成长,请勿来打扰。	나무와 풀을 아낍시다.
344	小心落水	익수주의
345	沿此路返回	이 길이 되돌아가는 길입니다.
346	易碎物品,轻拿轻放	파손 우려가 있으니 취급 주의
347	1.2米以下儿童免票	1.2m 미만 어린이는 무료 입장입니다.
348	1米以下儿童须家长陪同乘坐	1m 미만 어린이는 보호자와 동승해야 합니다.
349	游人止步	관광자 출입 금지
350	有佛事活动,请绕行	불교행사가 있으니 우회하세요.
351	在此刷卡;请刷卡——请重新刷卡	이 곳에 카드를 대세요/카드를 찍어 주세요.——카드를 다시 찍어 주세요.
352	注意落石	낙석주의

注1:条目中文"( )"中的内容是对中文内涵的补充说明。
注2:条目韩文"( )"中的内容是对韩文译写的解释或补充说明。